Advances in Environmental Applied Physics

Advances in Environmental Applied Physics

Editor

Francesco Caridi

Basel • Beijing • Wuhan • Barcelona • Belgrade • Novi Sad • Cluj • Manchester

Editor
Francesco Caridi
University of Messina
Messina, Italy

Editorial Office
MDPI
St. Alban-Anlage 66
4052 Basel, Switzerland

This is a reprint of articles from the Special Issue published online in the open access journal *Applied Sciences* (ISSN 2076-3417) (available at: https://www.mdpi.com/journal/applsci/special_issues/Environmental_Applied_Physics).

For citation purposes, cite each article independently as indicated on the article page online and as indicated below:

Lastname, A.A.; Lastname, B.B. Article Title. *Journal Name* **Year**, *Volume Number*, Page Range.

ISBN 978-3-0365-8500-0 (Hbk)
ISBN 978-3-0365-8501-7 (PDF)
doi.org/10.3390/books978-3-0365-8501-7

© 2023 by the authors. Articles in this book are Open Access and distributed under the Creative Commons Attribution (CC BY) license. The book as a whole is distributed by MDPI under the terms and conditions of the Creative Commons Attribution-NonCommercial-NoDerivs (CC BY-NC-ND) license.

Contents

About the Editor . . . . **vii**

Francesco Caridi
Special Issue on Advances in Environmental Applied Physics
Reprinted from: *Applied Sciences* **2023**, *13*, 6172, doi:10.3390/app13106172 . . . . **1**

**Francesco Caridi, Giuseppe Paladini, Santina Marguccio, Alberto Belvedere,
Maurizio D'Agostino, Maurizio Messina and et al.**
Evaluation of Radioactivity and Heavy Metals Content in a Basalt Aggregate for Concrete from Sicily, Southern Italy: A Case Study
Reprinted from: *Applied Sciences* **2023**, *13*, 4804, doi:10.3390/app13084804 . . . . **7**

Hiroshi Yasuda, Naoyuki Kurita and Kazuaki Yajima
Verification of Estimated Cosmic Neutron Intensities Using a Portable Neutron Monitoring System in Antarctica
Reprinted from: *Applied Sciences* **2023**, *13*, 3297, doi:10.3390/app13053297 . . . . **19**

**Francesco Caridi, Giuseppe Paladini, Antonio Francesco Mottese, Maurizio Messina,
Valentina Venuti and Domenico Majolino**
Multivariate Statistical Analyses and Potentially Toxic Elements Pollution Assessment of Pyroclastic Products from Mt. Etna, Sicily, Southern Italy
Reprinted from: *Applied Sciences* **2022**, *12*, 9889, doi:10.3390/app12199889 . . . . **31**

**Panagiota Makrantoni, Anastasia Tezari, Argyris N. Stassinakis, Pavlos Paschalis,
Maria Gerontidou, Pantelis Karaiskos and et al.**
Estimation of Cosmic-Ray-Induced Atmospheric Ionization and Radiation at Commercial Aviation Flight Altitudes
Reprinted from: *Applied Sciences* **2022**, *12*, 5297, doi:10.3390/ app12115297 . . . . **43**

**Francesco Caridi, Giuseppe Paladini, Valentina Venuti, Sebastiano Ettore Spoto,
Vincenza Crupi, Giovanna Belmusto and et al.**
Natural and Anthropogenic Radioactivity Content and Radiation Hazard Assessment of Baby Food Consumption in Italy
Reprinted from: *Applied Sciences* **2022**, *12*, 5244, doi:10.3390/app12105244 . . . . **57**

**Francesco Caridi, Giuseppe Paladini, Valentina Venuti, Vincenza Crupi,
Sebastiano Ettore Spoto, Santina Marguccio and et al.**
A New Methodological Approach for the Assessment of the ^{238}U Content in Drinking Water
Reprinted from: *Applied Sciences* **2022**, *12*, 3380, doi:10.3390/app12073380 . . . . **65**

**Spyridon A. Kalospyros, Violeta Gika, Zacharenia Nikitaki, Antigoni Kalamara,
Ioanna Kyriakou, Dimitris Emfietzoglou and et al.**
Monte Carlo Simulation-Based Calculations of Complex DNA Damage for Incidents of Environmental Ionizing Radiation Exposure
Reprinted from: *Applied Sciences* **2021**, *11*, 8985, doi:10.3390/app11198985 . . . . **75**

Dainius Jasaitis and Milda Pečiulienė
Natural Radioactivity and Radon Exhalation from Building Materials in Underground Parking Lots
Reprinted from: *Applied Sciences* **2021**, *11*, 7475, doi:10.3390/app11167475 . . . . **97**

Francesco Caridi, Giuseppe Acri, Alberto Belvedere, Vincenza Crupi, Maurizio D'Agostino, Santina Marguccio and et al.
Evaluation of the Radiological and Chemical Risk for Public Health from Flour Sample Investigation
Reprinted from: *Applied Sciences* **2021**, *11*, 3646, doi:10.3390/app11083646 . . . . **109**

Francesco Caridi, Marcella Di Bella, Giuseppe Sabatino, Giovanna Belmusto, Maria Rita Fede, Davide Romano and et al.
Assessment of Natural Radioactivity and Radiological Risks in River Sediments from Calabria (Southern Italy)
Reprinted from: *Applied Sciences* **2021**, *11*, 1729, doi:10.3390/app11041729 . . . . **123**

About the Editor

Francesco Caridi

Francesco Caridi is an Assistant Professor in Applied Physics (to Cultural Heritage, Environment, Biology and Medicine) at the Department of Mathematical and Computer Sciences, Physical and Earth Sciences of the University of Messina. He graduated in Physics cum laude in 2003 at the University of Messina and received his PhD in Physics in 2007 from the same University. He obtained National Scientific Qualifications as Full Professor of Experimental Physics in 2020 and as Full Professor of Applied Physics in 2022. He is co-author of 150 publications in ISI-rated journals and more than 100 invited talks/communications at national and international conferences and events in the field of physics applied to cultural and environmental heritage. Citations: 1426, H-index: 27 (Scopus database). His research interests include, but are not limited to: a) the application of invasive and non-invasive micro- and spectroscopic techniques for the analysis of materials largely employed in the field of cultural heritage, as well as their degradation forms; b) characterization of materials of particular historical artistic interest in terms of natural radioactivity content, in order to assess the radiological risk for humans; c) systematic implementation of operative strategies aimed at the evaluation of the radon exhalation rate in building materials; d) gamma spectrometry, alpha spectrometry, liquid scintillation counting (LSC), total alpha/beta counting, emanometry, and gas-filled detectors.

Editorial

Special Issue on Advances in Environmental Applied Physics

Francesco Caridi

Dipartimento di Scienze Matematiche e Informatiche, Scienze Fisiche e Scienze della Terra, Università degli Studi di Messina, Viale F. Stagno D'Alcontres 31, 98166 Messina, Italy; fcaridi@unime.it

Citation: Caridi, F. Special Issue on Advances in Environmental Applied Physics. *Appl. Sci.* **2023**, *13*, 6172. https://doi.org/10.3390/app13106172

Received: 11 May 2023
Accepted: 15 May 2023
Published: 18 May 2023

Copyright: © 2023 by the author. Licensee MDPI, Basel, Switzerland. This article is an open access article distributed under the terms and conditions of the Creative Commons Attribution (CC BY) license (https://creativecommons.org/licenses/by/4.0/).

This Special Issue, "Advances in Environmental Applied Physics", is dedicated to collecting original papers from eminent researchers in the field of environmental pollutants, which constitute a health risk to the population, increasing the likelihood of incurring cancer. It is noteworthy that, among the various analytical techniques for the assessment of physical and chemical pollutants in the environment, alpha as well as gamma spectrometry are employed to obtain the specific activity of alpha and gamma radionuclides, respectively; ICP-MS can be used to investigate metal concentrations; liquid scintillation counting (LSC) is employed to quantify the activity concentration of tritium, radon, and gross alpha as well as beta; total alpha/beta counting, with the thick-source method, can be used for gross alpha- and beta-specific activity evaluation; and emanometry, in a H_2O setup configuration, can be employed to estimate the gas radon activity concentration.

Furthermore, the main topic of the article titled "Evaluation of Radioactivity and Heavy Metals Content in a Basalt Aggregate for Concrete from Sicily, Southern Italy: A Case Study" is an investigation on the natural and anthropic radioactivity of as well as heavy metals content in a basalt aggregate for concrete from Sicily, Southern Italy, performed as a case study. In particular, the evaluation of the specific activity of radium-226, thorium-232, potassium-40, and caesium-137 radionuclides was performed by using high-purity germanium (HPGe) γ-ray spectrometry, together with the estimation of several indices developed to evaluate the radiological risk for the population related to radiation exposure, i.e., the alpha index (I_α), the radium equivalent activity (Ra_{eq}), the absorbed γ-dose rate (D), and the annual effective dose equivalent outdoors ($AEDE_{out}$) as well as indoors ($AEDE_{in}$). Moreover, measurements of the average heavy metals (arsenic, cadmium, copper, mercury, nickel, lead, antimony, thallium, and zinc) concentrations in the analyzed sample were performed by using inductively coupled plasma mass spectrometry (ICP-MS). Furthermore, with the aim to investigate any possible chemical pollution, the enrichment factor (EF), the geo-accumulation index (Igeo), the contamination factor (CF), and the pollution load index (PLI) were assessed. Finally, the identification of the source of the aforementioned radioisotopes of natural origin was carried out by X-ray diffraction (XRD), thus identifying the major mineralogical phases present in the investigated basalt aggregate for concrete [1–3].

The article titled "Verification of Estimated Cosmic Neutron Intensities Using a Portable Neutron Monitoring System in Antarctica" has the following featured application: a portable neutron-monitoring system that can be effectively applied to the verification of models used for estimating cosmic radiation intensities over a wide range of altitudes in a harsh environment, such as in Antarctica. Moreover, many ongoing studies for predicting the production rates of cosmogenic nuclides, forecasting changes in atmospheric compositions and climate, assessing the cosmic radiation exposure of aircraft crew and the effects on precise electronic devices, use numerical models that estimate cosmic radiation intensities in the atmosphere. Periodic verifications of these models are desirable to be performed for assuring the reliability of the study outcomes. Here, authors investigated an application of a portable neutron-monitoring system composed of an extended energy range neutron monitor and a small data logger for the monitoring of cosmic neutron intensities in a polar region. As a result of measurements in the East Antarctica region covering a wide range of altitudes (from 30 m to 3762 m), as well as comparisons with the model calculations performed with an analytical model based on comprehensive Monte Carlo simulations (PARMA), it was demonstrated that the portable neutron-monitoring system could be effectively applied to the periodic verification of cosmic neutron intensities that would improve the reliability of related studies [4,5].

In the research paper titled "Multivariate Statistical Analyses and Potentially Toxic Elements Pollution Assessment of Pyroclastic Products from Mt. Etna, Sicily, Southern Italy", potentially toxic element contamination, which represents a universal problem of major concern, due to several adverse health effects on human beings when permissible concentration levels are overcome, was investigated. In this sense, the assessment of potentially risky elements' contents in different environmental matrices plays a key role in the safeguarding of the quality of the environment, and thus of strictly correlated public health. In this article, measurements of the average potentially toxic element concentrations in pyroclastic products from Mt. Etna, Eastern Sicily, and Southern Italy were performed together with a comparison with the allowable levels set by Italian legislation, with the aim of evaluating the level of toxicity imposed on the ecosystem. For this purpose, inductively coupled plasma mass spectrometry (ICP-MS) measurements were performed to investigate any possible chemical pollution by potentially risky elements, via the application of different indices such as the enrichment factor (EF), the geo-accumulation index (I_{geo}), the contamination factor (CF), and the pollution load index (PLI). Finally, a multivariate statistical analysis was performed by processing potentially toxic element contents and pollution indices. It is worth noting that the approach used could be applied, in principle, to the evaluation of chemical risk due to the presence of potentially toxic elements in a large variety of samples of particular environmental interest, and can constitute a guideline for investigations focused on the monitoring of environmental quality [6–8].

In the article "Estimation of Cosmic-Ray-Induced Atmospheric Ionization and Radiation at Commercial Aviation Flight Altitudes", the main source of the ionization of the Earth's atmosphere, i.e., the cosmic radiation that depends on solar activity as well as geomagnetic activity, was investigated. Galactic cosmic rays constitute a permanent radiation background and contribute significantly to the radiation exposure inside the atmosphere. In this work, the cosmic-ray-induced ionization of the Earth's atmosphere, due to both solar and galactic cosmic radiation during the recent solar cycles, 23 (1996–2008) and 24 (2008–2019), was studied globally. Estimations of the ionization were based on the CRAC:CRII model produced by the University of Oulu. The use of this model allowed for extensive calculations from the Earth's surface (atmospheric depth of 1033 g/cm^2) to the upper limit of the atmosphere (atmospheric depth of 0 g/cm^2). Monte Carlo simulations were performed for the estimation quantities of radiobiological interest with the validated software DYASTIMA/DYASTIMA-R. This study was focused on specific altitudes of interest, such as the common flight levels used in commercial aviation [9,10].

The main topic of the article titled "Natural and Anthropogenic Radioactivity Content and Radiation Hazard Assessment of Baby Food Consumption in Italy" is the natural (^{40}K) and anthropogenic (^{137}Cs) radioactivity concentration in four different typologies of early childhood (up to two years old) foods, i.e., homogenized fruit, homogenized meat, childhood biscuits, and baby pasta, produced in Italy and sold in Italian large retailers, investigated via high-purity germanium (HPGe) gamma spectrometry. The present study was carried out with the aim of (i) evaluating the background levels of the investigated radionuclides in the analyzed early childhood foods, (ii) identifying whether the twenty analyzed samples were appropriate for infant consumption, and (iii) contributing to the construction of a database on the radioactivity of early childhood foods sold in Italy [11,12].

The paper "A New Methodological Approach for the Assessment of the ^{238}U Content in Drinking Water" deals with the radiological quality of drinking water, directly associated with the health of the population. Indeed, it is well known that the presence of radionuclides in drinking water constitutes a health risk for humans because the consumption of such water increases the likelihood of incurring cancer. For this reason, all of the studies aimed at developing new methodologies for the qualitative and quantitative analysis of the radioisotopic composition of drinking water are absolutely desired by the international scientific community, as well as by the institutes that deal with the protection of public health. In this paper, a new methodological approach was developed for the evaluation of ^{238}U content in drinking water. A sample from Paola, Calabria region, Southern Italy, was taken as a case study. The assessment was performed by using high-purity germanium (HPGe) gamma ray spectrometry, with the aim of quantifying the specific activity of the ^{234m}Pa radioisotope after a preconcentration procedure, and thus to assess the activity concentration of ^{238}U, in a hypothesis of the secular radioactive equilibrium between it and its daughter. The obtained results were validated via a comparison with the ^{238}U (µg/L) concentration as measured through inductively coupled plasma mass spectrometry (ICP-MS) [13,14].

In the paper "Monte Carlo Simulation-Based Calculations of Complex DNA Damage for Incidents of Environmental Ionizing Radiation Exposure", the authors present a useful Monte Carlo (MC)-based methodology that can be utilized to calculate the absorbed dose and the initial levels of complex DNA damage (such as double-strand breaks—DSBs) in cases of an environmental ionizing radiation (IR) exposure incident (REI), i.e., a nuclear accident. The objective was to assess the doses and complex DNA damage by isolating only one component of the total radiation released in the environment after an REI that will affect the health of an exposed individual; more specifically, the radiation emitted by radionuclide ^{137}Cs in the ground (under an individual's feet). The authors used a merging of the Monte Carlo N-particle transport (MCNP) code with the Monte Carlo damage simulation (MCDS) code. The DNA lesions were estimated through simulations for different surface activities of a ^{137}Cs ground-based γ radiation source. The energy spectrum of the emitted secondary electrons and the absorbed dose in typical mammalian cells were calculated via the use of the MCNP code, and these data are then used as an input in the MCDS code for the estimation of critical DNA damage levels and types. As a realistic application, the calculated dose was also used to assess the excess lifetime cancer risk (ELCR) for eight hypothetical individuals, living in different zones around the Chernobyl Nuclear Power Plant, exposed to different time periods on the days of the accident in 1986. The authors concluded that any exposition of an individual in the near zone of Chernobyl increases the risk of cancer at a moderate to high grade, also connected with the induction of complex DNA damage via radiation. Generally, this methodology has been proven to be useful for assessing γ-ray-induced complex DNA damage levels of the exposed population in the case of an REI, and for better understanding the long-term health effects of the exposure of the population to IR [15,16].

The article titled "Natural Radioactivity and Radon Exhalation from Building Materials in Underground Parking Lots" is focused on the change in natural ionizing radiation and the radon exhalation rates from typical building materials in underground parking lots. The activity concentration of natural radionuclides ^{232}Th, ^{226}Ra, and ^{40}K in six important types of construction materials, which are mostly used in Lithuania, were analyzed via the use of high-resolution gamma spectroscopy. The highest values were found in concrete and ferroconcrete samples, and a strong positive correlation (0.88) was observed between radium activity concentration and radon concentration. The activity indices (I_α and I_γ) and radium equivalent activity (Ra_{eq}), evaluating the suitability of materials for such constructions from the view of radiation safety, were determined. The average values of the calculated absorbed dose rate in samples ranged from 18.24 nGy h^{-1} in the sand to 87.26 nGy h^{-1} in ferroconcrete. The calculated annual effective dose was below the limit of 1.0 mSv y^{-1}. The values of the external and internal hazard indices (H_{ex} and H_{in}) were all below unity, and the values of I_γ and I_α were below the recommended levels of 0.5 and 1. A dosimetric analysis of underground parking lots was carried out. It was determined that the external equivalent dose rate caused by ^{222}Rn progeny radiation in the underground car parking lots varied from 17 to 30% of the total equivalent dose rate [17,18].

The main topic of the paper "Evaluation of the Radiological and Chemical Risk for Public Health from Flour Sample Investigation" is an investigation on flour, in terms of physical and chemical pollutants as well as mineral content; these are of great interest, in view of flour's high consumption for nutritional purposes. In this study, eleven types of flour (five samples for each one), from large retailers and employed by people for different food cooking purposes, were investigated through high-purity germanium (HPGe) gamma spectrometry in order to estimate natural (^{40}K)- and anthropogenic (^{137}Cs)-radioisotope-specific activity and, thus, to assess radiological risk due to flour ingestion. Inductively coupled plasma mass spectrometry (ICP-MS) and inductively coupled plasma emission spectroscopy (ICP-OES) were also employed to evaluate any possible heavy metal contamination and the mineral composition, as well as to perform a multivariate statistical analysis to deduce the flour authenticity. The evaluation of dose levels due to flour ingestion was performed for the age category higher than 17 years, taking into account the average yearly consumption in Italy and assuming this need to be satisfied from a single type of flour as a precaution. All of the obtained results are under the allowable level set by Italian legislation (1 mSv y^{-1}), thus excluding the risk of ionizing radiation effects on humans. As far as heavy metal contamination is concerned, Cd and Pb concentrations were seen to be lower than the threshold values, thus excluding their presence as pollutants. Finally, the multivariate statistical analysis allowed the unambiguous correlation of flour samples with their botanical origins, according to their elemental concentrations [19–21].

Finally, the research paper "Assessment of Natural Radioactivity and Radiological Risks in River Sediments from Calabria (Southern Italy)" was developed to carry out a comprehensive radiological assessment of natural radioactivity for river sediment samples from Calabria, Southern Italy, and to define a baseline background for the area on a radiation map. In the studied area, elevated levels of natural radionuclides were expected due to the outcropping acidic intrusive and metamorphic rocks from which the radioactive elements derive. To identify and quantify the natural radioisotopes, ninety river sediment samples from nine selected coastal sampling points (ten samples for each point) were collected as representative of the Ionian and the Tyrrhenian coastline of Calabria. The samples were analyzed via the use of a gamma ray spectrometer equipped with a high-purity germanium (HPGe) detector. The values of mean activity concentrations of ^{226}Ra, ^{232}Th, and ^{40}K measured for the studied samples are (21.3 ± 6.3) Bq kg^{-1}, (30.3 ± 4.5) Bq kg^{-1}, and (849 ± 79) Bq kg^{-1}, respectively. The calculated radiological hazard indices showed average values of 63 nGy h^{-1} (absorbed dose rate), 0.078 mSv y^{-1} (effective dose outdoors), 0.111 mSv y^{-1} (effective dose indoors), 63 Bq kg^{-1} (radium equivalent), 0.35 (Hex), 0.41 (Hin), 0.50 (activity concentration index), and 458 µSv y^{-1} (annual gonadal equivalent dose, AGED). In order to delineate the spatial distribution of natural radionuclides on the radiological map and to identify the areas with low, medium, and high radioactivity values, Surfer 10 software was employed. Finally, a multivariate statistical analysis was performed to deduce the interdependency and any existing relationships between the radiological indices and the concentrations of the radionuclides. The results of this study, also compared with values of other locations of the Italian Peninsula characterized by similar local geological conditions, can be used as a baseline for future investigations of the radioactivity backgrounds of investigated areas [22–24].

Conflicts of Interest: The author declares no conflict of interest.

References

1. Torrisi, L.; Caridi, F.; Giuffrida, L. Protons and ion acceleration from thick targets at 10^{10} W/cm^2 laser pulse intensity. *Las. and Part. Beams* **2011**, *29*, 29–37. [CrossRef]
2. Caridi, F.; Marguccio, S.; Durante, G.; Trozzo, R.; Fullone, F.; Belvedere, A.; D'Agostino, M.; Belmusto, G. Natural radioactivity measurements and dosimetric evaluations in soil samples with a high content of NORM. *Eur. Phys. J. Plus* **2017**, *132*, 56. [CrossRef]
3. Caridi, F.; Paladini, G.; Marguccio, S.; Belvedere, A.; D'Agostino, M.; Messina, M.; Crupi, V.; Venuti, V.; Majolino, D. Evaluation of Radioactivity and Heavy Metals Content in a Basalt Aggregate for Concrete from Sicily, Southern Italy: A Case Study. *Appl. Sci.* **2023**, *13*, 4804. [CrossRef]

4. Caridi, F.; Torrisi, L.; Mezzasalma, A.M.; Mondio, G.; Borrielli, A. Al$_2$O$_3$ plasma production during pulsed laser deposition. *Eur. Phys. Jour. D* **2009**, *54*, 467–472. [CrossRef]
5. Yasuda, H.; Kurita, N.; Yajima, K. Verification of Estimated Cosmic Neutron Intensities Using a Portable Neutron Monitoring System in Antarctica. *Appl. Sci.* **2023**, *13*, 3297. [CrossRef]
6. Caridi, F.; D'Agostino, M.; Messina, M.; Marcianò, G.; Grioli, L.; Belvedere, A.; Marguccio, S.; Belmusto, G. Lichens as environmental risk detectors. *Eur. Phys. J. Plus* **2017**, *132*, 189. [CrossRef]
7. Caridi, F.; Paladini, G.; Venuti, V.; Procopio, S.; Iannone, M.; Crupi, V.; Majolino, D. A New Radiological Risk Containment Procedure in Potentially Contaminated Areas. *Appl. Sci.* **2022**, *12*, 32. [CrossRef]
8. Caridi, F.; Paladini, G.; Mottese, A.F.; Messina, M.; Venuti, V.; Majolino, D. Multivariate Statistical Analyses and Potentially Toxic Elements Pollution Assessment of Pyroclastic Products from Mt. Etna, Sicily, Southern Italy. *Appl. Sci.* **2022**, *12*, 9889. [CrossRef]
9. Margarone, D.; Torrisi, L.; Borrielli, A.; Caridi, F. Silver plasma by pulsed laser ablation. *Pl. Sour. Sci. and Techn.* **2008**, *17*, 035019. [CrossRef]
10. Makrantoni, P.; Tezari, A.; Stassinakis, A.N.; Paschalis, P.; Gerontidou, M.; Karaiskos, P.; Georgakilas, A.G.; Mavromichalaki, H.; Usoskin, I.G.; Crosby, N.; et al. Estimation of Cosmic-Ray-Induced Atmospheric Ionization and Ra-diation at Commercial Aviation Flight Altitudes. *Appl. Sci.* **2022**, *12*, 5297. [CrossRef]
11. Mottese, A.F.; Fede, M.R.; Caridi, F.; Sabatino, G.; Marcianò, G.; Calabrese, G.; Albergamo, A.; Dugo, G. Chemometrics and innovative multidimensional data analysis (MDA) based on multi-element screening to protect the Italian porcino (Boletus sect. Boletus) from fraud. *Food Control.* **2020**, *110*, 107004. [CrossRef]
12. Caridi, F.; Paladini, G.; Venuti, V.; Spoto, S.E.; Crupi, V.; Belmusto, G.; Majolino, D. Natural and Anthropogenic Radioactivity Content and Radiation Hazard Assessment of Baby Food Consumption in Italy. *Appl. Sci.* **2022**, *12*, 5244. [CrossRef]
13. Caridi, F.; Messina, M.; D'Agostino, M. An investigation about natural radioactivity, hydrochemistry, and metal pollution in groundwater from Calabrian selected areas, southern Italy. *Environ. Earth Sci.* **2017**, *76*, 668. [CrossRef]
14. Caridi, F.; Paladini, G.; Venuti, V.; Crupi, V.; Spoto, S.E.; Marguccio, S.; D'Agostino, M.; Belvedere, A.; Majolino, D. A New Methodological Approach for the Assessment of the ^{238}U Content in Drinking Water. *Appl. Sci.* **2022**, *12*, 3380. [CrossRef]
15. Caridi, F.; Torrisi, L.; Margarone, D.; Borrielli, A. Investigations on low temperature laser-generated plasmas. *Las. and Part. Beams* **2008**, *26*, 265–271. [CrossRef]
16. Kalospyros, S.A.; Gika, V.; Nikitaki, Z.; Kalamara, A.; Kyriakou, I.; Emfietzoglou, D.; Kokkoris, M.; Georgakilas, A.G. Monte Carlo Simulation-Based Calculations of Complex DNA Damage for Incidents of Environmental Ionizing Radiation Exposure. *Appl. Sci.* **2021**, *11*, 8985. [CrossRef]
17. Torrisi, L.; Margarone, D.; Borrielli, A.; Caridi, F. Ion and photon emission from laser-generated titanium-plasma. *Appl. Surf. Sci.* **2008**, *254*, 4007–4012. [CrossRef]
18. Jasaitis, D.; Pečiulienė, M. Natural Radioactivity and Radon Exhalation from Building Materials in Underground Parking Lots. *Appl. Sci.* **2021**, *11*, 7475. [CrossRef]
19. Albergamo, A.; Mottese, A.F.; Bua, G.D.; Caridi, F.; Sabatino, G.; Barrega, L.; Costa, R.; Dugo, G. Discrimination of the Sicilian Prickly Pear (*Opuntia ficus-indica* L., CV. Muscaredda) According to the Provenance by Testing Unsupervised and Supervised Chemometrics. *J. Food Sci.* **2018**, *83*, 2933–2942. [CrossRef]
20. Torrisi, L.; Caridi, F.; Margarone, D.; Borrielli, A. Plasma-laser characterization by electrostatic mass quadrupole analyzer. *Nucl. Instr. and Meth. B* **2008**, *266*, 308–315. [CrossRef]
21. Caridi, F.; Acri, G.; Belvedere, A.; Crupi, V.; D'agostino, M.; Marguccio, S.; Messina, M.; Paladini, G.; Venuti, V.; Majolino, D. Evaluation of the Radiological and Chemical Risk for Public Health from Flour Sample Investigation. *Appl. Sci.* **2021**, *11*, 3646. [CrossRef]
22. Picciotto, A.; Krasa, J.; Laska, L.; Rohlena, K.; Torrisi, L.; Gammino, S.; Mezzasalma, A.M.; Caridi, F. Plasma temperature and ion current analysis of gold ablation at different laser power rates. *Nucl. Instr. and Meth. B* **2006**, *247*, 261–267. [CrossRef]
23. Caridi, F.; Marguccio, S.; Belvedere, A.; Belmusto, G.; Marcianò, G.; Sabatino, G.; Mottese, A. Natural radioactivity and elemental composition of beach sands in the Calabria region, south of Italy. *Environ. Earth Sci.* **2016**, *75*, 629. [CrossRef]
24. Caridi, F.; Di Bella, M.; Sabatino, G.; Belmusto, G.; Fede, M.R.; Romano, D.; Italiano, F.; Mottese, A.F. Assessment of Natural Radioactivity and Radiological Risks in River Sediments from Calabria (Southern Italy). *Appl. Sci.* **2021**, *11*, 1729. [CrossRef]

Disclaimer/Publisher's Note: The statements, opinions and data contained in all publications are solely those of the individual author(s) and contributor(s) and not of MDPI and/or the editor(s). MDPI and/or the editor(s) disclaim responsibility for any injury to people or property resulting from any ideas, methods, instructions or products referred to in the content.

Article

Evaluation of Radioactivity and Heavy Metals Content in a Basalt Aggregate for Concrete from Sicily, Southern Italy: A Case Study

Francesco Caridi [1,*], Giuseppe Paladini [1], Santina Marguccio [2], Alberto Belvedere [2], Maurizio D'Agostino [2], Maurizio Messina [2], Vincenza Crupi [1], Valentina Venuti [1,*] and Domenico Majolino [1]

[1] Dipartimento di Scienze Matematiche e Informatiche, Scienze Fisiche e Scienze della Terra, Università degli Studi di Messina, Viale F. Stagno D'Alcontres 31, 98166 Messina, Italy; gpaladini@unime.it (G.P.); vcrupi@unime.it (V.C.); dmajolino@unime.it (D.M.)

[2] Agenzia Regionale per la Protezione dell'Ambiente della Calabria (ARPACal)-Dipartimento di Reggio Calabria, Via Troncovito SNC, 89135 Reggio Calabria, Italy; s.marguccio@arpacal.it (S.M.); a.belvedere@arpacal.it (A.B.); m.dagostino@arpacal.it (M.D.); m.messina@arpacal.it (M.M.)

* Correspondence: fcaridi@unime.it (F.C.); vvenuti@unime.it (V.V.)

Abstract: In the present paper, an investigation on the natural and anthropic radioactivity and heavy metals content in a basalt aggregate for concrete from Sicily, Southern Italy, was performed as a case study. In particular, the evaluation of the specific activity of radium-226, thorium-232, potassium-40 and caesium-137 radionuclides was performed by using High-Purity Germanium (HPGe) γ-ray spectrometry, together with the estimation of several indexes developed to evaluate the radiological risk for the population related to radiation exposure, i.e., the alpha index (I_α), the radium equivalent activity (Ra_{eq}), the absorbed γ-dose rate (D) and the annual effective dose equivalent outdoor ($AEDE_{out}$) and indoor ($AEDE_{in}$). Moreover, measurements of the average heavy metals (arsenic, cadmium, copper, mercury, nickel, lead, antimony, thallium and zinc) concentrations in the analyzed sample were performed by using Inductively Coupled Plasma Mass Spectrometry (ICP-MS). Furthermore, with the aim to investigate any possible chemical pollution, the Enrichment Factor (EF), Geo-accumulation Index (I_{geo}), Contamination Factor (CF) and Pollution Load Index (PLI) were assessed. Finally, the identification of the source of the aforementioned radioisotopes of natural origin was carried out by X-ray diffraction (XRD), thus identifying the major mineralogical phases present in the investigated basalt aggregate for concrete.

Keywords: basalt aggregate for concrete; radioactivity; radiological risk; mineralogy; HPGe γ-ray spectrometry; heavy metals; pollution; inductively coupled plasma mass spectrometry; X-ray diffraction

Citation: Caridi, F.; Paladini, G.; Marguccio, S.; Belvedere, A.; D'Agostino, M.; Messina, M.; Crupi, V.; Venuti, V.; Majolino, D. Evaluation of Radioactivity and Heavy Metals Content in a Basalt Aggregate for Concrete from Sicily, Southern Italy: A Case Study. *Appl. Sci.* **2023**, *13*, 4804. https://doi.org/10.3390/app13084804

Academic Editor: Nikolaos Koukouzas

Received: 13 March 2023
Revised: 4 April 2023
Accepted: 8 April 2023
Published: 11 April 2023

Copyright: © 2023 by the authors. Licensee MDPI, Basel, Switzerland. This article is an open access article distributed under the terms and conditions of the Creative Commons Attribution (CC BY) license (https://creativecommons.org/licenses/by/4.0/).

1. Introduction

Basalt is the most widespread magmatic or igneous effusive rock. With andesite, another type of volcanic rock, it makes up almost all, about 98%, of the rocks made up of the lava that erupted on the Earth's surface and was then subjected to a process of crystallization. Generally, when not greatly weathered, basalt has colorations that from dark gray can tend to black [1]. For several years, it has been employed in casting procedures to produce ceramic plates and panels for architectural purposes [2]. In addition, fused basalt coatings for iron pipes show an extremely high abrasion strength in manufacturing operations [3]. Basalt is also used in many countries in the construction of highway and airport pavements [4], and it also finds application in organic farming, in the form of micronized rock flour, to revitalize and nourish soils and plants that have lost fertility, such as intensive and extensive farming that deplete soils of natural elements [5].

Furthermore, fragmented basalt aggregates, which are compact, finely grained, very dark green or black rocks produced when melted lava from the depths of the Earth's crust ascends and crystallizes, are also recognized as a natural resource for the manufacturing of cheap and eco-friendly construction materials with acceptable strength and durability features, well suited to the framework of sustainable development [6,7]. In detail, the partial replacement of Portland cement with basalt aggregates in concrete, when available, can lead to a more cost-efficient solution [8].

Basaltic rock in Italy can be found close to the Mt. Etna volcano (eastern Sicily, Southern Italy) [9], the edifice of which grew on a sedimentary substrate more than 1.5 km thick [10]. The origin of Mt. Etna's magmatism is probably related to extensive melting of the mantle, according to what is reported in [11].

In the present paper, a multi-technique approach including the use of High-Purity Germanium (HPGe) γ-ray spectrometry, Inductively Coupled Plasma Mass Spectrometry (ICP-MS) and X-ray diffraction (XRD) was employed with the aim to evaluate the radioactivity (radium-226, thorium-232, potassium-40 and caesium-137) and the heavy metals (arsenic, cadmium, copper, mercury, nickel, lead, antimony, thallium and zinc) content of the investigated basalt aggregate for concrete, picked up in a surrounding area of the Mt. Etna volcano [12], and to relate the natural radionuclides' specific activity to its mineralogical composition.

Furthermore, in order to assess any possible radiological hazard for the population, the calculation of the alpha index (I_α), the radium equivalent activity (Ra_{eq}), the absorbed γ-dose rate (D) and the annual effective dose equivalent outdoor ($AEDE_{out}$) and indoor ($AEDE_{in}$) was performed [13–15]. Of note, in Italy, the current legislation states that building materials or additives of natural igneous origin are subject to radiometric checking before being placed on the commercial market [16].

Finally, with the aim to estimate the level of environmental chemical pollution by the heavy metals, the Enrichment Factor (EF), Geo-accumulation Index (I_{geo}), Contamination Factor (CF) and Pollution Load Index (PLI) were assessed [17,18].

2. Materials and Methods

2.1. Sample Collection

The GPS coordinates of the specimen location are 37.53247 (latitude) and 15.037817 (longitude) (Figure 1).

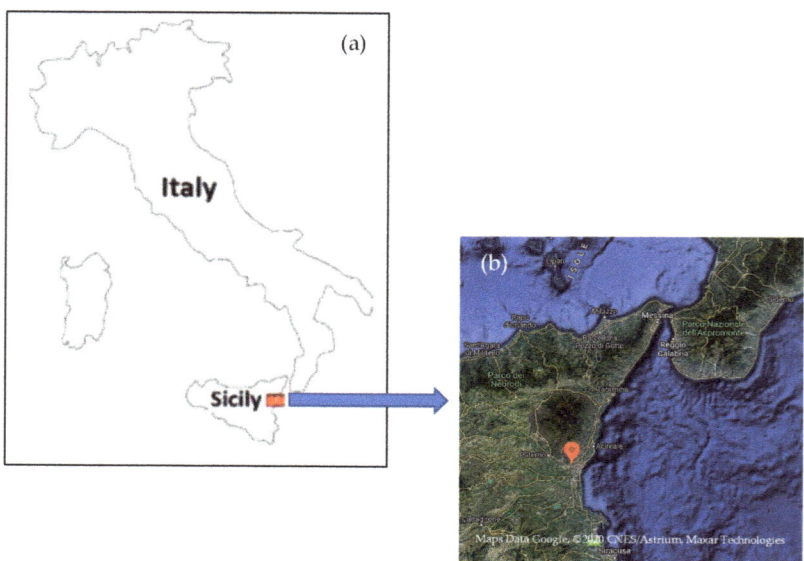

Figure 1. The sampling area (**a**), with the specimen location indicated (**b**).

Five aliquots of the basalt aggregate for concrete were collected in February 2022, from basalt outcrops, at depths of a few centimeters, and reduced to a coarse grain size by mechanical procedures. The sampling was performed from a relatively flat, clean, dry, hard surface, avoiding locations where surface dust or salts are likely to have accumulated.

After the collection, they were stored in labeled plastic containers, with proper precautions taken to avoid contamination [19], and subsequently transported to the laboratory.

2.2. HPGE γ-ray Spectrometry Measurements

Each aliquot of the basalt aggregate for concrete was first dried, in order to completely remove the moisture and to obtain constant mass. After, it was inserted into a Marinelli hermetically sealed container of 250 mL capacity. After 40 days, the secular radioactive equilibrium between ^{226}Ra and its daughter products was reached, and then the sample was ready for gamma spectrometry measurement with a live time of 70,000 s. Spectra were analyzed with the aim to assess the activity concentration of ^{226}Ra, ^{232}Th, ^{40}K and ^{137}Cs. In detail, the ^{226}Ra activity concentration was calculated by using the 295.21 keV and 351.92 keV ^{214}Pb and 1120.29 keV ^{214}Bi gamma-ray lines, and the ^{232}Th-specific activity was determined by using the 911.21 keV and 968.97 keV ^{228}Ac γ-ray lines. In particular, for the ^{214}Bi radionuclide, the TCS coincidence summation correction was applied [20] by using the MEFFTRAN code [21]. Continuing, for ^{40}K, the evaluation was performed from its γ-line at 1460.8 keV and, finally, in order to investigate the anthropic radioactivity content, the ^{137}Cs-specific activity was evaluated through its γ-line at 661.66 keV.

The experimental set-up was composed of a positive biased Ortec HPGe detector (GEM), whose operating parameters are reported in Table 1 [22].

Table 1. The HPGe GEM operating parameters.

HPGe GEM	
Parameter	Value
Full Width at Half Maximum	1.85 keV
Peak-to-Compton ratio	64:1
Relative Efficiency	40% (at the 1.33 MeV ^{60}Co γ-line)
Bias Voltage	4500 V
Energy Range	50 keV–2 MeV

The detector was located inside lead wells to screen the environmental background radioactivity and, for efficiency and energy settings, a multi-peak Marinelli γ-source (BC-4464) of 250 mL capacity, energy range 60–1836 keV, custom made to replicate the exact designs of the specimens in a water-equivalent epoxy–resin matrix, was employed.

The Gamma Vision (Ortec) software was used for data acquisition and analysis [22].

The specific activity (Bq kg^{-1} dry weight, d.w.) of the investigated radioisotopes was calculated as follows [23]:

$$C = \frac{N_E}{\varepsilon_E t \gamma_d M} \quad (1)$$

where N_E is the net area of a peak at energy E; ε_E and γ_d are the efficiency and yield of the photopeak at energy E, respectively; M is the mass of the sample (kg); and t is the live time (s) [24]. Moreover, with the density of the basalt aggregate for concrete being higher than 1.1, the self-absorption correction on the activity concentration value was performed according to [25,26].

The Italian Accreditation Body (ACCREDIA) certified the quality of the γ-ray spectrometry experimental results [27], thus ensuring continuous verification that the performance properties of the method are preserved [28].

2.3. Evaluation of the Radiological Health Risk

Several indexes developed over the years to evaluate the radiological risk for the human beings related to radiation exposure, i.e., the alpha index (I_α), the radium equivalent activity (Ra_{eq}), the absorbed γ-dose rate (D) and the annual effective dose equivalent outdoor ($AEDE_{out}$) and indoor ($AEDE_{in}$), were calculated to estimate the potential radiation risk to humans.

2.3.1. Alpha Index

The alpha index was calculated with the following formula [29]:

$$I_\alpha = C_{Ra}/200 \qquad (2)$$

where C_{Ra} is the mean activity concentrations of radium-226 in the basalt aggregate for concrete.

The alpha index allows to assess the alpha radiation exposure to the indoor radon exhaled from construction materials. The activity concentration of radium-226 must be lower than 200 Bq kg^{-1}, to prevent exposure to indoor radon-specific activity higher than the threshold value of 200 Bq m^{-3} [16], and then I_α must be less than unity for the risk of exposure to radiation to be minimal.

2.3.2. Radium Equivalent Activity

The radium equivalent activity is an index that describes the specific activities of radium-226, thorium-232 and potassium-40 in a single term [30,31]:

$$Ra_{eq} \text{ (Bq kg}^{-1}) = C_{Ra} + 1.43 C_{Th} + 0.077 C_K \qquad (3)$$

where C_{Ra}, C_{Th} and C_K are the mean activity concentrations of radium-226, thorium-232 and potassium-40 in the basalt aggregate for concrete, respectively.

This index must be lower than 370 Bq kg^{-1} for the safe utilization of the basalt aggregate for concrete as building material [32].

2.3.3. Absorbed γ-Dose Rate

This parameter was calculated with the following formula [33]:

$$D \text{ (nGy h}^{-1}) = 0.462 C_{Ra} + 0.604 C_{Th} + 0.0417 C_K \qquad (4)$$

2.3.4. Annual Effective Dose Equivalent Outdoor and Indoor

The annual effective dose equivalent for an individual was calculated using the equations below, with occupation factors of 20% and 80% for outdoor and indoor environments, respectively [34]:

$$AEDE_{out} \text{ (mSv y}^{-1}) = D \text{ (nGy h}^{-1}) \times 8760 \text{ h} \times 0.7 \text{ Sv Gy}^{-1} \times 0.2 \times 10^{-6} \qquad (5)$$

$$AEDE_{in} \text{ (mSv y}^{-1}) = D \text{ (nGy h}^{-1}) \times 8760 \text{ h} \times 0.7 \text{ Sv Gy}^{-1} \times 0.8 \times 10^{-6} \qquad (6)$$

Both must be lower than 1 mSv y^{-1} for the radiological health risk to be negligible [16].

2.4. Inductively Coupled Plasma Mass Spectrometry (ICP-MS) Measurements

For the ICP-MS analysis, approximately 0.5–1.0 g of sample, together with 3 mL of ultrapure (for trace analysis) HNO_3 (67–69%) and 9 mL of ultrapure (for trace analysis) HCl (32–35%) (aqua regia), was directly introduced into a 100 mL TFM vessel. A Milestone microwave system, Ethos 1, was used for the acid digestion, as follows: (i) 15 min at 1500 W and 180 °C; (ii) 10 min at 1500 W and 180 °C; (iii) 10 min at 1000 W and 120 °C, with 20 min cooling [35]. The mixture was filtered and filled to 50 mL with distilled H_2O and diluted

10 times. Opportune dilutions of two certified materials were employed in order to prepare calibration solutions for the analytes in 0.5 % (v/v) HNO_3 and 0.5 % (v/v) HCl [18].

For the measurements, a Thermo Scientific iCAP Qc ICP-MS was used [36]. The instrument was operated in a single collision cell mode, with kinetic energy discrimination (KED), using pure He as the collision gas. All samples were presented for analysis using a Cetac ASX-520.

2.5. Evaluation of the Level of Heavy Metals Contamination

In order to assess the level of heavy metals contamination in the basalt aggregate for concrete, the pollution indices reported in the following were calculated.

2.5.1. The Enrichment Factor

This index was evaluated as follows [37]:

$$\text{EF} = \frac{\{C_x/C_{Fe}\}\text{sample}}{\{C_x/C_{Fe}\}\text{reference}} \quad (7)$$

where C_x is the concentration of the potential enrichment element and C_{Fe} is the concentration of the normalizing element, usually iron [37].

2.5.2. The Geo-Accumulation Index

This pollution index is [38]:

$$I_{geo} = \text{Log}_2[C_n/(kB_n)] \quad (8)$$

where C_n is the concentration of the potential harmful element in the sample, B_n is the geochemical background value in the average shale of element n and k is the correction factor of the background matrix [38].

2.5.3. The Contamination Factor

This index is given by [39]

$$\text{CF} = C_{metal}/C_{background} \quad (9)$$

where C_{metal} and $C_{background}$ are the heavy metals concentration and background values, respectively [38].

2.5.4. The Pollution Load Index

The n-th root of the product of the Contamination Factor of heavy metals is the Pollution Load Index [40]:

$$\text{PLI} = (\text{CF}_1 \times \text{CF}_2 \times \text{CF}_3 \times \ldots \times \text{CF}_n)^{1/n} \quad (10)$$

where n is the number of metals [40].

2.6. XRD Analysis

X-ray diffraction analyses were performed by using a Panalytical Empyrean Diffractometer with Cu K_α radiation on a Bragg–Brentano theta-theta goniometer, equipped with a solid-state detector, PIXcel [41].

The generator settings were 40 kV and 40 mA. The measurements were performed in glass slide holders ensuring a uniform dispersion of properly compressed specimens. The continuous scan mode was employed in order to span the 2Θ incidence angle from 5° to 60° with a scan velocity of 1.2° per minute. The total runtime for each analysis was about 45 min.

The observed peak positions were then compared with reference spectra from RRUFF database, with the aim to identify the crystalline mineralogical constituents of the analyzed basalt aggregate for concrete [42].

3. Results and Discussion

3.1. The Specific Activity of the Radioisotopes

The average specific activity (the mean value of the 5 analyzed aliquots) of radium-226, thorium-232, potassium-40 and caesium-137, in the investigated basalt aggregate for concrete, was found to be (58.6 ± 6.6) Bq kg^{-1} dry weight (d.w.), (40.7 ± 5.3) Bq kg^{-1} d.w., (498 ± 57) Bq kg^{-1} d.w. and lower than the minimum detectable activity (0.24 Bq kg^{-1} d.w.), respectively. Table 2 reports the radium-226-, thorium-232-, potassium-40- and caesium-137-specific activity in the five analyzed aliquots, together with the average values.

Table 2. The specific activity C_{Ra}, C_{Th}, C_K and C_{Cs} of, respectively, ^{226}Ra, ^{232}Th, ^{40}K and ^{137}Cs, in the five analyzed aliquots, together with the average values.

Aliquot ID	C_{Ra} (Bq kg^{-1} d.w.)	C_{Th} (Bq kg^{-1} d.w.)	C_K (Bq kg^{-1} d.w.)	C_{Cs} (Bq kg^{-1} d.w.)
1	53.6 ± 6.1	36.4 ± 4.9	498 ± 57	<0.18
2	63.6 ± 7.1	44.9 ± 5.7	510 ± 66	<0.24
3	58.6 ± 6.6	35.7 ± 5.1	491 ± 50	<0.21
4	61.9 ± 6.8	45.7 ± 5.5	505 ± 64	<0.27
5	55.3 ± 6.4	40.7 ± 5.3	486 ± 48	<0.30
Average	58.6 ± 6.6	40.7 ± 5.3	498 ± 57	<0.24

The worldwide average specific activity of radium-226, thorium-232 and potassium-40 is 35, 30 and 400 Bq kg^{-1}, respectively [32]. In light of this, the experimental results here reported show that, in our case, the average specific activity of all the detected radioisotopes is higher than the average worldwide value. These results need a more critical interpretation, which will be provided further below in terms of the mineralogical composition of the basalt aggregate for concrete itself.

Regarding caesium-137, the mean specific activity turned out to be lower than the minimum detectable activity, ruling out an anthropic contamination.

3.2. Radiological Hazard Effects Assessment

With reference to the values of the radiological hazard indices, the alpha index, obtained by using Equation (2), was found to be 0.29, less than unity and thus avoiding exposure to the indoor radon concentration of more than 200 Bq m^{-3}. The radium equivalent activity was calculated through Equation (3) with the aim to ascertain the suitability of the investigated basalt aggregate for concrete for use as a structural material component. The obtained value was 155 Bq kg^{-1}, lower than 370 Bq kg^{-1}, set as the threshold limit for building materials, thus ensuring again that the analyzed sample may not be harmful if employed for civil construction.

The absorbed γ-dose rate, as obtained through Equation (4), was found to be equal to 65.3 nGy h^{-1}, a value attributable to the lithologic component of the sampling site [43], and it was used to evaluate, through Equations (5) and (6), the annual effective dose equivalent outdoor and indoor due to the activities of the radium-226, thorium-232 and potassium-40 in the investigated sample. The obtained values were 88.8 μSv y^{-1} and 355 μSv y^{-1}, respectively, lower than the threshold value of 1 mSv y^{-1} [16].

3.3. Heavy Metals Content

Table 3 reports the heavy metals content (mg kg^{-1} d.w.) for the analyzed basalt aggregate for concrete.

Table 3. Heavy metals content (mg kg^{-1} d.w.) for the analyzed basalt aggregate for concrete.

	ICP-MS Analysis	
		Threshold limit
C_{As}	0.87	20
C_{Cd}	0.03	2
C_{Cu}	70.8	120
C_{Hg}	0.04	1
C_{Ni}	9.09	120
C_{Pb}	8.90	100
C_{Sb}	0.06	10
C_{Tl}	0.02	1
C_{Zn}	50.1	150

Of note, the obtained results are lower than the threshold limits [44]; hence, they can be regarded as no pollutants and do not compromise the well-being of the environment.

3.4. Evaluation of the Heavy Metals Contamination Level

3.4.1. EF

In agreement with [45], an EF < 2 indicates minimal enrichment. In particular, 0.5 < EF < 1.5 shows a natural-origin metal, while EF > 1.5 suggests a more likely anthropic one [45]. Moreover, the values between 2 and 5 indicate moderate enrichment; between 5 and 20, significant enrichment; between 20 and 40, high enrichment; and an EF higher than 40, extremely high enrichment.

The obtained EF values, reported in Table 4, were found to be <2 in all cases, indicating no or minimal enrichment.

Table 4. Calculated values of EF, I_{geo}, CF and PLI for the investigated sample.

Metal	Index of Contamination			
	EF	I_{geo}	CF	PLI
As	0.07	−4.49	0.07	
Cd	0.10	−3.91	0.10	
Cu	1.58	0.07	1.57	
Hg	0.10	−3.91	0.10	
Ni	0.13	−3.49	0.13	0.14
Pb	0.45	−1.75	0.45	
Sb	0.04	−5.23	0.04	
Tl	0.01	−6.71	0.01	
Zn	0.53	−1.51	0.53	

3.4.2. I_{geo}

The I_{geo} values must be interpreted as follows [46]:

$I_{geo} \leq 0$ denotes no contamination;
For $0 < I_{geo} \leq 1$, no/a medium degree of contamination;
For $1 < I_{geo} \leq 2$, a medium degree of contamination;
For $2 < I_{geo} \leq 3$, a medium/high degree of contamination;
For $3 < I_{geo} \leq 4$, a high degree of contamination;
For $4 < I_{geo} \leq 5$, a high/very high degree of contamination;
$I_{geo} > 5$, a very high degree of contamination.

The obtained I_{geo} values, reported in Table 4, were found to be <0 with the only exception being copper, probably because it is often used as a soil defense product, as well as the soil texture and its high pH [46,47].

3.4.3. CF

According to [47], a CF ≤ 1 indicates no contamination; 1 < CF ≤ 3, a low or medium degree of contamination; 3 < CF ≤ 6, a high degree of contamination; and CF > 6, a very high degree of contamination.

The obtained CF values, reported in Table 4, are <1 in all cases except copper, showing again a very moderate degree of contamination for this metal.

3.4.4. PLI

According to [48], a PLI value higher than 1 indicates chemical pollution.

In our case, the PLI was found to be <1, thus revealing no pollution by the investigated heavy metals.

3.5. XRD Analysis

The X-ray diffraction analysis result is shown in Figure 2.

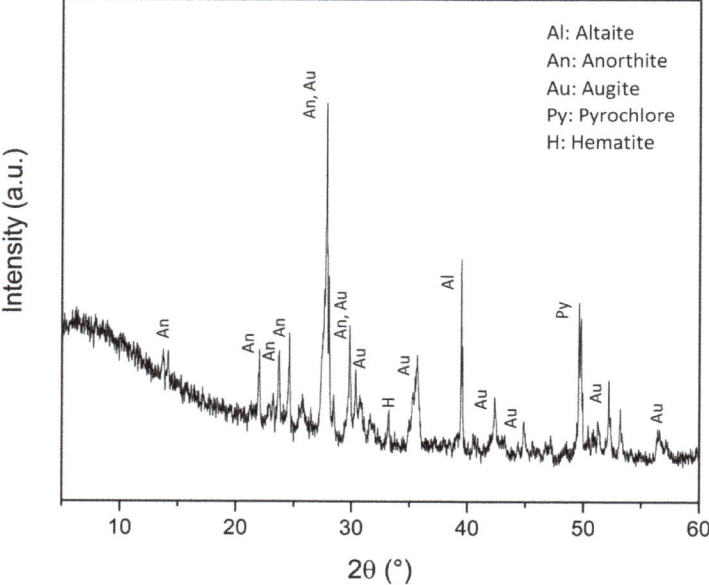

Figure 2. The X-ray diffraction analysis of the investigated basalt aggregate for concrete.

Minerals recognition was performed by comparing the measured diffraction peak positions to the RRUFF database. An XRD analysis put in evidence the presence of Altaite (PbTe, RRUFF ID: R060939), Anorthite (Ca(Al$_2$Si$_2$O$_8$), RRUFF ID: R040059), Augite ((Ca,Mg,Fe)$_2$Si$_2$O$_6$, RRUFF ID: R061108), Pyrochlore ((Na,Ca)2Nb2O6(OH,F), RRUFF ID: R060151) and Hematite (Fe$_2$O$_3$, RRUFF ID: R040024), superimposed to a glassy groundmass, in the investigated basalt aggregate for concrete.

Of note, we can reliably hold the detected mineralogical phases to account for the radionuclides content previously discussed. In particular, the high specific activity of radium-226, thorium-232 and potassium-40 radioisotopes, if compared with the average worldwide value, can be explained taking into account that, from the diffractogram, it is possible to evince in particular the presence of pyrochlore, in the composition of which

Niobium appears. This REE represents an element that, from a geochemical point of view, is a marker of occurrence of crustal contamination, i.e., a migration of isotopes of various elements from the Earth's crust to the magma, which then solidified and became basalt [49,50]. Therefore, in light of this, it is possible to justify the specific activity values of the detected natural radioisotopes, which are higher than the average worldwide value in all cases [51].

4. Conclusions

The natural and anthropic radioactivity content of a basalt aggregate for concrete from Sicily, Southern Italy, was analyzed through High-Purity Germanium (HPGe) γ-ray spectrometry. Moreover, calculations of the alpha index (I_α), the radium equivalent activity (Ra_{eq}), the absorbed γ-dose rate (D) and the annual effective dose equivalent outdoor ($AEDE_{out}$) and indoor ($AEDE_{in}$) were performed in order to estimate the radiological hazard for human beings. Of note, the obtained values turned out to be lower than the maximum recommended ones for humans, thereby rationally excluding any significant health impact related to exposure to ionizing radiation. Additionally, the mean specific activity of caesium-137 turned out to be lower than the minimum detectable activity.

Next, the concentration levels of the heavy metals in the analyzed basalt aggregate for concrete were investigated through Inductively Coupled Plasma Mass Spectrometry (ICP-MS). The resulting values were found to be below the threshold levels established by Italian legislation and thus do not reasonably represent a health risk to humans. In addition, the calculation of various pollution indices was carried out in order to assess the ecological risk from heavy metals imposed on the ecology of the ecosystem. The obtained results show a very minimal enrichment only for copper, probably due to the use of this metal as a soil defense product, as well as the soil texture and its high pH, and in general no pollution by the assessed heavy metals.

Finally, X-ray diffraction (XRD) was applied to recognize the mineralogical/geochemical composition of the investigated sample and to relate it to the natural radioactivity content. From the results, we can conclude that the analyzed basalt aggregate for concrete was characterized by the presence of Altaite, Anorthite, Augite, Pyrochlore and Hematite, superimposed to a glassy groundmass. Moreover, the natural radionuclides' specific activity reported in the present study underlined a high value of the activity concentration of radium-226, thorium-232 and potassium-40 radionuclides with respect to the average worldwide value. This can be explained by the occurrence of crustal contamination, put in evidence by the presence, in the diffractogram, of pyrochlore, in the composition of which Niobium appears.

Author Contributions: Conceptualization, F.C. and V.V.; methodology, F.C. and G.P.; validation, D.M.; formal analysis, A.B., M.D., S.M. and M.M.; investigation, F.C. and V.V.; resources, F.C. and V.C.; data curation, F.C.; writing—original draft preparation, F.C.; supervision, D.M. and V.V. All authors have read and agreed to the published version of the manuscript.

Funding: This research received no external funding.

Institutional Review Board Statement: Not applicable.

Informed Consent Statement: Not applicable.

Conflicts of Interest: Authors declare no conflict of interest.

References

1. Reino, W.; Pucha, G.; Recalde, C.; Tene, T.; Cadena, P. Occurrence of radioactive materials in pyroclastic flows of Tungurahua volcano using gamma spectrometry. *AIP Conf. Proc.* **2018**, *2003*, 020014. [CrossRef]
2. Kerur, B.; Tanakanti, R.; Basappa, D.; Kumar, A.; Narayani, K.; Rekha, A.; Hanumaiah, B. Radioactivity levels in rocks of North Karnataka, India. *Indian J. Pure Appl. Phys.* **2010**, *48*, 809–812.
3. Malczewski, D.; Dziurowicz, M.; Kalab, Z.; Rösnerová, M. Natural radioactivity of rocks from the historic Jeroným Mine in the Czech Republic. *Environ. Earth Sci.* **2021**, *80*, 650. [CrossRef]

4. Faanu, A.; Adukpo, O.K.; Tettey-Larbi, L.; Lawluvi, H.; Kpeglo, D.O.; Darko, E.O.; Emi-Reynolds, G.; Awudu, R.A.; Kansaana, C.; Amoah, P.A.; et al. Natural radioactivity levels in soils, rocks and water at a mining concession of Perseus gold mine and surrounding towns in Central Region of Ghana. *Springerplus* **2016**, *5*, 98. [CrossRef]
5. Conceição, L.T.; Silva, G.N.; Holsback, H.M.S.; Oliveira, C.d.F.; Marcante, N.C.; Martins, É.d.S.; Santos, F.L.d.S.; Santos, E.F. Potential of basalt dust to improve soil fertility and crop nutrition. *J. Agric. Food Res.* **2022**, *10*, 100443. [CrossRef]
6. Caridi, F.; Torrisi, L.; Mezzasalma, A.M.; Mondio, G.; Borrielli, A. Al$_2$O$_3$ plasma production during pulsed laser deposition. *Eur. Phys. Journ. D* **2009**, *54*, 467–472. [CrossRef]
7. Zagorodnyuk, L.H.; Mestnikov, A.E.; Makhortov, D.S.; Akhmed, A.A.A. Mixed binders with the use of volcanic ash. *Lect. Notes Civ. Eng.* **2021**, *95*, 9–15. [CrossRef]
8. Ahmedai, M.A.; Ahmed, S.A.; Ahmed, Y.H.; Ibrahiem, E.S.M. Tagabo Volcanic Ash as Cement Replacing Materials. *FES J. Eng. Sci.* **2021**, *9*, 35–39. [CrossRef]
9. Chester, D.K.; Duncan, A.M.; Guest, J.E.; Kilburn, C.R.J. Mount Etna. The Anatomy of a Volcano. *Geol. Mag.* **1986**, *123*, 463–464. [CrossRef]
10. Tanguy, J.-C.; Condomines, M.; Kieffer, G. Evolution of the Mount Etna magma: Constraints on the present feeding system and eruptive mechanism. *J. Volcanol. Geotherm. Res.* **1997**, *75*, 221–250. [CrossRef]
11. Gvirtzman, Z.; Nur, A. The formation of Mount Etna as the consequence of slab rollback. *Nature* **1999**, *401*, 782–785. [CrossRef]
12. Kozłowska, B.; Walencik-łata, A.; Giammanco, S.; Immè, G.; Catalano, R.; Mangano, G. Radioactivity of mt. Etna volcano and radionuclides transfer to groundwater. *Ann. Geophys.* **2019**, *62*, 1–12. [CrossRef]
13. Caridi, F.; D'Agostino, M.; Messina, M.; Marcianò, G.; Grioli, L.; Belvedere, A.; Marguccio, S.; Belmusto, G. Lichens as environmental risk detectors. *Eur. Phys. J. Plus* **2017**, *132*, 189. [CrossRef]
14. Caridi, F.; D'Agostino, M.; Belvedere, A.; Marguccio, S.; Belmusto, G. Radon radioactivity in groundwater from the Calabria region, south of Italy. *J. Instrum.* **2016**, *11*, P05012. [CrossRef]
15. Avwiri, G.O.; Egieya, J.M. Radiometric assay of hazard indices and excess lifetime cancer risk due to natural radioactivity in soil profile in Ogba/Egbema/Ndoni local government area of Rivers state, Nigeria. *Acad. Res. Int.* **2013**, *4*, 54–65.
16. Italian Legislation D.Lgs. 101/20. Available online: https://www.normattiva.it/ (accessed on 20 February 2023).
17. Caridi, F.; Messina, M.; D'Agostino, M. An investigation about natural radioactivity, hydrochemistry, and metal pollution in groundwater from Calabrian selected areas, southern Italy. *Environ. Earth Sci.* **2017**, *76*, 668. [CrossRef]
18. Mottese, A.F.; Fede, M.R.; Caridi, F.; Sabatino, G.; Marcianò, G.; Calabrese, G.; Albergamo, A.; Dugo, G. Chemometrics and innovative multidimensional data analysis (MDA) based on multi-element screening to protect the Italian porcino (Boletus sect. Boletus) from fraud. *Food Control* **2020**, *110*, 107004. [CrossRef]
19. Stewart, C.; Horwell, C.; Plumlee, G.; Cronin, S.; Delmelle, P.; Baxter, P.; Calkins, J.; Damby, D.; Morman, S.; Oppenheimer, C. *Protocol for Analysis of Volcanic Ash Samples for Assessment of Hazards from Leachable Elements*; International Volcanic Health Hazard Network Publisher: Durham, UK, 2013; pp. 1–22.
20. Agarwal, C.; Chaudhury, S.; Goswami, A.; Gathibandhe, M. True coincidence summing corrections in point and extended sources. *J. Radioanal. Nucl. Chem.* **2011**, *289*, 773–780. [CrossRef]
21. Available online: https://efftran.github.io/ (accessed on 20 February 2023).
22. Caridi, F.; Marguccio, S.; Durante, G.; Trozzo, R.; Fullone, F.; Belvedere, A.; D'Agostino, M.; Belmusto, G. Natural radioactivity measurements and dosimetric evaluations in soil samples with a high content of NORM. *Eur. Phys. J. Plus* **2017**, *132*, 56. [CrossRef]
23. Caridi, F.; Messina, M.; Belvedere, A.; D'Agostino, M.; Marguccio, S.; Settineri, L.; Belmusto, G. Food salt characterization in terms of radioactivity and metals contamination. *Appl. Sci.* **2019**, *9*, 2882. [CrossRef]
24. Caridi, F.; Di Bella, M.; Sabatino, G.; Belmusto, G.; Fede, M.R.; Romano, D.; Italiano, F.; Mottese, A.F. Assessment of Natural Radioactivity and Radiological Risks in River Sediments from Calabria (Southern Italy). *Appl. Sci.* **2021**, *11*, 1729. [CrossRef]
25. Caridi, F.; Marguccio, S.; Belvedere, A.; D'Agostino, M.; Belmusto, G. A methodological approach to a radioactive sample analysis with low-level γ-ray spectrometry. *J. Instrum.* **2018**, *13*, P09022. [CrossRef]
26. Torrisi, L.; Caridi, F.; Margarone, D.; Borrielli, A. Plasma-laser characterization by electrostatic mass quadrupole analyzer. *Nucl. Instr. Meth. Phys. Res. B* **2008**, *266*, 308–315. [CrossRef]
27. ACCREDIA. Available online: https://www.accredia.it/ (accessed on 13 February 2023).
28. Caridi, F.; D'Agostino, M.; Belvedere, A. Radioactivity in calabrian (Southern Italy) wild boar meat. *Appl. Sci.* **2020**, *10*, 3580. [CrossRef]
29. Xinwei, L. Radioactivity level in Chinese building ceramic tile. *Radiat. Prot. Dosim.* **2004**, *112*, 323–327. [CrossRef]
30. Caridi, F.; Testagrossa, B.; Acri, G. Elemental composition and natural radioactivity of refractory materials. *Environ. Earth Sci.* **2021**, *80*, 170. [CrossRef]
31. Caridi, F.; Paladini, G.; Venuti, V.; Crupi, V.; Procopio, S.; Belvedere, A.; D'agostino, M.; Faggio, G.; Grillo, R.; Marguccio, S.; et al. Radioactivity, metals pollution and mineralogy assessment of a beach stretch from the ionian coast of calabria (Southern italy). *Int. J. Environ. Res. Public Health* **2021**, *18*, 12147. [CrossRef]
32. United Nations Scientific Committee on the Effects of Atomic Radiation. *Sources and Effects of Ionizing Radiation: Report to the General Assembly, with Scientific Annexes*; United Nations Scientific Committee on the Effects of Atomic Radiation: Vienna, Austria, 2000; Volume I, ISBN 92-1-142238-8.

33. Caridi, F.; Marguccio, S.; Belvedere, A.; Belmusto, G.; Marcianò, G.; Sabatino, G.; Mottese, A. Natural radioactivity and elemental composition of beach sands in the Calabria region, south of Italy. *Environ. Earth Sci.* **2016**, *75*, 629. [CrossRef]
34. Caridi, F.; D'Agostino, M.; Belvedere, A.; Marguccio, S.; Belmusto, G.; Gatto, M.F. Diagnostics techniques and dosimetric evaluations for environmental radioactivity investigations. *J. Instrum.* **2016**, *11*, C10012. [CrossRef]
35. Hassan, N.M.; Rasmussen, P.E.; Dabek-Zlotorzynska, E.; Celo, V.; Chen, H. Analysis of Environmental Samples Using Microwave-Assisted Acid Digestion and Inductively Coupled Plasma Mass Spectrometry: Maximizing Total Element Recoveries. *Water. Air. Soil Pollut.* **2007**, *178*, 323–334. [CrossRef]
36. Thermo Fisher. *iCAP Q Operating Manual*; Thermo Fisher: Waltham, MS, USA, 2012.
37. Turekian, K.K.; Haven, N.; Hans, K.; Universitat, W.M. Der Distribution of the Elements in Some Major Units of the Earth's Crust. *America* **1961**, *72*, 175–192.
38. Håkanson, L. An Ecological Risk Index for Aquatic Pollution Control—A Sedimentological Approach. *Water Res.* **1980**, *14*, 975–1001. [CrossRef]
39. Chandrasekaran, A.; Ravisankar, R.; Harikrishnan, N.; Satapathy, K.K.; Prasad, M.V.R.; Kanagasabapathy, K.V. Multivariate statistical analysis of heavy metal concentration in soils of Yelagiri Hills, Tamilnadu, India–Spectroscopical approach. *Spectrochim. Acta Part A Mol. Biomol. Spectrosc.* **2015**, *137*, 589–600. [CrossRef]
40. Ramasamy, V.; Meenakshisundaram, V.; Venkatachalapathy, R.; Ponnusamy, V. Influence of mineralogical and heavy metal composition on natural radionuclide concentrations in the river sediments. *Appl. Radiat. Isot.* **2011**, *69*, 1466–1474. [CrossRef]
41. Malvern Panalytical. *Empyrean Diffractometer User Manual*; Malvern Panalytical: Malvern, UK, 2013.
42. Available online: https://rruff.info (accessed on 20 February 2023).
43. Morelli, D.; Immé, G.; Cammisa, S.; Catalano, R.; Mangano, G.; La Delfa, S.; Patanè, G. Radioactivity measurements in volcano-tectonic area for geodynamic process study. *Eur. Phys. J. Web Conf.* **2012**, *24*, 05009.
44. D. Lgs. 152/2006. Available online: https://www.normattiva.it/ (accessed on 20 February 2023).
45. Zheng, L.-G.; Liu, G.-J.; Kang, Y.; Yang, R.-K. Some potential hazardous trace elements contamination and their ecological risk in sediments of western Chaohu Lake, China. *Environ. Monit. Assess.* **2010**, *166*, 379–386. [CrossRef]
46. Karimi, B.; Masson, V.; Guilland, C.; Leroy, E.; Pellegrinelli, S.; Giboulot, E.; Maron, P.-A.; Ranjard, L. Ecotoxicity of copper input and accumulation for soil biodiversity in vineyards. *Environ. Chem. Lett.* **2021**, *19*, 2013–2030. [CrossRef]
47. Pietrzak, U.; McPhail, D.C. Copper accumulation, distribution and fractionation in vineyard soils of Victoria, Australia. *Geoderma* **2004**, *122*, 151–166. [CrossRef]
48. Naji, A.; Ismail, A. Assessment of Metals Contamination in Klang River Surface Sediments by using Different Indexes. *Environ. Asia* **2011**, *4*, 30–38. [CrossRef]
49. Gołuchowska, K.; Barker, A.K.; Manecki, M.; Majka, J.; Kośmińska, K.; Ellam, R.M.; Bazarnik, J.; Faehnrich, K.; Czerny, J. The role of crustal contamination in magma evolution of Neoproterozoic metaigneous rocks from Southwest Svalbard. *Precambrian Res.* **2022**, *370*, 106521. [CrossRef]
50. Catalano, S.; Torrisi, S.; Ferlito, C. The relationship between Late Quaternary deformation and volcanism of Mt. Etna (eastern Sicily): New evidence from the sedimentary substratum in the Catania region. *J. Volcanol. Geotherm. Res.* **2004**, *132*, 311–334. [CrossRef]
51. Li, X.; Li, J.; Bader, T.; Mo, X.; Scheltens, M.; Chen, Z.; Xu, J.; Yu, X.; Huang, X. Evidence for crustal contamination in intra-continental OIB-like basalts from West Qinling, central China: A Re–Os perspective. *J. Asian Earth Sci.* **2015**, *98*, 436–445. [CrossRef]

Disclaimer/Publisher's Note: The statements, opinions and data contained in all publications are solely those of the individual author(s) and contributor(s) and not of MDPI and/or the editor(s). MDPI and/or the editor(s) disclaim responsibility for any injury to people or property resulting from any ideas, methods, instructions or products referred to in the content.

Article

Verification of Estimated Cosmic Neutron Intensities Using a Portable Neutron Monitoring System in Antarctica

Hiroshi Yasuda [1,*], Naoyuki Kurita [2] and Kazuaki Yajima [3]

[1] Department of Radiation Biophysics, Research Institute for Radiation Biology and Medicine, Hiroshima University, Hiroshima 734-8553, Japan
[2] Institute for Space-Earth Environmental Research, Nagoya University, Nagoya 464-8601, Japan
[3] National Institutes of Quantum Science and Technology, National Institute of Radiological Sciences (QST–NIRS), Chiba 263-8555, Japan
* Correspondence: hyasuda@hiroshima-u.ac.jp

Featured Application: A portable neutron-monitoring system can be effectively applied to verification of the models used for estimating cosmic radiation intensities over a wide range of altitudes in a harsh environment such as in Antarctica.

Abstract: Many ongoing studies for predicting the production rates of cosmogenic nuclides, forecasting changes of atmospheric compositions and climate, assessing the cosmic-radiation exposure of aircraft crew, and the effects on precise electronic devices use numerical models that estimate cosmic-radiation intensities in the atmosphere. Periodic verifications of those models are desirable to be performed for assuring the reliability of the study outcomes. Here, we investigated an application of a portable neutron-monitoring system composed of an extended-energy-range neutron monitor and a small data logger for monitoring of cosmic-neutron intensities in a polar region. As a result of measurements in the east Antarctica region covering a wide range of altitudes (from 30 m to 3762 m) and comparisons with the model calculations performed with an analytical model based on comprehensive Monte Carlo simulations (PARMA), it was demonstrated that the portable neutron-monitoring system could be effectively applied for periodic verification of cosmic-neutron intensities that would improve the reliability of related studies.

Keywords: Antarctica; cosmic rays; atmosphere; radiation detector; neutron measurement; portable monitoring system

1. Introduction

Primary cosmic radiations or cosmic rays are composed of highly energetic particles, mainly protons. Those particles can be classified by origin to two main components: galactic cosmic rays (GCRs) that come from outside our solar system and solar energetic particles (SEPs) that originate from an eruptive process on the sun. The high-energy cosmic-ray particles that enter the Earth's atmosphere cause nuclear spallation reactions with atmospheric atoms, mainly oxygen or nitrogen atoms, in the stratosphere and the upper troposphere. The electromagnetic cascades produce various secondary radiations such as electrons, pions, neutrons, etc.

These nuclear reactions also produce many cosmogenic nuclides such as ^{3}H, ^{7}Be, ^{10}Be, ^{14}C, and ^{36}Cl that fall out onto the ground with almost constant rates. Those nuclides provide useful information related to geoscience, and much research has actively been performed in the relevant field [1–5]. Particularly, cosmogenic nuclides in snow and ice in polar regions at high geomagnetic latitudes can tell us about the long history of solar activities, including extreme solar particle events that affect cosmic radiation intensities and resultant cosmogenic production rates [6–8]. Production rates of cosmogenic nuclides in the earth's atmosphere have been estimated by model calculations, and many models have been developed for this purpose over the past 70 years. The first models [9–11] were based on simplified functions expressing the cosmic-ray-induced cascade process. Since the 1980s, Monte Carlo simulation codes were developed to describe the stochastic process of the spallation reactions in more detail [12–17]. In addition, an analytical model based on comprehensive Monte Carlo simulations has been lately developed [18,19].

Cosmic radiation can change the physical–chemical properties of the atmosphere, such as ion balance and temperature, and may subsequently affect regional climate variability [20–23]. It has been considered that ionizations induced by cosmic radiation in the atmosphere contribute to the production of many ions that are followed by various reaction processes that may cause different climate parameters. More accurate prediction of long-term climate change needs a more reliable model that can precisely describe the atmospheric ionization processes in the atmosphere, especially in the polar regions.

Aside from the effects on the atmospheric compositions, direct exposure of humans to cosmic radiation at high altitude has become a subject in view of health [24]. According to the fact that the dose level of the cosmic radiation is elevated with altitude and reaches a level about 100 times higher at the cruising altitude of a commercial jet aircraft than that on the ground, the International Commission on Radiological Protection (ICRP) has recommended that exposure to cosmic radiation of aircraft crew should be managed as an occupational exposure [25,26]. ICRP recommended in a recent publication [27] that frequent flyers also be informed of their dose levels in aviation. Following these recommendations, the individual doses received from cosmic radiation onboard aircraft have been assessed by using numerical models. Several easy-to-use program tools for aviation-dose calculations were developed based on those models and have been provided by different groups. Those are CARI [28], PCAIRE [29], SIEVERT [30], AVIDOS [31], EPCARD [32], JISCARD EX [33], and other models [34]. Periodic verification of the accuracies of those programs including intercomparisons [35,36] is crucially important for reliable dose assessments of aircraft crew and frequent flyers.

Furthermore, there are concerns about possible errors by many avionic electronic systems during a flight due to the hits by cosmic radiation, particularly high-energy neutrons [37,38]. A secondary high-energy neutron collides with an atom of the semiconductor, which produces an ionization charge that can cause an unfavorable reaction of a semiconductor device. To prepare adequately for such errors, a reliable, well-verified model that can predict the probabilities of the hits is needed.

Regarding observations of cosmic radiation intensities related to the fields above, ground-based neutron monitors have played an important role for up to 70 years. The ground-based neutron monitors detect secondary particles produced in the atmosphere as a product of spallation reactions caused by primary cosmic-ray particles. While two types of standardized detectors (IGY and NM64) are generally operated, both types consist of gas-filled proportional counters surrounded by a moderator, lead producer, and reflector [39]. The incident cosmic protons and neutrons cause nuclear reactions in the lead, and the secondary neutrons slow down by the moderator, and thermal-energy neutrons are detected by the proportional counter tubes. Many stations of the ground-based neutron monitors were built worldwide since the 1950s and have been operated for space sciences and space weather applications [40]. The monitoring data acquired at these stations are publicly available in some repositories and data sources to observe the cosmic-ray variations and incident energetic solar particles, and also to estimate the global-scale change of cut-off rigidity, i.e., the minimum magnetic rigidity that a vertically incident particle can have and still reach a given location above the Earth [18].

While the ground-based neutron monitors have provided accurate and stable data, these large-scale instruments can hardly be carried and thus have been employed for fixed-point observations. It should be noted that, in addition to the solar activities and global geomagnetic field condition, local meteorological factors as well as the atmospheric pressure, such as clouds and snowfall, could affect the cosmic-radiation intensities at a specific site. Moreover, a notable change in the Earth's geomagnetic field originating from the core has lately been observed [41,42]. According to the awareness on the spatial variation of cosmic-radiation intensity, we have investigated the application of a portable neutron-monitoring system composed of an extended-energy-range neutron monitor and a small data logger for model verifications, with the on-site measurements covering a wide area of interest. The designed monitoring system is preferably to be tested in a polar region where the cosmic-radiation intensities are the highest on the Earth.

2. Materials and Methods
2.1. Locations of Measurements

Measurements of cosmic neutrons were performed from a coastal to a plateau region in East Antarctica where the Japanese crew usually conducts their activities. A snow vehicle with the instruments for neutron measurement left Syowa Station (69.0° S, 39.6° E) in the coastal area in November 2018, moved to Dome Fuji Station (77.5° S, 37.5° E) at 3765 m in altitude in the inland area, and then back to the Syowa Station in January 2019. This period was in the solar minimum. The neutron measurements along the inward (coast to inland) route were performed at 16 locations from 17 November 2018 to 7 December 2018, and those along the outward route were performed at 17 locations from 31 December 2018 to 19 January 2019. The time for monitoring at each location ranged from 7.2 h to 88 h. The locations of these measurements are shown with circle points in Figure 1.

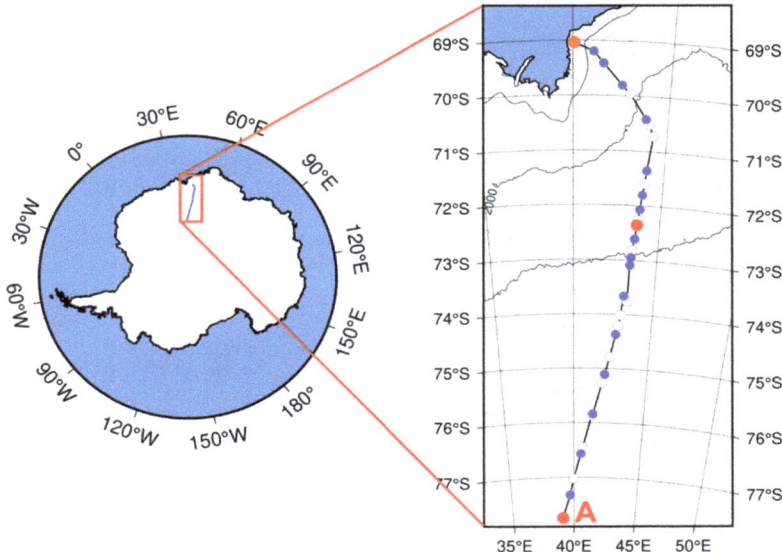

Figure 1. Locations in the Antarctica Continent where the measurements of cosmic neutrons were performed with a portable neutron monitor (WENDI-II) from November 2018 to January 2019. The points on the inward route are indicated with blue, those on the outward with white. The time for monitoring at each location was more than 7 h. Long-term stays were made at three points shown in red; among them, a continuous neutron monitoring for about 20 days was performed at the end of the inward route near Dome Fuji Station (location A).

In addition to the repetitive measurements along the inward and outward routes, long-term monitoring for about 20 days was performed at the end point of the route (location A in Figure 1); the measured data were recorded with 12 h intervals at these fixed-point measurements.

2.2. Methods of Measurements

For cosmic-neutron measurements, we employed an extended energy-range rem meter coupled with a tungsten-powder-mixed moderator (FHT762 Wendi-2, Thermo Fisher Scientific K.K., Franklin, MA, USA). WENDI-II has functions of continuously counting the pulses generated from the ^{3}He(n, α)Li reaction with moderated thermal neutrons and calculating the hourly rate of 1 cm ambient dose equivalent, H*(10), multiplying the one-hour integrated pulse counts and a constant conversion coefficient. Selected properties of WENDI-II are indicated in Table 1. More details on the dosimetric properties of WENDI-II were presented by Olsher et al. [43,44].

Table 1. Selected properties of the portable neutron monitor WENDI-II.

Detector	φ2.5 cm ^{3}He Proportional Counter
Moderator	Polyethylene with tungsten powder shell
Applicable neutron energy	0.025 eV to 5 GeV
Applicable temperature range	−30 °C to 50 °C
Applicable atmospheric pressure	500 hPa to 1500 hPa
Dimensions	φ23 cm × H32 cm
Weight	13.5 kg

WENDI-II has been employed by the authors for measurements of cosmic neutrons on high mountains and onboard aircraft [45–49] and was carefully calibrated with the monitoring data acquired through the repeated neutron measurements at the high-altitude station at Mt. Fuji (altitude: 3776 m) in Japan [46,48]. It was confirmed that WENDI-II had negligibly low sensitivity to photons from ^{60}Co and ^{137}Cs sources and thus its threshold for n/γ discrimination was set as a default value. In addition, its negligible response to energetic protons (~230 MeV) was roughly confirmed at the Heavy Ion Medical Accelerator in Chiba (HIMAC) in Japan.

WENDI-II was connected to a small, battery-powered data logger (NM10) with dimensions of W21 cm × H6.6 cm × D16 cm and weight of 2.4 kg. NM10 was originally made by the authors for long-term mobile use in recording the pulse counts from WENDI-II with adjustable time intervals [45,49]. A set of WENDI-II and NM10 was placed on the desk near a front window of the snow vehicle (Figure 2) over the whole monitoring period. The signals of neutron-induced pulses from WENDI-II were automatically recorded by NM10 with 1 h intervals and converted to the hourly H*(10) rates. The temperature at the location where the neutron-monitoring system was placed varied from −10 °C to 20 °C during the measurement period (i.e., November 2018 to January 2019); this variation was within the temperature-applicable range of WENDI-II (−30 °C to 50 °C) indicated in Table 1.

Figure 2. A photograph of the snow vehicle (left) and the portable neutron monitor (WENDI-II) connected to an exclusive data logger (NM10) (right) originally made for mobile use. The neutron monitor was placed near the front window inside the snow vehicle.

2.3. Model Calculation

For discussion about the effectiveness of the portable neutron-monitoring system in comparison with model estimates, we employed a recent model named "PHITS-based Analytical Radiation Model in the Atmosphere (PARMA)" [18,19], which was originally developed in Japan and has been incorporated into the program (JISCARD EX) for calculating the crew doses of selected Japanese airlines [33]. Those companies have responsibility for calculations of individual doses of aircraft crew from cosmic radiation to keep their annual doses below 5 mSv y^{-1} by voluntary efforts; they are also requested to prepare for an additional dose increase due to a solar flare by utilizing possible prediction measures such as space weather forecasts.

The PARMA comprises several theoretical or empirical functions with parameters whose numerical values were fitted through the least square method to the results of the comprehensive Monte Carlo air-shower simulations performed by using the Particle and Heavy Ion Transport code System (PHITS) [50] coupled with the Japanese Evaluated Nuclear Data Library/High Energy file (JENDL/HE), which contains differential cross-sections of neutrons and protons over a wide range of energy up to 3 GeV [51]. In the air-shower simulation, cosmic rays were assumed to be incident from the top of the Earth's atmosphere, i.e., from the altitude of 86 km. Though the atmospheric atoms slightly exist over 86 km actually, it was judged that the effects of such a high-altitude atmosphere had little influence on the spallation reactions. As incident particles, the protons and heavy ions of galactic cosmic rays (GCRs) with energies up to 1 TeV per nucleon and charges up to 28 (nickel) were considered. The GCR fluxes at 1 astronomical unit (1 AU, around the Earth) were obtained from their local interstellar (LIS) fluxes considering the modulation due to the solar-wind magnetic field, so-called solar modulation. Effects of the solar modulation were evaluated from the count rates of several neutron monitors located all over the world, using the force-field formalism.

According to its analytical calculation procedures, PARMA can instantaneously estimate terrestrial cosmic-ray fluxes of neutrons, protons, and ions with charge up to 28 (nickel), muons, electrons, positrons, and photons anywhere in the Earth's atmosphere; the covered energy ranges are from 0.01 eV to 100 GeV for neutrons and from 1 keV to 100 GeV for other major particles such as protons, helium ions (per nucleon), muons, electrons, positrons, and photons. While the first version of PARMA was applicable to 20 km or lower in altitude [18], the lately updated version can deal with a wider altitude of nearly the top of the atmosphere [19].

3. Results and Discussions

3.1. Time Change of Neutron Dose Rates

Figure 3 shows the time change of atmospheric pressure measured with a barometer and neutron-dose rates measured with WENDI-II near Dome Fuji Station (77.735° S, 39.114° E, 3762 m in altitude; location A in Figure 1). Each plot was obtained as an average of continuous measurements at the same location for 12 h. Total counts of neutron pulses at each location were around 7000, and thus the standard deviation of each value was derived as less than 2%. A clear, inverse correlation was observed between the neutron-dose rate and atmospheric pressure, which was considered to result from the nuclear spallation reactions with atmospheric atoms such as nitrogen and oxygen. The fact that this relationship was confirmed even for a small fluctuation (~10 hPa) of atmospheric pressure indicates that the employed portable system (WENDI-II and NM10) can be appropriately used for on-site monitoring of cosmic neutrons in Antarctica.

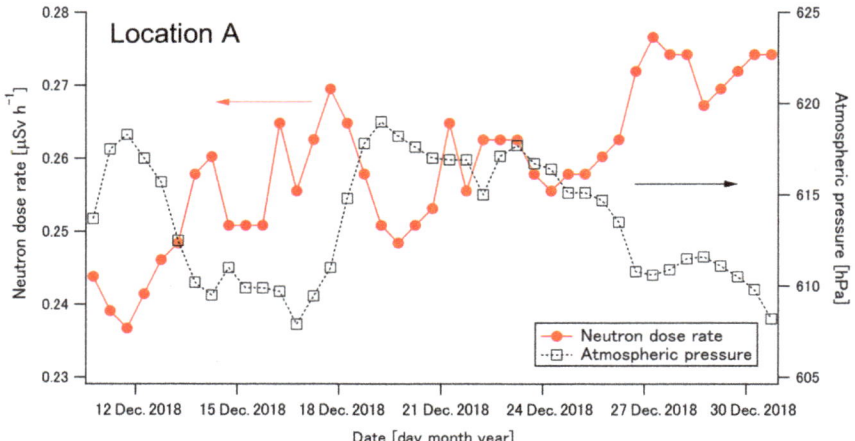

Figure 3. Time course of the neutron dose rate measured with WENDI-II (circle marker/solid line) and atmospheric pressure (square marker/dotted line) measured with a barometer near Dome Fuji Station (location A in Figure 1) at 3762 m in altitude in December 2018. The standard deviation of each dose-rate plot was less than 2%.

3.2. Neutron Dose Rates as a Function of Atmospheric Pressure

Figure 4 shows the relationships of the measured neutron dose rates versus the barometric atmospheric pressures along the inward and outward routes between the areas near Syowa Station and near Dome Fuji Station in the period from 18 November 2018 to 23 January 2019. The counts of neutron signals obtained at each plot ranged from 1300 (for 7.2 h) to 25,000 (for 35 h), and thus the standard deviation of each point was calculated to be less than 3%.

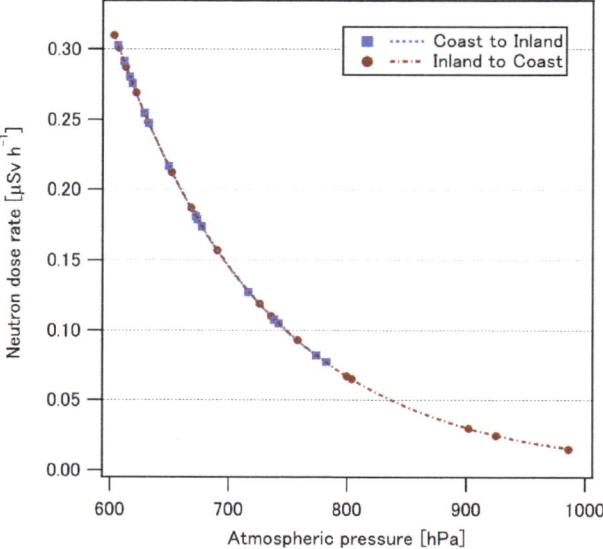

Figure 4. Relationship of the measured neutron-dose rates and barometric atmospheric pressures along the routes between the coastal and inland areas (shown in Figure 1) in the period from November 2018 to January 2019. The standard deviation of each dose-rate plot was less than 3%.

As seen in the figure, the quite reproducible relationships were obtained between the cosmic-neutron intensities and atmospheric pressures, regardless of the measurement timings; as mentioned above, there was a time interval of about 20 days between the end of the inward route measurements and the start of the outward route ones. These results imply that the employed portable system can stably work for measuring the cosmic- neutron intensities with good accuracy even in a harsh environment such as Antarctica.

3.3. Comparison with Model Calculation

The relationships between the neutron-dose rates calculated by using the analytical model (PARMA) and those measured with the portable neutron-monitoring system are plotted in Figure 5. Overall good agreements of the calculated and measured neutron-dose rates were produced for both routes covering a wide range of altitudes. Since the model calculations did not consider the shielding effects of the structure of the snow vehicle and onboard equipment, it was assumed that the slightly smaller measured values in the range of low dose rates (i.e., at lower altitudes) were due to the attenuation of the lower-energy secondary cosmic radiation inside the vehicle.

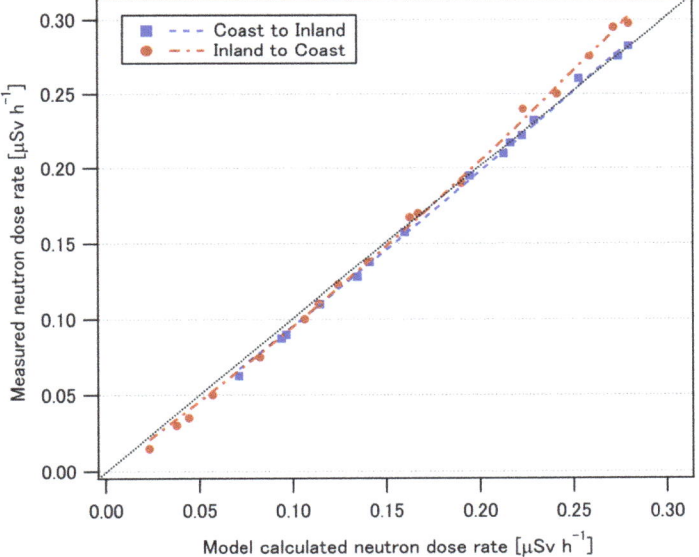

Figure 5. Relationship between the calculated neutron-dose rates (X-axis) using PARMA [18,19] and the measured neutron-dose rates (Y-axis) along the routes shown in Figure 1 for the period from November 2018 to January 2019. The standard deviation of each plot was less than 3%.

On the other hand, some discrepancies (~10%) were seen at the high dose rates, i.e., at high-altitude areas. Since no major space weather events were reported in the respective period (i.e., from late December 2018 to January 2019) [52], this discrepancy is attributable to short-term changes of environmental factors such as atmospheric parameters (other than barometric pressure), heliospheric modulation by the solar wind, and geomagnetic cutoff rigidity at the monitoring location.

It can be pointed out that the chronological variations of meteorological conditions such as clouds and snowfall affected the energy spectra of the cosmic neutrons, and those changes altered the responses of the neutron detector as the efficiency of WENDI-II varied depending on the neutron energy [44,45]. However, this possibility is low since it is known that the shapes of cosmic-neutron-energy spectra in the atmosphere do not notably change with altitude. In a previous monitoring performed at Mt. Fuji, Japan, covering similar altitudes (40 to 3700 m) [53], the energy spectra of cosmic neutrons measured by using a Bonner multi-sphere neutron spectrometer were quite identical in their shapes, irrelevant to the altitude. This finding has been well-reflected in our model calculations. For example, the neutron-energy spectra calculated by PARMA at three locations along the routes (indicated with red points in Figure 1) are shown in Figure 6. It is seen that the shapes of neutron-energy spectra are nearly the same while the overall level of neutron flux decreases with increasing atmospheric pressure, i.e., decreasing altitude. Thus, the relative response of WENDI-II would be stable, regardless of the atmospheric pressure.

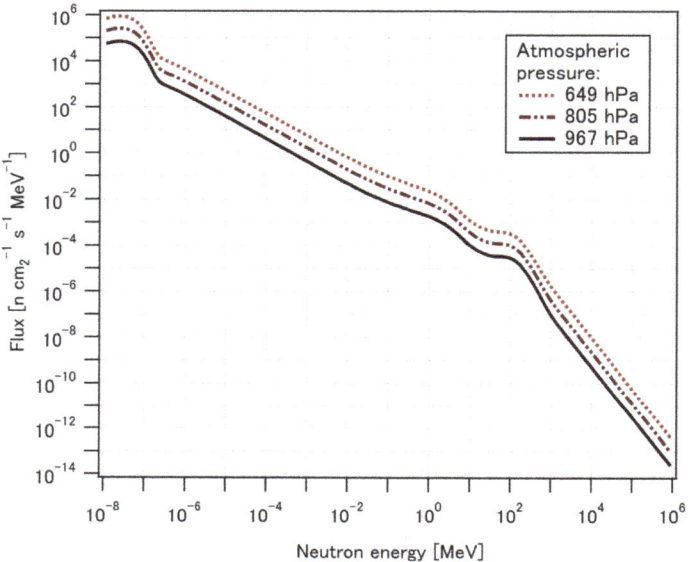

Figure 6. The neutron-energy spectra calculated by the model PARMA [18,19] at three locations along the route (indicated with red points in Figure 1) in the period from December 2018 to January 2019.

Regarding the effect of geomagnetic-field variation surrounding the Earth, it was confirmed that the count rates of the ground-based neutron monitors (South Pole: SOPO and South Pole Bare: SOPB) placed at 90.0° S reduced by a few percent during the respective period [52]. As PARMA simply described the azimuth and zenith dependences of the cut-off rigidities assuming a dipole magnet [19], it can be assumed that, as a result of such simplification of the model structure, the observed count reductions of ground-based neutron monitors were overly reflected in evaluation of solar activities expressed as the values of heliocentric or force field potential, i.e., they caused the smaller cosmic-neutron intensities at the high-latitude and high-altitude area. This possibility should thoroughly be investigated with more comprehensive data in further research.

These findings indicate the need for further studies for improving the reliability of model calculations of cosmic-radiation intensities in the atmosphere and imply that the portable neutron-monitoring system employed in the present study would be useful for achieving this task.

4. Conclusions

In the present study, we confirmed that cosmic-neutron intensities could be measured over a wide range of altitude (from 30 m to 3762 m) in Antarctica by using a portable neutron-monitoring system composed of an extended-energy neutron detector and an originally made data logger. While the cosmic-neutron intensities measured for more than two months agreed well with those calculated with one of the most recent models overall, some discrepancy (~10%) was observed at a high-altitude area, which implies further need for improving the reliability of the model calculations of cosmic-radiation intensities in the atmosphere.

In view of technological application, it is considered that the employed portable system for neutron monitoring will be effectively applied to verifications of the models that describe the nuclear spallation reactions in the atmosphere. It is expected that the data from such on-site measurements covering a wide area at different altitudes in harsh environments will improve the soundness of many ongoing studies on various subjects, such as the production of cosmogenic nuclides, changes in atmospheric properties/climate, the cosmic-radiation exposure of aircraft crew, and the stability of precise electronic devices, that rely on models for calculating the complex nuclear reactions in the atmosphere. More investigations to explain the reasons of observed discrepancies between the measurements and the model calculations are to be conducted in future studies.

Author Contributions: Conceptualization, N.K. and H.Y.; material preparation and maintenance, K.Y. and H.Y.; transporting and measurements, N.K.; data curation, N.K.; data analysis, H.Y.; model validation, H.Y.; writing—original draft preparation, H.Y.; writing—review and editing, N.K. and K.Y.; funding acquisition, N.K. and H.Y. All authors have read and agreed to the published version of the manuscript.

Funding: This research was supported by JSPS KAKENHI Grant Number 18K19851, the joint research program of the Institute for Space–Earth Environmental Research (ISEE), Nagoya University, and the Program of the Network-type joint Usage/Research Center for Radiation Disaster Medical Science funded by the Ministry of Education, Culture, Sports, Science, and Technology (MEXT) of Japan and Hiroshima University.

Institutional Review Board Statement: Not applicable.

Informed Consent Statement: Not applicable.

Data Availability Statement: Not applicable.

Conflicts of Interest: The authors declare no conflict of interest.

References

1. Asvestari, E.; Gil, A.; Kovaltsov, G.A.; Usoskin, I.G. Neutron monitors and cosmogenic isotopes as cosmic ray energy-integration detectors: Effective yield functions, effective energy, and its dependence on the local interstellar spectrum. *J. Geophys. Res. Space Phys.* **2017**, *122*, 9790–9802. [CrossRef]
2. Palcsu, L.; Morgenstern, U.; Sültenfuss, J.; Koltai, G.; László, E.; Temovski, M.; Major, Z.; Nagy, J.T.; Papp, L.; Varlam, C.; et al. Modulation of cosmogenic tritium in meteoric precipitation by the 11-year cycle of solar magnetic field activity. *Sci. Rep.* **2018**, *8*, 12813. [CrossRef]
3. Arce-Chamorro, C.; Sanjurjo-Sánchez, J.; Vidal-Romaní, J.R. Chronology of coastal alluvial deposits in the Ria de Coruña (NW Spain) linked to the upper pleistocene sea level regression. *Appl. Sci.* **2022**, *12*, 9982. [CrossRef]
4. Narazaki, Y.; Sakoda, A.; Akata, N.; Itoh, H.; Momoshima, N. Analysis of Factors Contributing to the Increase in 7Be Activity Concentrations in the Atmosphere. *Int. J. Environ. Res. Public Health* **2022**, *19*, 10128. [CrossRef] [PubMed]
5. Schaefer, J.M.; Codilean, A.T.; Willenbring, J.K.; Lu, Z.-T.; Keisling, B.; Fülöp, R.-H.; Val, P. Cosmogenic nuclide techniques. *Nat. Rev. Methods Prim.* **2022**, *2*, 18. [CrossRef]
6. Fourré, E.; Landais, A.; Cauquoin, A.; Jean-Baptiste, P.; Lipenkov, V.; Petit, J.R. Tritium records to trace stratospheric moisture inputs in Antarctica. *J. Geophys. Res. Atmos.* **2018**, *123*, 3009–3018. [CrossRef]
7. Spector, P.; Balco, G. Exposure-age data from across Antarctica reveal mid-Miocene establishment of polar desert climate. *Geology* **2021**, *49*, 91–95. [CrossRef]
8. Horiuchi, K.; Kato, S.; Ohtani, K.; Kurita, N.; Tsutaki, S.; Nakazawa, F.; Motoyama, H.; Kawamura, K.; Tazoe, H.; Akata, N.; et al. Spatial variations of 10Be in surface snow along the inland traverse route of Japanese Antarctic Research Expeditions. *Nucl. Instrum. Methods Phys. Res. Sect. B* **2022**, *533*, 61–65. [CrossRef]
9. Fireman, E.L. Measurement of the (n, H3) cross section in nitrogen and its relationship to the tritium production in the atmosphere. *Phys. Rev.* **1953**, *91*, 922–926. [CrossRef]
10. Nir, A.; Kruger, S.T.; Lingenfelter, R.E.; Flamm, E.J. Natural tritium. *Rev. Geophys.* **1966**, *4*, 441–456. [CrossRef]
11. O'Brien, K. Secular variations in the production of cosmogenic isotopes in the Earth's atmosphere. *J. Geophys. Res.* **1979**, *84*, 423–431. [CrossRef]
12. Masarik, J.; Beer, J. Simulation of particle fluxes and cosmogenic nuclide production in the Earth's atmosphere. *J. Geophys. Res.* **1999**, *104*, 12099–12112. [CrossRef]

13. Webber, W.R.; Higbie, P.R.; McCracken, K.G. Production of the cosmogenic isotopes ^{3}H, ^{7}Be, ^{10}Be, and ^{36}Cl in the Earth's atmosphere by solar and galactic cosmic rays. *J. Geophys. Res.* **2007**, *112*, A10106. [CrossRef]
14. Masarik, J.; Beer, J. An updated simulation of particle fluxes and cosmogenic nuclide production in the Earth's atmosphere. *J. Geophys. Res.* **2009**, *114*, D11103. [CrossRef]
15. Usoskin, I.G.; Kovaltsov, G.A.; Mironova, I.A. Cosmic ray induced ionization model CRAC: CRII: An extension to the upper atmosphere. *J. Geophys. Res.* **2010**, *115*, D10302. [CrossRef]
16. Poluianov, S.V.; Kovaltsov, G.A.; Mishev, A.L.; Usoskin, I.G. Production of cosmogenic isotopes ^{7}Be, ^{10}Be, ^{14}C, ^{22}Na, and ^{36}Cl in the atmosphere: Altitudinal profiles of yield functions. *J. Geophys. Res. Atmos.* **2016**, *121*, 8125–8136. [CrossRef]
17. Poluianov, S.V.; Kovaltsov, G.A.; Usoskin, I.G. A New Full 3-D Model of Cosmogenic Tritium ^{3}H production in the atmosphere (CRAC:3H). *J. Geophys. Res. Atmos.* **2020**, *125*, e2020JD033147. [CrossRef]
18. Sato, T.; Yasuda, H.; Niita, K.; Endo, A.; Sihver, L. Development of PARMA: PHITS-based Analytical Radiation Model in the Atmosphere. *Radiat. Res.* **2008**, *170*, 244–259. [CrossRef] [PubMed]
19. Sato, T. Analytical Model for Estimating Terrestrial Cosmic Ray Fluxes Nearly Anytime and Anywhere in the World: Extension of PARMA/EXPACS. *PLoS ONE* **2015**, *10*, e0144679. [CrossRef]
20. Velinov, P.I.Y.; Mateev, L. Analytical approach for cosmic ray proton ionization in the lower ionosphere and middle atmosphere. *Comptes Rendus l'Academie Bulg. Sci.* **2005**, *58*, 511–516.
21. Calisto, M.; Usoskin, I.; Rozanov, E.; Peter, T. Influence of Galactic Cosmic Rays on atmospheric composition and dynamics. *Atmos. Chem. Phys.* **2011**, *11*, 4547–4556. [CrossRef]
22. Semeniuk, K.; Fomichev, V.I.; McConnell, J.C.; Fu, C.; Melo, S.M.L.; Usoskin, I.G. Middle atmosphere response to the solar cycle in irradiance and ionizing particle precipitation. *Atmos. Chem. Phys.* **2011**, *11*, 5045–5077. [CrossRef]
23. Mironova, I.A.; Aplin, K.L.; Arnold, F.; Bazilevskaya, G.A.; Harrison, R.G.; Krivolutsky, A.A.; Nicoll, K.A.; Rozanov, E.V.; Turunen, E.; Usoskin, I.G. Energetic Particle Influence on the Earth's Atmosphere. *Space Sci. Rev.* **2015**, *194*, 1–96. [CrossRef]
24. Ortiz, E.; Mendoza, B.; Gay, C.; Mendoza, V.M.; Pazos, M.; Garduño, R. Simulation and Evaluation of the Radiation Dose Deposited in Human Tissues by Atmospheric Neutrons. *Appl. Sci.* **2021**, *11*, 8338. [CrossRef]
25. International Commission on Radiological Protection (ICRP). *1990 Recommendations of the International Commission on Radiological Protection*; ICRP Publication 60; Ann. ICRP 21, Pergamon Press: London, UK, 1991.
26. International Commission on Radiological Protection (ICRP). *The 2007 Recommendations of the International Commission on Radiological Protection*; ICRP Publication 103; Ann. ICRP 37, Elsevier: London, UK, 2007.
27. International Commission on Radiological Protection. *Radiological Protection from Cosmic Radiation in Aviation*; ICRP Publication 132; Ann. ICRP 45, SAGE: London, UK, 2016.
28. Copeland, K. CARI-7A: Development and validation. *Radiat. Prot. Dosim.* **2017**, *175*, 419–431. [CrossRef] [PubMed]
29. Lewis, B.J.; Bennett, L.G.I.; Green, A.R.; Butler, A.; Desormeaux, M.; Kitching, F.; McCall, M.J.; Ellaschuk, B.; Pierre, M. Aircrew dosimetry using the predictive code for aircrew radiation exposure (PCAIRE). *Radiat. Prot. Dosim.* **2005**, *116*, 320–326. [CrossRef] [PubMed]
30. Bottollier-Depois, J.F.; Blanchard, P.; Clairand, I.; Dessarps, P.; Fuller, N.; Lantos, P.; Saint-Lô, D.; Trompier, F. An operational approach for aircraft crew dosimetry: The SIEVERT system. *Radiat. Prot. Dosim.* **2007**, *125*, 421–424. [CrossRef] [PubMed]
31. Latocha, M.; Beck, P.; Rollet, S. AVIDOS—A software package for European accredited aviation dosimetry. *Radiat. Prot. Dosim.* **2009**, *136*, 286–290. [CrossRef]
32. Mares, V.; Maczka, T.; Leuthold, G.; Ruhm, W. Air crew dosimetry with a new version of EPCARD. *Radiat. Prot. Dosim.* **2009**, *136*, 262–266. [CrossRef] [PubMed]
33. Yasuda, H.; Sato, T.; Yonehara, H.; Kosako, T.; Fujitaka, K.; Sasaki, Y. Management of cosmic radiation exposure for aircraft crew in Japan. *Radiat. Prot. Dosim.* **2011**, *146*, 123–125. [CrossRef]
34. Makrantoni, P.; Tezari, A.; Stassinakis, A.N.; Paschalis, P.; Gerontidou, M.; Karaiskos, P.; Georgakilas, A.G.; Mavromichalaki, H.; Usoskin, I.G.; Crosby, N.; et al. Estimation of Cosmic-Ray-Induced Atmospheric Ionization and Radiation at Commercial Aviation Flight Altitudes. *Appl. Sci.* **2022**, *12*, 5297. [CrossRef]
35. Mares, V.; Yasuda, H. Aviation route doses calculated with EPCARD.Net and JISCARD EX. *Radiat. Meas.* **2010**, *45*, 1553–1556. [CrossRef]
36. Zhou, D.; O'Sullivan, D.; Xu, B.; Flood, E. Cosmic ray measurements at aircraft altitudes and comparison with predictions of computer codes. *Adv. Space Res.* **2003**, *32*, 47–52. [CrossRef]
37. Chiang, Y.; Tan, C.M.; Chao, T.-C.; Lee, C.-C.; Tung, C.-J. Investigate the Equivalence of Neutrons and Protons in Single Event Effects Testing: A Geant4 Study. *Appl. Sci.* **2020**, *10*, 3234. [CrossRef]
38. Leray, J.L. Effects of atmospheric neutrons on devices, at sea level and in avionics embedded systems. *Microelectron. Reliab.* **2007**, *47*, 1827–1835. [CrossRef]
39. Bütikofer, R. *Neutron Monitors–Study of Solar and Galactic Cosmic Rays*; Activity Report; International Foundation HFSJG: Bern, Switzerland, 2018; pp. 50–52.
40. Väisänen, P.; Usoskin, I.; Mursula, K. Seven Decades of Neutron Monitors (1951–2019): Overview and Evaluation of Data Sources. *J. Geophys. Res. Space Phys.* **2021**, *126*, e2020JA028941. [CrossRef]
41. Gillet, N.; Gerick, F.; Angappan, R.; Jault, D. A Dynamical Prospective on Interannual Geomagnetic Field Changes. *Surv. Geophys.* **2022**, *43*, 71–105. [CrossRef]

42. Nicolas, Q.; Buffett, B. Excitation of high-latitude MAC waves in Earth's core. *Geophys. J. Int.* **2023**, *233*, 1961–1973. [CrossRef]
43. Olsher, R.H.; Hsu, H.-H.; Beverding, A.; Kleck, J.H.; Casson, W.H.; Vasilik, D.G.; Devine, R.T. WENDI: An improved neutron rem meter. *Health Phys.* **2000**, *79*, 170–181. [CrossRef]
44. Olsher, R.H.; McLean, T.D. High-energy response of the PRESCILA and WENDI-II neutron rem meters. *Radiat. Prot. Dosim.* **2008**, *130*, 510–513. [CrossRef]
45. Yasuda, H.; Yajima, K.; Sato, T.; Takada, M.; Nakamura, T. Responses Of Selected Neutron Monitors To Cosmic Radiation At Aviation Altitudes. *Health Phys.* **2009**, *96*, 655–660. [CrossRef]
46. Yasuda, H.; Yajima, K. Characterization of Radiation Instruments at the Summit of Mt. Fuji. *Radiat. Meas.* **2010**, *45*, 1600–1604. [CrossRef]
47. Yasuda, H.; Lee, J.; Yajima, K.; Hwang, J.A.; Sakai, K. Measurement of cosmic-ray neutron dose onboard a polar route flight from New York to Seoul. *Radiat. Prot. Dosim.* **2011**, *146*, 213–216. [CrossRef]
48. Yasuda, H.; Yajima, K.; Yoshida, S. Dosimetry of cosmic radiation in the troposphere based on the measurements at the summit of Mt. Fuji. *Proc. Radiochem.* **2011**, *1*, 67–70. [CrossRef]
49. Yasuda, H.; Yajima, K. Verification of cosmic neutron doses in long-haul flights from Japan. *Radiat. Meas.* **2018**, *119*, 6–11. [CrossRef]
50. Niita, K.; Sato, T.; Iwase, H.; Nose, H.; Nakashima, H.; Sihver, L. PHITS—A particle and heavy ion transport code system. *Radiat. Meas.* **2006**, *41*, 1080–1090. [CrossRef]
51. Watanabe, Y.; Kosako, K.; Kunieda, S.; Chiba, S.; Fujimoto, R.; Harada, H.; Kawai, M.; Maekawa, F.; Murata, T.; Nakashima, H.; et al. Status of JENDL High Energy File. *J. Korean Phys. Soc.* **2011**, *59*, 1040–1045. [CrossRef]
52. Neutron Monitor Database (NMDB). NMDB Event Search Tool (NEST). Available online: https://www.nmdb.eu/nest/ (accessed on 24 February 2023).
53. Kowatari, M.; Nagaoka, K.; Satoh, S.; Ohta, Y.; Abukawa, J.; Tachimori, S.; Nakamura, T. Evaluation of the altitude variation of the cosmic-ray induced environmental neutrons in the Mt. Fuji area. *J. Nucl. Sci. Technol.* **2005**, *42*, 495–502. [CrossRef]

Disclaimer/Publisher's Note: The statements, opinions and data contained in all publications are solely those of the individual author(s) and contributor(s) and not of MDPI and/or the editor(s). MDPI and/or the editor(s) disclaim responsibility for any injury to people or property resulting from any ideas, methods, instructions or products referred to in the content.

Article

Multivariate Statistical Analyses and Potentially Toxic Elements Pollution Assessment of Pyroclastic Products from Mt. Etna, Sicily, Southern Italy

Francesco Caridi [1,*], Giuseppe Paladini [1], Antonio Francesco Mottese [1], Maurizio Messina [2], Valentina Venuti [1,*] and Domenico Majolino [1]

[1] Dipartimento di Scienze Matematiche e Informatiche, Scienze Fisiche e Scienze Della Terra, Università Degli Studi di Messina, V.le F. Stagno D'Alcontres, 31, 98166 Messina, Italy

[2] Dipartimento di Reggio Calabria, Agenzia Regionale per la Protezione dell'Ambiente della Calabria (ARPACal), Via Troncovito SNC, 89135 Reggio Calabria, Italy

* Correspondence: fcaridi@unime.it (F.C.); vvenuti@unime.it (V.V.)

Abstract: Potentially toxic elements contamination represents a universal problem of major concern, due to several adverse health effects on human beings when permissible concentration levels are overcome. In this sense, the assessment of potentially risky elements content in different environmental matrices plays a key role in the safeguarding of the quality of the environment, and thus of the strictly correlated public health. In this article, measurements of the average potentially toxic elements concentrations in pyroclastic products from Mt. Etna, Eastern Sicily and Southern Italy were performed together with a comparison with the allowable levels set by Italian legislation, with the aim to evaluate the level of toxicity imposed on the ecosystem. For this purpose, Inductively-Coupled Plasma Mass Spectrometry (ICP-MS) measurements were performed to investigate any possible chemical pollution by potentially risky elements, by applying different indices such as Enrichment Factor (EF), Geo-accumulation Index (I_{geo}), Contamination Factor (CF) and Pollution Load Index (PLI). Finally, the multivariate statistical analysis was performed by processing potentially toxic elements content and pollution indices. It is worth noting that the used approach could be applied, in principle, for the evaluation of the chemical risk due to the presence of potentially toxic elements in a large variety of samples of particular environmental interest, and can constitute a guideline for investigations focused on the monitoring of the environmental quality.

Keywords: pyroclastic products; potentially toxic elements; pollution; inductively-coupled plasma mass spectrometry; multivariate statistics

1. Introduction

The rapid industrialization and the uncontrolled urbanization in many cities and coastal areas led to an alarming level of chemical contaminants around these environments [1,2]. Among these pollutants, heavy metals are of major concern, being characterized by a persistent and bio-accumulative character [3,4]. In order to address the extent of contamination, the knowledge of the potentially risky elements' sources is of particular importance, together with the contamination mechanisms of systems where toxicity levels of concentration are reached [5–7].

The environmental pollution by potentially toxic elements (including heavy metals) is by now a universal problem, especially for the toxic effects on living organisms when permissible concentration levels are exceeded [4]. In fact, under such circumstances, a decline in the mental, cognitive and physical health of the individual could appear [8,9].

Moreover, the potentially toxic elements abundance in soils, waters and biota can be indicative of the presence of natural/anthropogenic sources, as reported in the literature [10,11]. In this sense, geochemical and mineralogical studies of soils can be, in particular, helpful in order to understand, on one side, the elemental distribution patterns and the environmental conditions existing in a specific area [12], and on the other side, the geological history of the transport and sorting process [13].

In the view of a sustainable development, pyroclastic products are considered as natural resources for the production of building materials [14,15]. In addition, in countries where active volcanoes exist, pyroclastic products could be employed to supply nutrients and reduce CO_2 from the atmosphere [16].

In the present study, Inductively-Coupled Plasma Mass Spectrometry (ICP-MS) was employed to measure the potentially toxic elements content, i.e., arsenic (As), cadmium (Cd), copper (Cu), mercury (Hg), nickel (Ni), lead (Pb), antimony (Sb), thallium (Tl), and zinc (Zn), of pyroclastic products sampled in a surrounding area of the Mt. Etna (Eastern Sicily, Southern Italy) [17–19]. With the aim of estimating the level of toxicity imposed on the ecosystem by the potentially risky elements, different pollution indices, such as Enrichment Factor (EF), Geo-accumulation Index (I_{geo}), Contamination Factor (CF) and Pollution Load Index (PLI) were also calculated. Finally, with the aim to analyze the chemical pollution, Pearson correlation, Principal Component Analysis (PCA), Hierarchical Cluster Analysis (HCA), and Multidimensional Data Analysis (MDA), were conducted with the aim of finding out any possible relationship among the variables [20,21].

2. Materials and Methods

2.1. Samples Collection

Table 1 reports the Identification (IDs) and the Global Positioning System (GPS) coordinates of the sampling sites (fifty samples of pyroclastic products in total, five for each site).

Table 1. The Identification (IDs) and the Global Positioning System (GPS) latitude and longitude coordinates of the investigated pyroclastic products sampling sites.

Site ID	GPS Coordinates	
	Latitude	Longitude
1	37.68864	15.09499
2	37.64975	15.05663
3	37.71456	15.11615
4	37.68809	15.13123
5	37.61574	15.09846
6	37.57984	15.09326
7	37.61873	15.05600
8	37.69899	15.00120
9	37.65249	15.09540
10	37.69900	15.05389

Figure 1 shows the map of the sampling area, with the site IDs (1–10) indicated.

Pyroclastic products were collected according to [22]. In particular, in the ID 1, 4, 5, 7 and 9 sites, freshly erupted air-fall pyroclastic products were sampled, while in the remaining ID 2, 3, 6, 8 and 10 sites, samples from heaps of pyroclastic wastes from previous volcanic activities were collected [22]. The samples were stored into labeled plastic vials, with adequate caution taken in order to prevent their contamination.

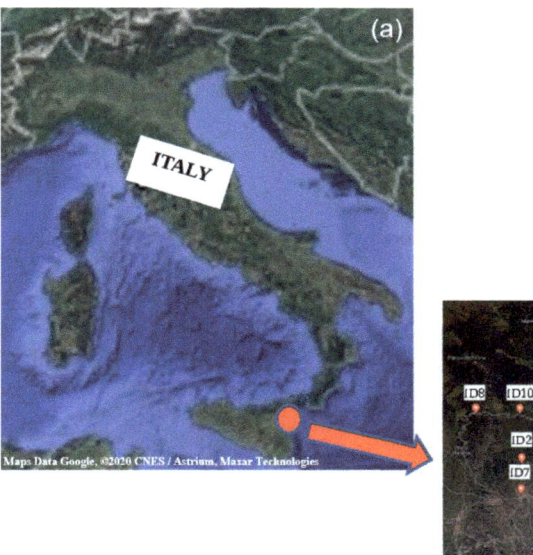

Figure 1. The map of the sampling area (**a**), with the site IDs (1–10) indicated (**b**).

2.2. Inductively Coupled Plasma Mass Spectrometry (ICP-MS) Measurements

For the ICP-MS analysis, approximately 0.5–1.0 g of sample, together with 3 mL of ultrapure (for trace analysis) HNO$_3$ (67–69%) and 9 mL of ultrapure (for trace analysis) HCl (32–35%) (aqua regia), were directly introduced into a 100 mL TFM vessel, according to [23].

For the measurements a Thermo Scientific (Waltham, MA, USA) iCAP Qc ICP-MS was used [24,25], according to [26]. The sample introduction system consisted of a Peltier cooled (3 °C), baffled cyclonic spray chamber, PFA nebulizer and quartz torch with a 2.5 mm i.e., removable quartz injector. The instrument was operated in a single collision cell mode, with kinetic energy discrimination (KED), using pure Helium as the collision gas. All samples were presented for analysis using a Cetac ASX-520 (Teledyne Cetac Technologies, Omaha, NE, USA) and for each one, data were recorded in duplicate.

The quality of the ICP-MS experimental results was certified by the Italian Accreditation Body (ACCREDIA) [27]. This implies the continued verification (with annual periodicity) of the maintenance of the ICP-MS method performance characteristics.

2.3. Level of Potentially Toxic Elements Pollution Assessment

The level of potentially toxic elements pollution was evaluated by calculating the pollution indices reported in the following.

2.3.1. The Enrichment Factor

The Enrichment Factor is

$$\mathrm{EF} = \frac{\{C_x/C_{Fe}\}\mathrm{sample}}{\{C_x/C_{Fe}\}\mathrm{reference}} \quad (1)$$

where C_x is the concentration of the potentially enrichment element and C_{Fe} is the concentration of the normalizing element, usually Fe [28]. Considering that the regional geochemical background values for these elements are not available, the world average elemental concentrations reported by [28] in the Earth's crust were used as reference.

2.3.2. The Geo-Accumulation Index

The Geo-accumulation Index is

$$I_{geo} = \text{Log}_2[C_n/(kB_n)] \tag{2}$$

where C_n is the concentration of the potentially hazardous trace element in the sample, B_n is the geochemical background value in average shale of the element n, and k is the background matrix correction factor [28,29].

2.3.3. The Contamination Factor

The Contamination Factor is

$$CF = C_{metal}/C_{background} \tag{3}$$

where C_{metal} and $C_{background}$ are the concentration and the background values for each heavy metal, respectively [30].

2.3.4. The Pollution Load Index

The Pollution Load Index is defined as the n-th root of the product of the Contamination Factor of potentially risky elements

$$PLI = (CF_1 \times CF_2 \times CF_3 \times \ldots \times CF_n)^{1/n} \tag{4}$$

where n is the number of metals [31,32].

2.4. Statistical Analysis

The XLSTAT statistical software for Windows was used for all statistical calculations [33].

With the aim to individuate the presence of the relationships among the original variables (Pearson correlation analysis), an exploratory method (PCA) was performed. The PCA elaboration ensures the reduction of the data dimensionality, whereas the combinations of variables identified by the Principal Components (PCs) provide the greatest contribution to sample variability [34]. Moreover, in order to add a further degree of detail to the implemented statistical approaches, the Hierarchical Clusters Analysis (HCA) [35] and a new innovative statistical technique called Multidimensional Data Analysis (MDA) [36], which merges the calculation algorithms of PCA with those of HCA, were also employed.

3. Results and Discussion

3.1. Potentially Toxic Elements Analysis

Table 2 reports the potentially toxic elements content (mg kg^{-1} dry weight, d.w.) for the analyzed pyroclastic products, as obtained through ICP-MS analysis.

Table 2. Potentially toxic elements content (mg kg^{-1} dry weight, d.w.), as obtained through ICP-MS analysis for the analyzed samples.

	ICP-MS Analysis										
	Site ID										
	1	2	3	4	5	6	7	8	9	10	Threshold Limit
C_{As}	1.73	1.74	1.72	2.09	1.85	2.11	1.98	2.32	1.97	2.14	20
C_{Cd}	0.10	0.15	0.10	0.11	0.10	0.13	0.10	0.11	0.12	0.12	2
C_{Cu}	76.91	76.83	76.04	74.02	82.61	87.23	82.45	85.23	85.08	92.91	120
C_{Hg}	0.03	0.03	0.03	0.03	0.03	0.03	0.03	0.03	0.04	0.04	1
C_{Ni}	16.61	14.95	14.32	15.06	15.91	17.45	17.81	21.95	18.82	18.32	120
C_{Pb}	4.93	5.02	4.67	5.17	5.18	5.55	5.23	5.16	5.02	5.46	100
C_{Sb}	0.08	0.08	0.08	0.15	0.09	0.12	0.09	0.11	0.35	0.10	10
C_{Tl}	0.11	0.09	0.08	0.07	0.08	0.09	0.09	0.08	0.09	0.09	1
C_{Zn}	62.15	58.45	56.56	58.41	62.32	69.32	63.39	80.23	68.65	69.05	150

Worth noting is that the obtained concentrations are lower than the threshold limits [37], also reported in Table 2, for all detected metals. Therefore, they cannot be considered as pollutants, and thus do not compromise the welfare of the environment. For this reason, they do not constitute a risk to human health.

3.2. Estimation of the Level of Potentially Toxic Elements Pollution

3.2.1. EF

Table 3 reports the calculated EF values.

Table 3. Calculated values of the Enrichment Factor (EF), Geo-accumulation Index (Igeo), Contamination Factor (CF) and Pollution Load Index (PLI) for all the investigated sites.

Site ID	Metal	EF	I_{geo}	CF	PLI	Site ID	Metal	EF	I_{geo}	CF	PLI	Site ID	Metal	EF	I_{geo}	CF	PLI
1	As	0.14	−3.49	0.13	0.21	2	As	0.15	−3.49	0.13	0.22	3	As	0.15	−3.50	0.13	0.20
	Cd	0.34	−2.19	0.33			Cd	0.54	−1.58	0.50			Cd	0.37	−2.17	0.33	
	Cu	1.80	0.19	1.71			Cu	1.85	0.19	1.71			Cu	1.89	0.17	1.69	
	Hg	0.07	−4.48	0.07			Hg	0.07	−4.48	0.07			Hg	0.08	−4.48	0.07	
	Ni	0.26	−2.62	0.24			Ni	0.24	−2.78	0.22			Ni	0.24	−2.83	0.21	
	Pb	0.26	−2.61	0.25			Pb	0.27	−2.58	0.25			Pb	0.26	−2.68	0.23	
	Sb	0.06	−4.79	0.05			Sb	0.06	−4.81	0.05			Sb	0.06	−4.81	0.05	
	Tl	0.08	−4.25	0.08			Tl	0.07	−4.54	0.06			Tl	0.06	−4.71	0.06	
	Zn	0.69	−1.20	0.65			Zn	0.67	−1.29	0.61			Zn	0.67	−1.33	0.59	
4	As	0.19	−3.22	0.16	0.22	5	As	0.15	−3.40	0.14	0.21	6	As	0.16	−3.21	0.16	0.24
	Cd	0.42	−2.03	0.37			Cd	0.36	−2.17	0.33			Cd	0.43	−1.79	0.43	
	Cu	1.89	0.13	1.64			Cu	1.97	0.29	1.84			Cu	1.90	0.37	1.94	
	Hg	0.08	−4.48	0.07			Hg	0.07	−4.48	0.07			Hg	0.07	−4.48	0.07	
	Ni	0.25	−2.77	0.22			Ni	0.25	−2.68	0.23			Ni	0.25	−2.55	0.26	
	Pb	0.30	−2.54	0.26			Pb	0.28	−2.53	0.26			Pb	0.27	−2.43	0.28	
	Sb	0.12	−3.91	0.10			Sb	0.06	−4.64	0.06			Sb	0.08	−4.23	0.08	
	Tl	0.06	−4.91	0.05			Tl	0.06	−4.71	0.06			Tl	0.06	−4.54	0.06	
	Zn	0.71	−1.29	0.61			Zn	0.70	−1.19	0.66			Zn	0.72	−1.04	0.73	
7	As	0.16	−3.30	0.15	0.22	8	As	0.18	−3.07	0.18	0.24	9	As	0.16	−3.31	0.15	0.28
	Cd	0.35	−2.17	0.33			Cd	0.36	−2.03	0.37			Cd	0.42	−1.91	0.40	
	Cu	1.94	0.29	1.83			Cu	1.86	0.34	1.89			Cu	1.98	0.33	1.89	
	Hg	0.07	−4.48	0.07			Hg	0.07	−4.48	0.07			Hg	0.11	−3.91	0.10	
	Ni	0.28	−2.52	0.26			Ni	0.32	−2.22	0.32			Ni	0.29	−2.44	0.28	
	Pb	0.28	−2.52	0.26			Pb	0.25	−2.54	0.26			Pb	0.27	−2.58	0.25	
	Sb	0.06	−4.64	0.06			Sb	0.07	−4.35	0.07			Sb	0.25	−2.68	0.23	
	Tl	0.07	−4.54	0.06			Tl	0.06	−4.71	0.06			Tl	0.07	−4.54	0.06	
	Zn	0.71	−1.17	0.67			Zn	0.83	−0.83	0.84			Zn	0.76	−1.05	0.72	
10	As	0.17	−3.19	0.16	0.25												
	Cd	0.40	−1.91	0.40													
	Cu	2.00	0.46	2.06													
	Hg	0.10	−3.91	0.10													
	Ni	0.27	−2.48	0.27													
	Pb	0.27	−2.46	0.27													
	Sb	0.07	−4.49	0.07													
	Tl	0.06	−4.54	0.06													
	Zn	0.73	−1.05	0.73													

According to the literature [38], EF values < 2 indicate deficient to minimal enrichment. In particular, values between 0.5 and 1.5 indicate an entirely crustal material/natural origin metal, while EF > 1.5 suggests a more likely anthropogenic one [39]. Moreover, $2 \leq EF < 5$ means moderate enrichment; $5 \leq EF < 20$ significant enrichment; $20 \leq EF \leq 40$ high enrichment and EF > 40 extremely high enrichment.

In our case, the obtained EF values are lower than 2 for all investigated sites, indicating no or minimal enrichment.

3.2.2. I_{geo}

Obtained I_{geo} values are presented in Table 3.

According to previous literature [40], the I_{geo} values were interpreted as follows: $I_{geo} \leq 0$ indicates no contamination; $0 < I_{geo} \leq 1$ no/moderate contamination; $1 < I_{geo} \leq 2$ moderate contamination; $2 < I_{geo} \leq 3$ moderate/strong contamination; $3 < I_{geo} \leq 4$ strong contamination; $4 < I_{geo} \leq 5$ strong/extreme contamination; and $I_{geo} > 5$ extreme contamination.

In our case, all values were found to be lower than 0, with the only exception of copper (Cu), indicating a very moderate contamination by Cu for all the investigated samples in all sampling sites. This occurrence can be justified, in agreement with [41,42], considering that this metal is typically employed as a soil defense product, the soil texture and high pH—all factors that can contribute to Cu accumulation.

3.2.3. CF

Table 3 reports the assessed CF values.

According to [43], $CF \leq 1$ implies no contamination, $1 < CF \leq 3$ low or moderate contamination, $3 < CF \leq 6$ high contamination and $CF > 6$ very high contamination.

In our case, all values are <1 in all cases except of Cu, once again indicating a moderate contamination in all the sampling sites.

3.2.4. PLI

PLI values are presented in Table 3.

According to [44], the PLI value > 1 indicates the presence of pollution, whereas PLI value < 1 indicates no pollution. PLI turned out to be lower than 1 in all cases, thus revealing no pollution by the assessed potentially risky elements.

3.3. Statistical Features

The sphericity (or Bartlett) test was preliminarily conducted with the aim of making multivariate treatments more reliable and statistically significant, furnishing a *p*-value equal to 0.04. Thus, considering that a high statistical significance of the data is ensured for *p*-values < 0.05, it follows that starting from reliable data, the results of the calculation algorithms will also be trustworthy [45]. Furthermore, in order to understand any possible relationship between the different variables, expressed as concentrations of the detected potentially toxic elements, the Pearson correlation matrix was calculated.

The results of the Pearson's correlation coefficients are presented in Table 4.

Table 4. Pearson correlation matrix among the considered variables. Values in bold are different from 0 at the significance level $\alpha = 0.05$.

Variables	C_{As}	C_{Cd}	C_{Cu}	C_{Hg}	C_{Ni}	C_{Pb}	C_{Sb}	C_{Tl}	C_{Zn}
C_{As}	**1.00**	0.03	0.61	0.43	**0.76**	**0.67**	0.19	−0.15	**0.80**
C_{Cd}	0.03	**1.00**	0.15	0.13	−0.05	0.24	0.16	−0.04	0.04
C_{Cu}	0.61	0.15	**1.00**	0.68	0.68	**0.71**	0.18	0.27	**0.72**
C_{Hg}	0.43	0.13	0.68	**1.00**	0.44	0.30	0.55	0.01	0.45
C_{Ni}	**0.76**	−0.05	0.68	0.44	**1.00**	0.39	0.28	0.23	**0.97**
C_{Pb}	**0.67**	0.24	**0.71**	0.30	0.39	**1.00**	−0.03	0.16	0.48
C_{Sb}	0.19	0.16	0.18	0.55	0.28	−0.03	**1.00**	−0.08	0.22
C_{Tl}	−0.15	−0.04	0.27	0.01	0.23	0.16	−0.08	**1.00**	0.18
C_{Zn}	**0.80**	0.04	**0.72**	0.45	**0.97**	0.48	0.22	0.18	**1.00**

All positive correlations were detected, with the exception of C_{Sb}-C_{Tl} (−0.08), C_{Cd}-C_{Ni} (−0.05), C_{Cd}-C_{Tl} (−0.04), C_{Pb}-C_{Sb} (−0.03).

As far as the PCA algorithm is concerned, ten variables (Site IDs, C_{As}, C_{cd}, C_{Cu}, C_{Hg}, C_{Ni}, C_{Pb}, C_{Sb}, C_{Tl} and C_{Zn}) were processed, also performing the Varimax rotation [46]. The obtained results are reported in Figure 2.

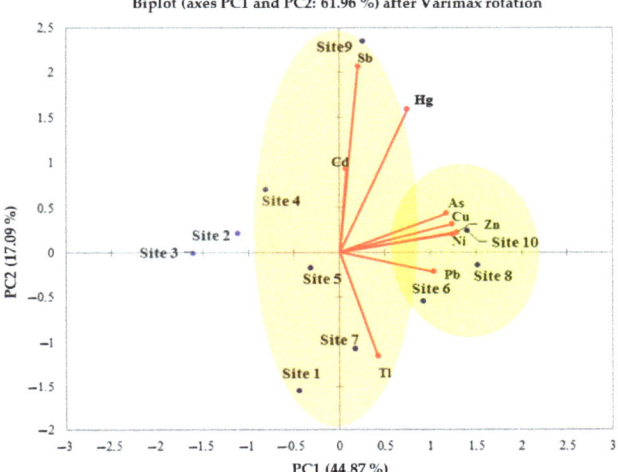

Figure 2. 2D plots of the first two PCs obtained through PCA elaboration after the Varimax rotation.

As can be seen from a first inspection of the figure, the PCA and Pearson matrix results appear to be coherent with each other. In particular, PCA elaboration allowed us to clearly discriminate three groups of samples. The first is formed by pyroclastic products from ID 6, 8 and 10 sites (yellow area in Figure 2), and it is clearly separated from the others on the first main component (PC1). The second group contains pyroclastic products from ID 1, 4, 5, 7 and 9 sites (salmon area in Figure 2) whose variance is more justified by the PC2. The last ideal group seems to be formed by pyroclastic wastes from ID 2 and 3 sites (light-blue area in Figure 2).

It is worth noting that the difference in the behavior of samples of the same type, i.e., pyroclastic wastes from previous volcanic activities, may depend on the different residence time of the pyroclastic products in the soil, and on the possible differential pollution that the pyroclastic waste samples have undergone [47].

Figure 3 shows the outcome dendrogram of the HCA. The dotted line represents the cut automatically made by the calculation algorithm, which allows us to identify the formation of three clusters (C1, C2 and C3).

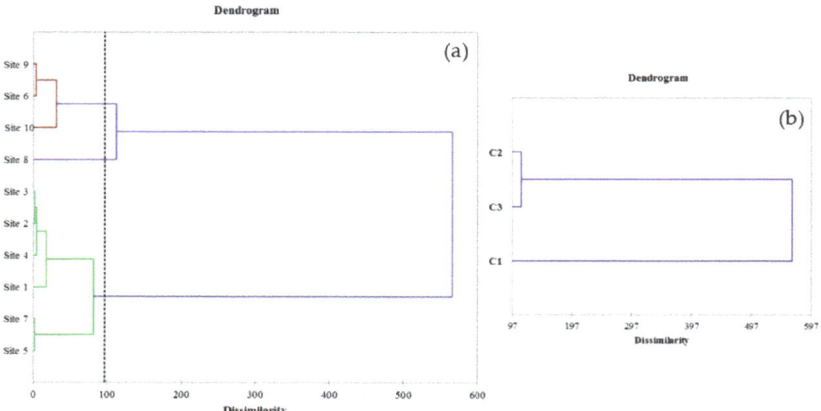

Figure 3. Results, before (**a**) and after (**b**) the automatic cut.

The C1 cluster (green color in Figure 3) is made up of 60% of the samples (ID 1, 2, 3, 4, 5 and 7 sites), while 30% of the pyroclastic products fall within the C2 cluster (blue color in Figure 3) and come from the ID 6, 9 and 10 sites. The last cluster (C3) is instead formed by samples from the ID 8 site.

Noteworthy, the similar behavior of samples collected as "fresh eruption" and "pyroclastic wastes" could be probably due to the fact that pyroclastic wastes have not—or have negligibly—undergone contamination processes.

With reference to the MDA, the outcome graph is shown in Figure 4. The graphical interface consists of the results previously obtained from the PCA, with the superimposition of a contour map comprising different colors in relation to the degree of similarity that the analyzed samples highlight. The interpretation of the results is made clearer by the presence of circular, elliptical or square vectors capable of explaining the differences observed in multidimensional space. Obviously, a greater degree of difference observed between the considered samples will correspond to a lower degree of similarity [48].

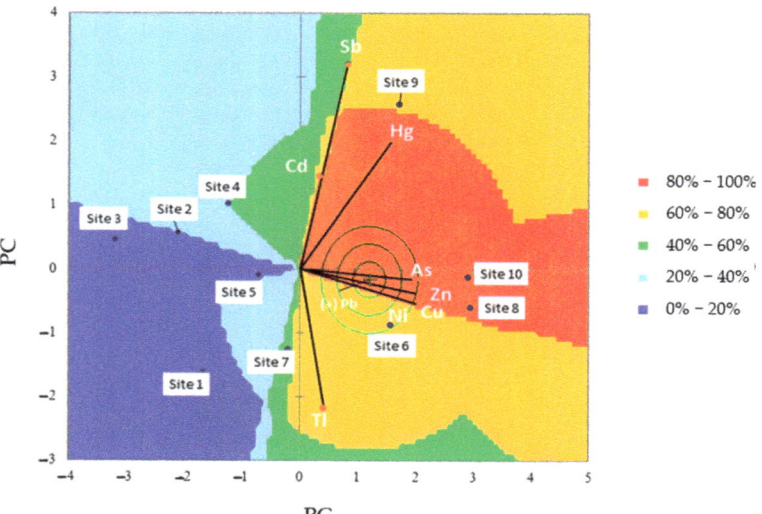

Figure 4. MDA contour plot as obtained by combining PCA and HCA results. Different colors account for the degree of similarity between the analyzed samples.

The results of the MDA approach confirm what was suggested by the previous analyses (PCA and HCA). In fact, it is possible to identify three groups, which respectively include:

1. Samples from the ID 8 and 10 sites, with a degree of similarity equal to 100%, and samples from the ID 6 and 9 sites, with a degree of similarity equal to 78%. These pyroclastic products can be ideally grouped within the same cluster. However, while samples from the ID 6, 8 and 10 sites are pyroclastic wastes, those from the ID 9 site were collected as a fresh eruption sample;
2. All other samples are placed in the quadrants on the left side of the MDA graph. In particular, samples from ID 7 site have a degree of similarity of 56% (green color), and belong to the category of freshly erupted air-fall pyroclastic products;
3. The remaining samples show heterogeneous degrees of similarity, but commonly less than 40% for all of them. This last hypothetical cluster seems to consist of the remaining fresh eruption samples (ID 1, 4 and 5 sites) and the pyroclastic waste samples (ID 2 and 3 sites), which probably have undergone pollution phenomena capable of determining potentially toxic elements concentrations similar to those shown by the fresh eruption pyroclastic samples.

4. Conclusions

The concentration levels of potentially toxic elements in pyroclastic products from Mt. Etna, Sicily, Southern Italy, were investigated through ICP-MS. The obtained values were found to be lower than the threshold limits set by the Italian legislation, and for this reason they do not constitute a risk to human health.

Moreover, the calculation of different pollution indices was performed to evaluate the ecological risk imposed on the ecosystem by potentially risky elements. In particular, EF values indicate no or minimal enrichment in all cases, suggesting an anthropogenic origin for Cu only. Furthermore, the obtained I_{geo} and CF data indicate a moderate Cu contamination for all the investigated samples, probably due to the use of this metal as a soil defense product, to the soil texture and high pH. Finally, the PLI values indicated no pollution by the assessed potentially risky elements.

Statistical analyses, i.e., Pearson correlation, PCA, HCA and MDA, were also performed by processing measured potentially toxic elements contents with the aim to determine their correlation with the sampling locations. In detail, the calculated PCA biplot identifies three different clusters, into which the analyzed pyroclastic products can be grouped. Furthermore, results of HCA and MDA turned out to be in good agreement with those produced by the PCA with a high degree of accuracy, validating the use of such statical approaches for the analysis of the relationship between chemical contaminants and sampling sites.

Finally, the approach reported in this paper could be applied, in principle, for the evaluation of the chemical risk due to the presence of potentially toxic elements in a large variety of environmental samples, by constituting a guideline for investigations focused on the monitoring of the environmental quality.

Author Contributions: Conceptualization, F.C. and V.V.; methodology, F.C. and G.P.; validation, D.M.; formal analysis, A.F.M. and M.M.; investigation, F.C. and V.V.; resources, F.C. and D.M.; data curation, F.C.; writing–original draft preparation, F.C.; and supervision, D.M. and V.V. All authors have read and agreed to the published version of the manuscript.

Funding: This research received no external funding.

Institutional Review Board Statement: Not applicable.

Informed Consent Statement: Not applicable.

Acknowledgments: Authors are grateful to Sebastiano Ettore Spoto for providing us with the samples used in this study.

Conflicts of Interest: The authors declare no conflict of interest.

References

1. Liang, L.; Gong, P. Urban and air pollution: A multi-city study of long-term effects of urban landscape patterns on air quality trends. *Sci. Rep.* **2020**, *10*, 18618. [CrossRef]
2. Masindi, V.; Liang, L.; Gong, P. Environmental Contamination by Heavy Metals. *Heavy Metals* **2018**, *10*, 115–132.
3. Ali, H.; Khan, E.; Ilahi, I. Environmental Chemistry and Ecotoxicology of Hazardous Heavy Metals: Environmental Persistence, Toxicity, and Bioaccumulation. *J. Chem.* **2019**, *2019*, 6730305. [CrossRef]
4. Briffa, J.; Sinagra, E.; Blundell, R. Heavy metal pollution in the environment and their toxicological effects on humans. *Heliyon* **2020**, *6*, e04691. [CrossRef] [PubMed]
5. Tchounwou, P.B.; Yedjou, C.G.; Patlolla, A.K.; Sutton, D.J. Heavy metal toxicity and the environment. *Exp. Suppl.* **2012**, *101*, 133–164. [CrossRef]
6. Torrisi, L.; Caridi, F.; Giuffrida, L. Protons and ion acceleration from thick targets at 10^{10} W/cm^2 laser pulse intensity. *Laser and Part. Beams.* **2011**, *29*, 29–37. [CrossRef]
7. Torrisi, L.; Visco, A.M.; Campo, N.; Caridi, F. Pulsed laser treatments of polyethylene films. *Nucl. Instr. and Meth. in Phys. Res. Sect. B* **2010**, *268*, 3117–3121. [CrossRef]
8. Jaishankar, M.; Tseten, T.; Anbalagan, N.; Mathew, B.B.; Beeregowda, K.N. Toxicity, mechanism and health effects of some heavy metals. *Interdiscip. Toxicol.* **2014**, *7*, 60–72. [CrossRef] [PubMed]
9. Saleh, M.Q.; Hamad, Z.A.; Hama, J.R. Assessment of some heavy metals in crude oil workers from Kurdistan Region, northern Iraq. *Environ. Monit. Assess.* **2021**, *193*, 49. [CrossRef]
10. Iwuoha, G.N.; Osuji, L.; Horsfall, M.J. Index model analysis approach to heavy metal pollution assessment in sediments of Nworie and Otamiri Rivers in Imo State of Nigeria. *Res. J. Chem. Sci.* **2012**, *2*, 1–8.
11. Caridi, F.; D'Agostino, M.; Belvedere, A.; Marguccio, S.; Belmusto, G.; Gatto, M.F. Diagnostics techniques and dosimetric evaluations for environmental radioactivity investigations. *J. Instrum.* **2016**, *11*, C10012. [CrossRef]
12. Caridi, F.; D'Agostino, M.; Messina, M.; Marcianò, G.; Grioli, L.; Belvedere, A.; Marguccio, S.; Belmusto, G. Lichens as environmental risk detectors. *Eur. Phys. J. Plus* **2017**, *132*, 189. [CrossRef]
13. Ravisankar, R.; Vanasundari, K.; Chandrasekaran, A.; Rajalakshmi, A.; Suganya, M.; Vijayagopal, P.; Meenakshisundaram, V. Measurement of natural radioactivity in building materials of Namakkal, Tamil Nadu, India using gamma-ray spectrometry. *Appl. Radiat. Isot.* **2012**, *70*, 699–704. [CrossRef]
14. Raja, S.L.; Marpaung, H.; Simanjuntak, S.; Simanjuntak, C.; Pudjadi, E. Distribution and risk assessment of natural radioactive elements in volcanic ashes, cold lava, river waters due to volcanic eruption of Mount Sinabung. *AIP Conf. Proc.* **2021**, *2342*, 020008. [CrossRef]
15. Zagorodnyuk, L.H.; Mestnikov, A.E.; Makhortov, D.S.; Akhmed, A.A.A. Mixed binders with the use of volcanic ash. *Lect. Notes Civ. Eng.* **2021**, *95*, 9–15. [CrossRef]
16. Ahmedai, M.A.; Ahmed, S.A.M.; Ahmed, Y.H.; Ibrahiem, E.-S.M. Tagabo Volcanic Ash as Cement Replacing Materials. *FES J. Eng. Sci.* **2021**, *9*, 35–39. [CrossRef]
17. Gvirtzman, Z.; Nur, A. The formation of Mount Etna as the consequence of slab rollback. *Nature* **1999**, *401*, 782–785. [CrossRef]
18. Tanguy, J.-C.; Condomines, M.; Kieffer, G. Evolution of the Mount Etna magma: Constraints on the present feeding system and eruptive mechanism. *J. Volcanol. Geotherm. Res.* **1997**, *75*, 221–250. [CrossRef]
19. Mezzasalma, A.M.; Mondio, G.; Serafino, T.; Caridi, F.; Torrisi, L. Electronic properties of thin films of laser-ablated Al_2O_3. *Appl. Surf. Sci.* **2009**, *255*, 4123–4128. [CrossRef]
20. Giorgia Potortì, A.; Francesco Mottese, A.; Rita Fede, M.; Sabatino, G.; Dugo, G.; Lo Turco, V.; Costa, R.; Caridi, F.; Di Bella, M.; Di Bella, G. Multielement and chemometric analysis for the traceability of the Pachino Protected Geographical Indication (PGI) cherry tomatoes. *Food Chem.* **2022**, *386*, 132746. [CrossRef] [PubMed]
21. Mottese, A.F.; Sabatino, G.; Di Bella, M.; Fede, M.R.; Parisi, F.; Marcianò, G.; Tripodo, A.; Italiano, F.; Dugo, G.; Caridi, F. Contribution of soil compositions, harvested times and varieties on chemical fingerprint of Italian and Turkish citrus cultivars. *Int. J. Food Sci. Technol.* **2021**, *56*, 2628–2639. [CrossRef]
22. Stewart, C.; Horwell, C.; Plumlee, G.; Cronin, S.; Delmelle, P.; Baxter, P.; Calkins, J.; Damby, D.; Morman, S.; Oppenheimer, C. Protocol for analysis of volcanic ash samples for assessment of hazards from leachable elements. *Int. Volcan. Health Hazards Netw. Publ.* **2013**, *1*, 1–22.
23. EPA METHOD 3051a:2007. 2007. Available online: https://www.epa.gov/sites/default/files/2015-12/documents/3051a.pdf (accessed on 1 September 2022).
24. Caridi, F.; Marguccio, S.; D'Agostino, M.; Belvedere, A.; Belmusto, G. Natural radioactivity and metal contamination of river sediments in the Calabria region, south of Italy. *Eur. Phys. J. Plus* **2016**, *131*, 155. [CrossRef]
25. Caridi, F.; Messina, M.; D'Agostino, M. An investigation about natural radioactivity, hydrochemistry, and metal pollution in groundwater from Calabrian selected areas, southern Italy. *Environ. Earth Sci.* **2017**, *76*, 668. [CrossRef]
26. EPA METHOD 6020a:2007. 2007. Available online: https://19january2017snapshot.epa.gov/sites/production/files/2015-07/documents/epa-6020a.pdf (accessed on 2 September 2022).
27. ACCREDIA. Available online: https://www.accredia.it/ (accessed on 2 September 2022).
28. Turekian, K.K.; Haven, N.; Hans, K.; Universitat, W.M. Der Distribution of the Elements in Some Major Units of the Earth's Crust. *America (NY)* **1961**, *1*, 175–192.

29. Caridi, F.; D'Agostino, M.; Marguccio, S.; Belvedere, A.; Belmusto, G.; Marcianò, G.; Sabatino, G.; Mottese, A. Radioactivity, granulometric and elemental analysis of river sediments samples from the coast of Calabria, south of Italy. *Eur. Phys. J. Plus* **2016**, *131*, 136. [CrossRef]
30. Håkanson, L. An Ecological Risk Index for Aquatic Pollution Control—A Sedimentological Approach. *Water Res.* **1980**, *14*, 975–1001. [CrossRef]
31. Chandrasekaran, A.; Ravisankar, R.; Harikrishnan, N.; Satapathy, K.K.; Prasad, M.V.R.; Kanagasabapathy, K.V. Multivariate statistical analysis of heavy metal concentration in soils of Yelagiri Hills, Tamilnadu, India—Spectroscopical approach. *Spectrochim. Acta Part A Mol. Biomol. Spectrosc.* **2015**, *137*, 589–600. [CrossRef]
32. Ramasamy, V.; Meenakshisundaram, V.; Venkatachalapathy, R.; Ponnusamy, V. Influence of mineralogical and heavy metal composition on natural radionuclide concentrations in the river sediments. *Appl. Radiat. Isot.* **2011**, *69*, 1466–1474. [CrossRef]
33. Caridi, F.; D'Agostino, M.; Belvedere, A.; Mottese, A.F. Multi-element Analysis and Geographical Origin Classification of Italian (Calabrian) Wines. *Curr. Nutr. Food Sci.* **2020**, *16*, 1259–1264. [CrossRef]
34. Caridi, F.; Acri, G.; Belvedere, A.; Crupi, V.; Agostino, M.D.; Marguccio, S.; Messina, M.; Paladini, G.; Venuti, V.; Majolino, D. Evaluation of the Radiological and Chemical Risk for Public Health from Flour Sample Investigation. *Appl. Sci.* **2021**, *11*, 3646. [CrossRef]
35. Mottese, A.F.; Fede, M.R.; Caridi, F.; Sabatino, G.; Marcianò, G.; Calabrese, G.; Albergamo, A.; Dugo, G. Chemometrics and innovative multidimensional data analysis (MDA) based on multi-element screening to protect the Italian porcino (Boletus sect. Boletus) from fraud. *Food Control* **2020**, *110*, 107004. [CrossRef]
36. Bondarev, A.E.; Galaktionov, V.A. Multidimensional data analysis and visualization for time-dependent CFD problems. *Program. Comput. Softw.* **2015**, *41*, 247–252. [CrossRef]
37. D. Lgs. 152/2006. Available online: https://www.normattiva.it/uri-res/N2Ls?urn:nir:stato:decreto.legislativo:2006-04-03;152 (accessed on 2 September 2022).
38. Hassan, N.M.; Rasmussen, P.E.; Dabek-Zlotorzynska, E.; Celo, V.; Chen, H. Analysis of Environmental Samples Using Microwave-Assisted Acid Digestion and Inductively Coupled Plasma Mass Spectrometry: Maximizing Total Element Recoveries. *Water. Air. Soil Pollut.* **2007**, *178*, 323–334. [CrossRef]
39. Zheng, L.-G.; Liu, G.-J.; Kang, Y.; Yang, R.-K. Some potential hazardous trace elements contamination and their ecological risk in sediments of western Chaohu Lake, China. *Environ. Monit. Assess.* **2010**, *166*, 379–386. [CrossRef]
40. Naji, A.; Ismail, A. Assessment of Metals Contamination in Klang River Surface Sediments by using Different Indexes. *EnvironmentAsia* **2011**, *4*, 30–38. [CrossRef]
41. Karimi, B.; Masson, V.; Guilland, C.; Leroy, E.; Pellegrinelli, S.; Giboulot, E.; Maron, P.-A.; Ranjard, L. Ecotoxicity of copper input and accumulation for soil biodiversity in vineyards. *Environ. Chem. Lett.* **2021**, *19*, 2013–2030. [CrossRef]
42. Pietrzak, U.; McPhail, D.C. Copper accumulation, distribution and fractionation in vineyard soils of Victoria, Australia. *Geoderma* **2004**, *122*, 151–166. [CrossRef]
43. Yuan, H.; Song, J.; Li, X.; Li, N.; Duan, L. Distribution and contamination of heavy metals in surface sediments of the South Yellow Sea. *Mar. Pollut. Bull.* **2012**, *64*, 2151–2159. [CrossRef]
44. Selvaraj, K.; Ram Mohan, V.; Szefer, P. Evaluation of metal contamination in coastal sediments of the Bay of Bengal, India: Geochemical and statistical approaches. *Mar. Pollut. Bull.* **2004**, *49*, 174–185. [CrossRef]
45. Mohd Razali, N.; Yap, B. Power comparisons of some selected normality tests. In Proceedings of the Regional Conference on Statistical Sciences 2010 (RCSS'10), Kota Bharu, Malaysia, 13–14 June 2010; Volume 1, pp. 126–138.
46. Weide, A.C.; Beauducel, A. Varimax Rotation Based on Gradient Projection Is a Feasible Alternative to SPSS. *Front. Psychol.* **2019**, *10*, 1–14. [CrossRef]
47. Paez, P.A.; Cogliati, M.G.; Caselli, A.T.; Monasterio, A.M. An analysis of volcanic SO_2 and ash emissions from Copahue volcano. *J. S. Am. Earth Sci.* **2021**, *110*, 103365. [CrossRef]
48. Fraire, M. Statistical methods for exploratory multidimensional data analysis on time use. *Statistica* **2013**, *69*, 317–341.

Article

Estimation of Cosmic-Ray-Induced Atmospheric Ionization and Radiation at Commercial Aviation Flight Altitudes

Panagiota Makrantoni [1], Anastasia Tezari [1,2], Argyris N. Stassinakis [1], Pavlos Paschalis [1], Maria Gerontidou [1], Pantelis Karaiskos [3], Alexandros G. Georgakilas [4], Helen Mavromichalaki [1,*], Ilya G. Usoskin [5], Norma Crosby [6] and Mark Dierckxsens [6]

[1] Athens Cosmic Ray Group, Faculty of Physics, National and Kapodistrian University of Athens, 15784 Athens, Greece; pmakrantoni@phys.uoa.gr (P.M.); anatez@med.uoa.gr (A.T.); a-stasinakis@phys.uoa.gr (A.N.S.); ppaschalis@phys.uoa.gr (P.P.); mgeront@phys.uoa.gr (M.G.)
[2] Eugenides Foundation, 17564 Athens, Greece
[3] Medical Physics Laboratory, Faculty of Medicine, National and Kapodistrian University of Athens, 11517 Athens, Greece; pkaraisk@med.uoa.gr
[4] DNA Damage Laboratory, Physics Department, School of Applied Mathematical and Physical Sciences, National Technical University of Athens (NTUA), Zografou, Athens 15780, Greece; alexg@mail.ntua.gr
[5] Space Physics and Astronomy Research Unit and Sodankylä Geophysical Observatory, University of Oulu, FIN-90014 Oulu, Finland; ilya.usoskin@oulu.fi
[6] Royal Belgian Institute for Space Aeronomy, 1180 Brussels, Belgium; norma.crosby@aeronomie.be (N.C.); mark.dierckxsens@aeronomie.be (M.D.)
* Correspondence: emavromi@phys.uoa.gr

Citation: Makrantoni, P.; Tezari, A.; Stassinakis, A.N.; Paschalis, P.; Gerontidou, M.; Karaiskos, P.; Georgakilas, A.G.; Mavromichalaki, H.; Usoskin, I.G.; Crosby, N.; et al. Estimation of Cosmic-Ray-Induced Atmospheric Ionization and Radiation at Commercial Aviation Flight Altitudes. *Appl. Sci.* 2022, 12, 5297. https://doi.org/10.3390/app12115297

Academic Editor: Francesco Caridi

Received: 9 May 2022
Accepted: 22 May 2022
Published: 24 May 2022

Publisher's Note: MDPI stays neutral with regard to jurisdictional claims in published maps and institutional affiliations.

Copyright: © 2022 by the authors. Licensee MDPI, Basel, Switzerland. This article is an open access article distributed under the terms and conditions of the Creative Commons Attribution (CC BY) license (https://creativecommons.org/licenses/by/4.0/).

Abstract: The main source of the ionization of the Earth's atmosphere is the cosmic radiation that depends on solar activity as well as geomagnetic activity. Galactic cosmic rays constitute a permanent radiation background and contribute significantly to the radiation exposure inside the atmosphere. In this work, the cosmic-ray-induced ionization of the Earth's atmosphere, due to both solar and galactic cosmic radiation during the recent solar cycles 23 (1996–2008) and 24 (2008–2019), was studied globally. Estimations of the ionization were based on the CRAC:CRII model by the University of Oulu. The use of this model allowed for extensive calculations from the Earth's surface (atmospheric depth 1033 g/cm^2) to the upper limit of the atmosphere (atmospheric depth 0 g/cm^2). Monte Carlo simulations were performed for the estimation quantities of radiobiological interest with the validated software DYASTIMA/DYASTIMA-R. This study was focused on specific altitudes of interest, such as the common flight levels used by commercial aviation.

Keywords: cosmic rays; ionization; radiation; atmosphere; solar cycle; flight level; aviation

1. Introduction

Cosmic rays are highly energetic particles of extraterrestrial origin. There are two main components of cosmic rays: galactic cosmic rays (GCRs), which originate from outside of our Solar System and Solar Energetic Particles (SEPs), which are accelerated during eruptive processes on the Sun [1]. As cosmic rays travel through the interplanetary space and reach the terrestrial atmosphere, (these rays are named primary cosmic rays), they penetrate by colliding with nuclei of atoms and ions of the atmosphere, thus creating nucleonic, muonic and electromagnetic cascades named secondary cosmic rays, as the primary particles are absorbed inside the atmosphere due to ionization losses. In this way, cosmic rays affect the physical–chemical properties of the atmosphere, i.e., its ion balance, [2,3] and may even affect the regional climate's variability [4]. The Earth's magnetic field acts as a charge discriminator and modulates the cosmic ray flux that reaches each location on the Earth.

Since cosmic rays are always present as a natural radiation background, they constitute a major factor in the ionization of the atmosphere. This process is called cosmic-ray-induced ionization (CRII). The GCRs affect the CRII by following an 11-year modulation oppositely correlated to the solar activity, i.e., the greater the solar activity, the lower the intensity of the CRII is. On the other hand, strong fluxes of the unpredictable SEPs produced in solar flares or coronal mass ejections (CMEs) most likely occur during periods of intense solar activity and mostly affect the polar regions and high altitudes, where the magnetic field lines are open and the energetic particles may deposit their energy, even at 20 km a.s.l. It is noteworthy that GCRs are referred to as the continuous flux of the charged particles which originate from different sources within the intergalactic space, while SEPs make up the solar component of cosmic rays, associated with an increase in particle fluxes released in the interplanetary space after great solar activity. SEPs also create hazards for satellites, spacecraft, high-altitude aircraft, as well as for the health of air crews and space crews, due to the enhanced radiation environment SEPs create [5,6].

As cosmic rays contribute to the production of ion pairs, which are involved in several atmospheric processes, numerous studies indicate that ionization induced by CRs may affect different climate parameters [7,8] and so the computation of CRII is considered necessary. Specifically, the atmospheric ionization may alter the physical and chemical properties of the atmosphere and affect several processes, such as aerosol and cloud formation, atmospheric transparency, cloud cover, cyclogenesis and precipitation, especially in regions of middle and high geographic latitudes. Therefore, several numerical models were created and validated via comparison with direct observations and measurements of the CRII, e.g., the Sofia model [8,9], the Bern model, also called ATMOCOSMIC [10,11] and the Oulu model, also called CRAC:CRII [12,13]. Results from the latter model [14] are used in this work.

Aside from cosmic rays affecting the composition of the atmosphere and contributing to climate configuration, they may also affect human health [15,16]. The way that CRII is modulated and distributed inside the atmosphere affects human exposure to radiation, suggesting that air crew members and frequent flyers of commercial flights should be treated in a specific way and extra safety measures and necessary regulations should be applied during their flights. Other than ones referring to the general public, specific regulations and safety measures do not yet exist for frequent flyers. However, the European Commission, as well as other entities such as the International Commission on Radiation Units and Measurements (ICRU) and the International Committee on Radiological Protection (ICRP), have adopted a series of recommendations and frameworks regarding the determination of the occupational exposure of aviation crews to cosmic radiation, as well as the most efficient measures and counteractions to ensure radiation protection [17–19]. For this reason, several studies on the problem have been performed [20–27], while various models and tools have also been developed by the scientific community in cooperation with the aviation industry. Some of these well-known models are the following: SIEVERT [28], AVIDOS [29], NAIRAS [30], CARI [31], CALVADOS [32] SPENVIS [33], CRAC:DOSE [23] and PLANETOCOSMICS [10].

Furthermore, ionization also affects the avionic electronic systems during a flight, with single event effects (SEEs) being a main factor in this [34,35]. To expand, a single secondary high-energy atmospheric neutron can collide with a nucleus of the semiconductor, causing an ionization charge that can affect a semiconductor device. The most common effects of SEEs are soft errors, firm errors and hard errors that decrease the performance and the availability of electronic systems. Furthermore, radiation can also affect optical components (i.e., LEDs, lasers and optical fibers), by changing their optical properties and causing displacement damage. Usually, the electronic and optoelectronic devices anneal after the irradiation has stopped but, in some cases, radiation can cause permanent damage [36–38]. Therefore, it is crucial to estimate the ionization and radiation levels during a flight in order to be able to maintain reliability standards.

In this work, the CRII was calculated for three different flight levels (FLs): FL310 (9.45 km a.s.l. or 31,000 ft), FL350 (10.67 km a.s.l. or 35,000 ft) and FL390 (11.89 km a.s.l. or 39,000 ft). The model used for the aforementioned calculations was the CRAC:CRII model in its extended version [12,13]. The CRII for these typical FLs is depicted in ionization maps (Figure 1), showing the distribution of CRII globally for specific phases of solar cycles 23 and 24 (i.e., solar maxima and minima). More to that, time profiles of the monthly distribution of CRII for selected magnetic cut-off rigidities for the same FLs during solar cycles 23 and 24 will be presented.

In addition, a similar study concerning the radiation assessment of occupational exposure to cosmic rays, specifically the estimation of the ambient equivalent dose rate for the typical FLs, was performed. For these calculations, the software application Dynamic Atmospheric Shower Tracking Interactive Model Application (DYASTIMA) [39,40] of the Athens Cosmic Ray Group was used. Finally, regarding the investigation in this work, a combined study was performed and a correlation between these two physical parameters is shown.

2. Technical Analysis and Data Selection

For the ionization induced by cosmic rays, the CRAC:CRII model of the Oulu University was used—a numerical model that computes the CRII from the sea level to up to 40 km in the atmosphere, for every location on Earth. This model uses the Monte Carlo CORSIKA tool (v.6.617 August 2007) [41], which provides a full development simulation of an electromagnetic–muon–nucleonic cascade in the atmosphere, as well as the FLUKA package for the low-energy interactions (v.2006.3b March 2007) [42] and is fully described in [12,13].

Moreover, concerning calculations of the CRII for specific latitudes, altitudes and time periods, considering both solar and galactic cosmic rays, the "Cosmic Ray Induced Ionization: Do-it-yourself kit" (http://cosmicrays.oulu.fi/CRII/CRII.html) (accessed on 5 May 2022) of the Oulu Cosmic Ray Station was used, and the monthly and annual values of the modulation parameter Phi (in MV), reconstructed from the ground-based cosmic ray data, are provided [43,44]. The modulation parameter corresponds to the local interstellar spectrum (LIS) of cosmic rays, as provided by [45].

In order to calculate the ambient dose equivalent rate $dH^*(10)/dt$, DYASTIMA was used [39]. Monte Carlo simulations of the secondary cascades taking place in the different atmospheric layers were performed with this independent GEANT4 software tool [46–48], which allowed for the determination of several characteristics of the cascade, such as the energy of the particles and the energy deposits at the different atmospheric layers. The FTFP_BERT_HP GEANT4 physics list was used, as it adequately describes all processes taking place due to secondary cascades. Then, several radiobiological quantities were calculated with the DYASTIMA-R extension. Specifically, the operational quantity $dH^*(10)/dt$ was estimated by taking into consideration the different radiation weighting factors that corresponded to the different types of secondary cosmic ray particles [9]. DYASTIMA/DYASTIMA-R is a validated tool [40,49,50], as it meets the criteria provided by the ICRU and ICRP documents [18,19] regarding radiation protection in the aviation sector. DYASTIMA software was provided through the portal of the Athens Neutron Monitor Station (A.Ne.Mo.S.) (http://cosray.phys.uoa.gr/index.php/dyastima) (accessed on 6 April 2022), while a database of selected simulated scenarios is available as a federated product on the ESA SWE Portal (https://swe.ssa.esa.int/dyastima-federated) (accessed on 6 April 2022).

The required input parameters for performing a simulation with DYASTIMA concern the characteristics of the planet and its atmosphere, as well as the differential spectrum of the incoming primary cosmic ray particles at the top of the atmosphere. As far as the simulations presented in this work are concerned, the atmospheric profile was based on the International Standard Atmosphere (ISA) model [51], while the ISO15390 model was used for the determination of the primary cosmic ray spectra [52]. To take into account the effect of the geomagnetic field, maps of the cut-off rigidity threshold values as a function of the geographic coordinates were used, based on the International Geomagnetic Reference Field (IGRF) [53–56]. The magnetic field components were obtained via the National Oceanic and

Atmospheric Administration portal (https://www.ngdc.noaa.gov/geomag/) (accessed on 24 March 2022).

3. Results

In this work, a study of cosmic-ray-induced ionization, computed via the CRAC:CRII model [12,13], along with the estimated ambient dose equivalent rate computed via the validated software DYASTIMA/DYASTIMA-R [39,40], was performed globally during the last two solar cycles (23 and 24) and focused on specific altitudes that corresponded to the most common commercial flight levels: FL310 (9.45 km a.s.l.), FL350 (10.67 km a.s.l.) and FL390 (11.89 km a.s.l.).

More specifically, the CRII at FL390 during the solar minima and solar maxima of solar cycles 23 and 24 is presented in Figure 1, globally, via ionization maps. Figure 1a depicts the CRII map that corresponds to the minimum of solar cycle 23 (in the year 1996), Figure 1b depicts the CRII map that corresponds to the maximum of solar cycle 23 (in the year 2001), Figure 1c depicts the CRII map that corresponds to the minimum of solar cycle 24 (in the year 2009) and Figure 1d depicts the CRII map that corresponds to the maximum of solar cycle 24 (in the year 2014). Comparing these four maps, it is clear that the ionization rate during the solar minima was greater than the ionization rate during the solar maxima of both cycles. This is due to the fact that the CRII followed the behavior of the cosmic ray intensity and was positively correlated with them, while it negatively correlated with the solar activity. In other words, the greater the solar activity, the lower the intensity of the CRII is [57–59].

Moreover, when comparing the solar minima and maxima of solar cycles 23 and 24, it is obvious that the CRII had greater values during solar cycle 24 than that of solar cycle 23, which was well expected, since solar cycle 24 is characterized as a relatively quiet solar cycle, unlike solar cycle 23, where the solar activity was greater. The minimum and maximum values for CRII and $dH^*(10)/dt$ obtained during this work for these specific time periods are presented in Table 1. Regarding the geographic coordinates, it was observed that, globally, the maximum ionization rate was found in polar regions while, at lower latitudes, the ionization rate reached minimum. This was due to the magnetic field of the Earth and the geomagnetic cut-off rigidity (Rc) that corresponded to each location, from 0 GV in polar regions to up to 17 GV in equatorial regions. The lower the geomagnetic cut-off rigidity (Rc), the more cosmic rays penetrated the magnetosphere and the atmosphere of the Earth; the CRs then ionized the atmosphere and created various effects [51]. Both the CRII and estimated ambient dose equivalent rate maps were generated based on the rigidity map of [53–56].

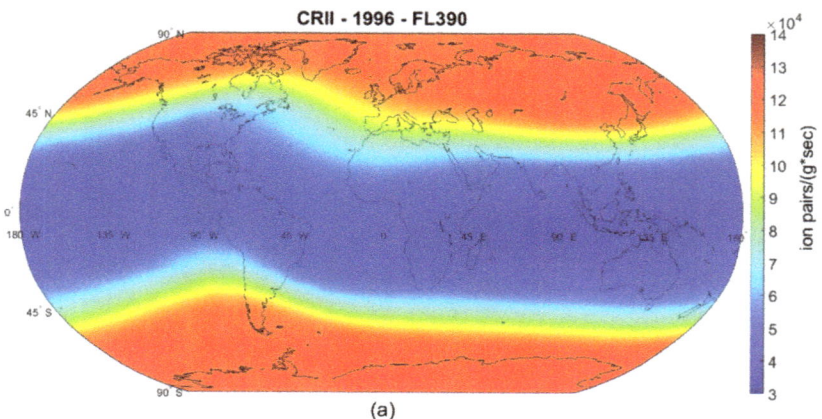

(a)

Figure 1. Cont.

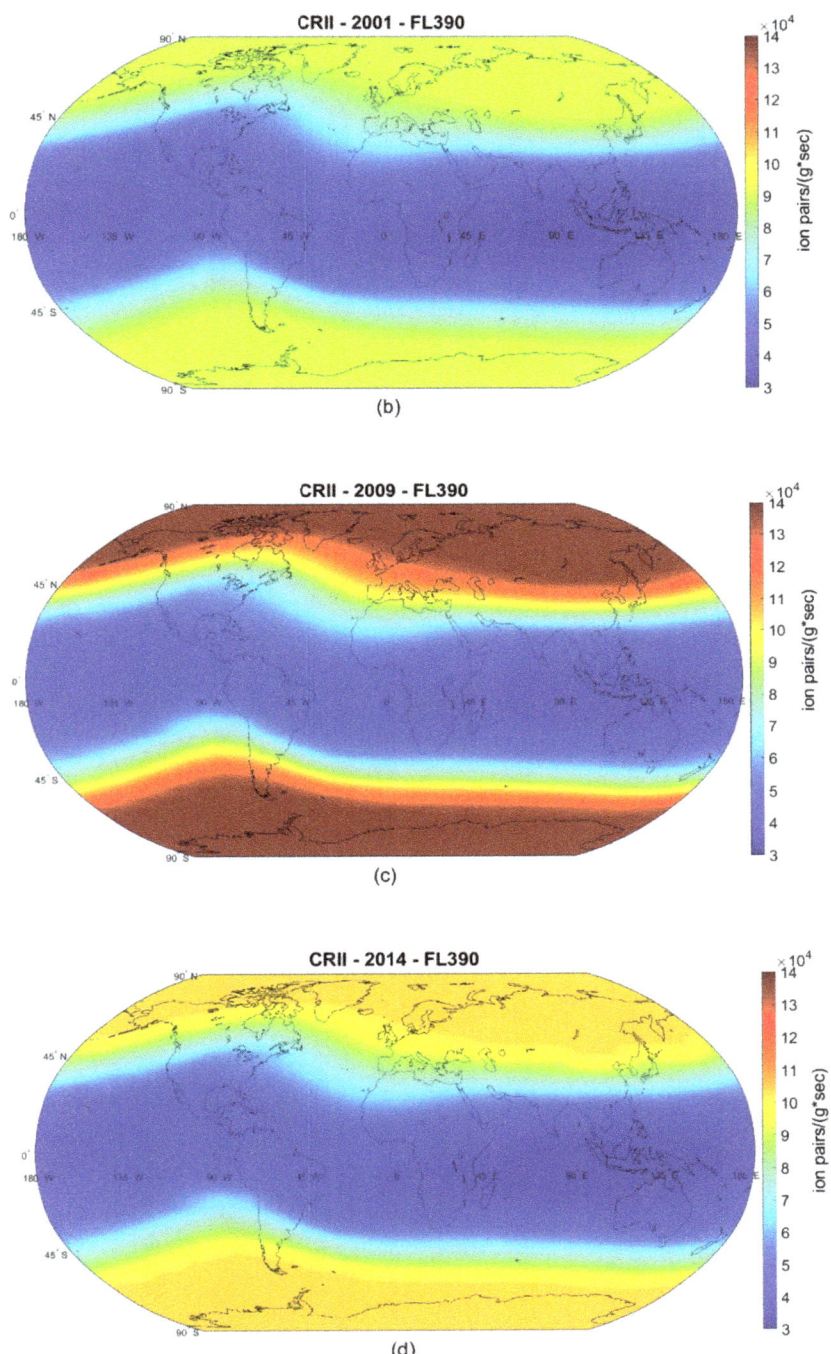

Figure 1. Maps of the CRII rate (ion pairs/(g*s)) at FL390: (**a**) during the minimum of solar cycle 23; (**b**) during the maximum of solar cycle 23; (**c**) during the minimum of solar cycle 24; (**d**) during the maximum of solar cycle 24.

Table 1. Minimum and maximum values of CRII and the estimated ambient dose equivalent rate during the minimum and maximum of solar cycles 23 and 24 at FL390.

YEARS	CRII (Ion Pairs/(g*s))		dH*(10)/dt (µSv/h)	
	Minimum Values ×10^4	Maximum Values ×10^4	Minimum Values	Maximum Values
1996 (SC23 min)	3.6	12.0	1.22	6.83
2009 (SC24 min)	3.7	13.6	1.24	7.05
2001 (SC23 max)	3.4	9.1	1.18	5.49
2014 (SC24 max)	3.5	11.0	1.19	5.50

With regard to the radiation exposure, the ambient dose equivalent rate at FL390 during the solar minima and solar maxima of solar cycles 23 and 24 is presented in Figure 2. A behavior similar to that of CRII was noticed. Greater values of the dH*(10)/dt were observed in the polar regions (Rc = 0–2 GV) and lower values near the equator (Rc = 15–17 GV), for both solar minima and maxima conditions. This was due to the dependence of the radiation levels at the atmospheric layers on the cosmic ray intensity [40,60]. As expected, the radiation exposure was greater during the solar minima compared to the solar maxima, due to the negative correlation between the solar activity and the intensity of the incoming cosmic ray particles. Greater values of dH*(10)/dt were also observed during the extended solar minimum in 2009 for both polar and equatorial regions, as compared to those observed during 1996. The observed differences can be characterized as relatively small, since the primary spectrum model used as input for the respective computations provided the estimation of the galactic component and did not take into account any SEPs which took place during this time period.

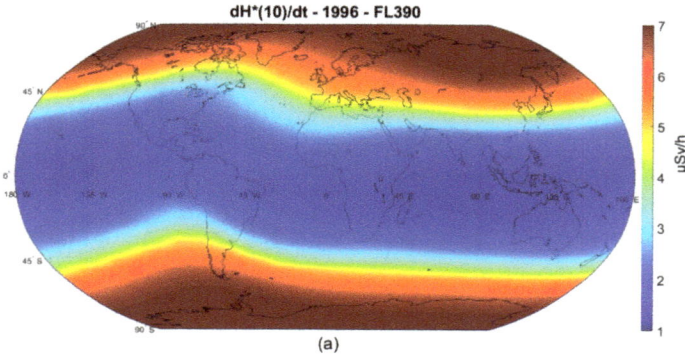

(a)

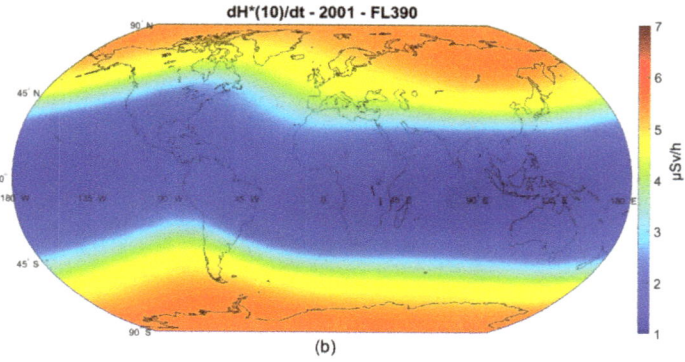

(b)

Figure 2. Cont.

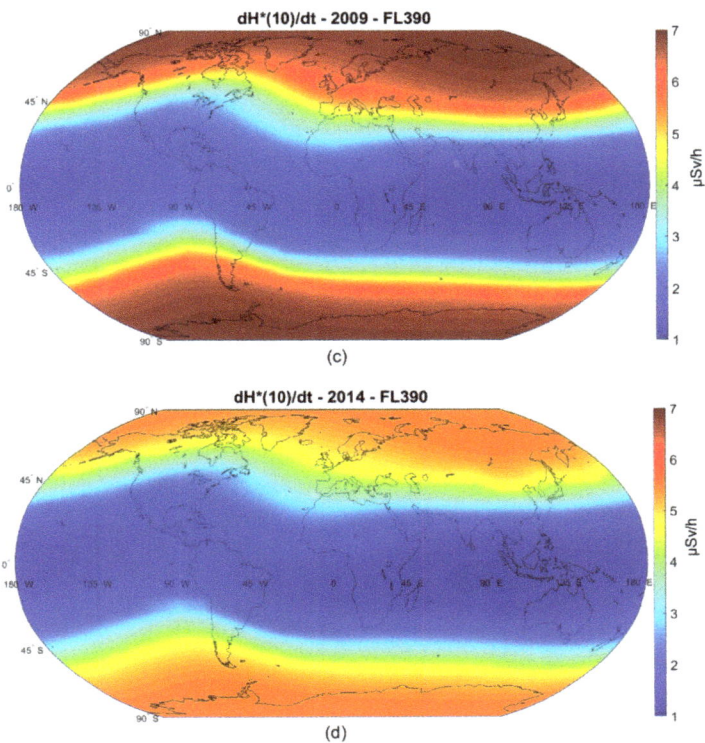

Figure 2. Maps of the estimated ambient dose equivalent rate (µSv/h) at FL390: (**a**) during the minimum of solar cycle 23; (**b**) during the maximum of solar cycle 23; (**c**) during the minimum of solar cycle 24; (**d**) during the maximum of solar cycle 24.

Time profiles of the yearly values of the CRII and the ambient dose equivalent rate from the year 1996 to the year 2019 (covering the last two solar cycles) are presented in Figures 3 and 4. Four different geomagnetic cut-off rigidity values were selected: 0.1 GV for the polar region (Figure 3a), 3.1 GV (Figure 3b), 8.5 GV, which corresponded to the middle geographic latitudes and specifically Athens, Greece (Figure 4a) and 14.9 GV for the equatorial region (Figure 4b). The results are provided for the three different atmospheric altitudes which corresponded to the usual flight levels of the commercial aircraft: FL310 (9.45 km a.s.l.), FL350 (10.67 km a.s.l.) and FL390 (11.89 km a.s.l.).

The CRII and dH*(10)/dt values for this time period and for all flight levels can be found in the Supplementary Material. It is interesting that both the CRII (left axis, blue lines) and ambient dose equivalent rate (right axis, red lines) followed a long-term modulation, specifically an 11-year one, at all the aforementioned locations, the same way the GCR intensity did [59–61], since the radiation exposure of aircraft crews was directly linked to the intensity of the cosmic radiation. Furthermore, comparing the time profiles of the three different FLs, it is obvious that the higher the aircraft flew, the higher the CRII and the estimated ambient dose equivalent rates were, since the shielding effect of the atmosphere was reduced and thus the radiation exposure of the aircrew and frequent flyers was higher. It was also observed that the difference among the values at the three FLs was greater as one reached lower rigidities, e.g., polar regions, and became smaller as one reached higher rigidities, e.g., equatorial regions. Since the magnetic field was weaker and more permeable in the polar regions, it allowed even primary cosmic ray particles of lower energies to reach the surface of the Earth, resulting in higher levels of cosmic radiation, unlike in the lower geographic latitudes where the magnetic lines were almost parallel to the Earth's surface, and therefore provided effective shielding.

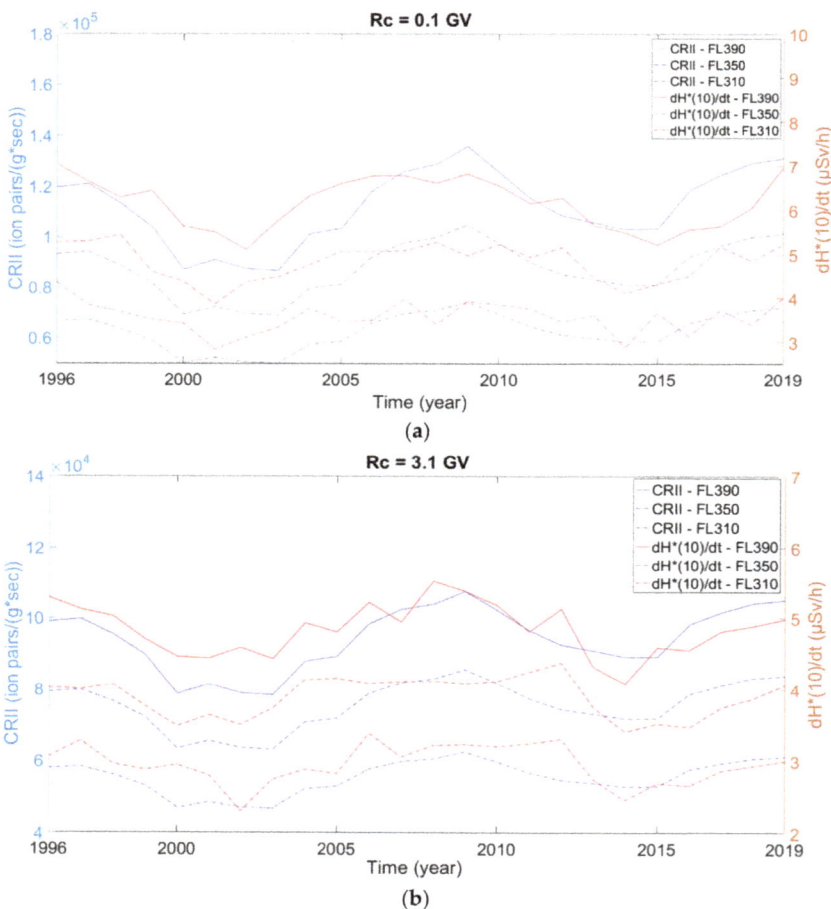

Figure 3. Yearly distribution of CRII rate (left axis, blue lines) and ambient dose equivalent rate (right axis, red lines) at three different flight levels (FL310, FL350, FL390), for the time period 1996–2019: (**a**) at a polar region with cut-off rigidity 0.1 GV; (**b**) a region with cut-off rigidity 3.1 GV.

Concerning the CRII, once again, it is noted that during all phases of solar cycle 24, which was a less active solar cycle, the values were greater than those of the respective phases of solar cycle 23, when the solar activity was intense. However, this difference became very small as we moved towards the equatorial regions, which showed that the solar activity mostly affected low-rigidity regions.

More precisely, the CRII decreased by 5.6% near the poles and 24.2% near the equator during SC23 and by 5.4% and 19.1% during SC24, respectively. Similarly, the dependence of the dH*(10)/dt on the solar cycle was most evident near the poles (Rc = 0.1 GV) and, to a lesser extent, near the equator (Rc = 14.9 GV), due to the geomagnetic field shielding, which reflected particles of lower energies. In addition, the dH*(10)/dt decreased by 3.3% near the poles and 19.6% near the equator during SC23 and by 4.1% and 22% during SC24, respectively.

Finally, the correlation between the yearly distribution of the CRII and the estimated ambient dose equivalent rate for all four rigidities mentioned above (0.1 GV, 3.1 GV, 8.5 GV and 14.9 GV), for all three FLs (FL310, FL350 and FL390), from 1996 to 2019, is illustrated in Figure 5. It is of great importance that a positive correlation between the two physical quantities was observed, with the correlation coefficient being $R^2 = 0.97$. This confirms that the cosmic-ray-induced ionization of the Earth's magnetosphere contributed to the radiation deposited at different locations and altitudes. The data of Figures 3 and 4 are given as Supplementary Material.

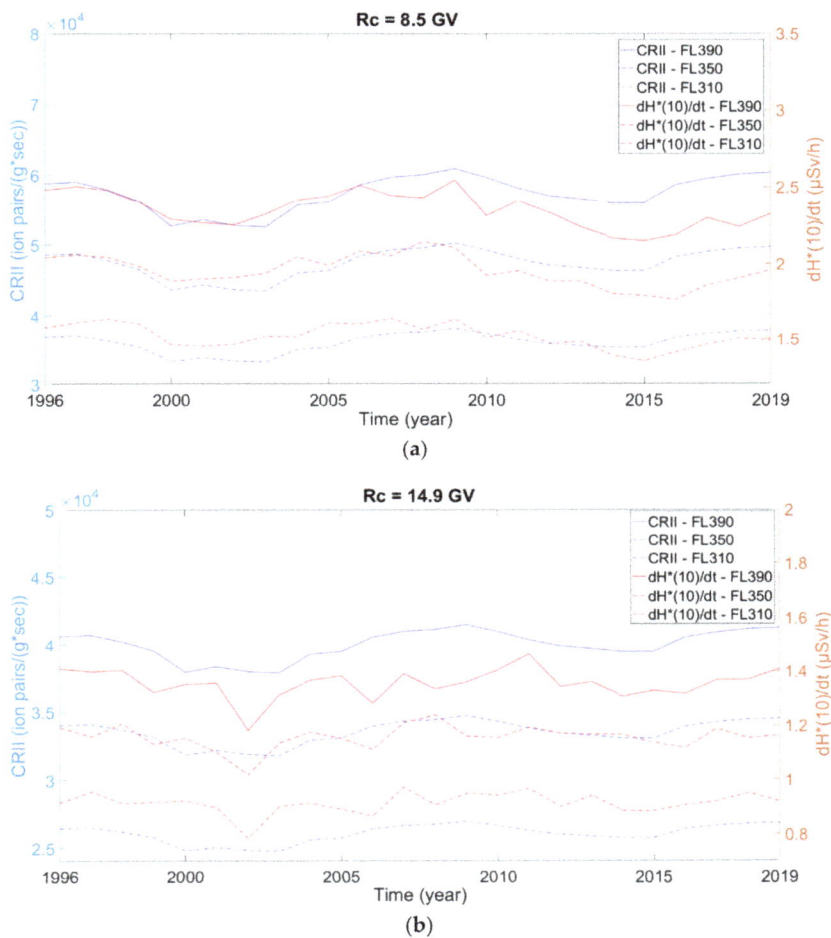

Figure 4. Yearly distribution of CRII rate (left axis, blue lines) and ambient dose equivalent rate (right axis, red lines) at three different flight levels (FL310, FL350, FL390), for the time period 1996–2019: (**a**) at a region with cut-off rigidity 8.5 GV; (**b**) an equatorial region with cut-off rigidity 14.9 GV.

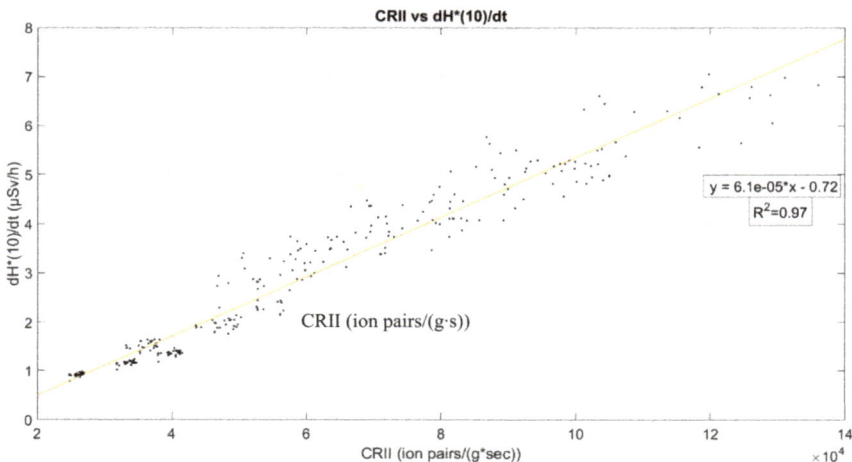

Figure 5. Scatter plot of the yearly distribution of the CRII and the ambient dose equivalent rate for the time period 1996–2019 for FL310, FL350, FL390.

4. Discussion and Conclusions

In this study, the estimated CRII rate and ambient dose equivalent rate distributions all over the globe were presented for the most common commercial flight levels (FL310, FL350 and FL390) during the recent two solar cycles 23 and 24 (1996–2019). For the calculation of the CRII and the dH*(10)/dt, the CRAC:CRII model of Oulu University [12,13] and the DYASTIMA/DYASTIMA-R software [39,40] were used, respectively. The distribution of both physical quantities was initially depicted in the maps, where the values during the minima and maxima of solar cycles 23 and 24 (for FL390) were illustrated for the entire Earth and all the cut-off rigidities (0–17 GV). The maximum values were observed during the solar minima and at polar regions (approximately 7 μSv/h at FL390), while the minimum values during the solar maxima and at the equatorial regions were approximately 1.2 μSv/h at FL390, due to the anticipated anticorrelation of the cosmic ray intensity with the solar activity, as well as due to the shielding of the geomagnetic field. Furthermore, a comparison between solar activity and ionization can be presented. Using the average sunspot number (ASN) as a measure of solar activity (8 for 1996, 180.3 for 2001, 8.4 for 2009 and 114 for 2014), we can get the following ratios: $ASN_{2001}/ASN_{2014} = 1.58$ and $ASN_{1996}/ASN_{2009} = 0.95$. By calculating the corresponding rations for the maximum values of CRII at FL390 for the same timestamps, we get the following results: $CRII_{2001}/CRII_{2014} = 0.83$ and $CRII_{1996}/CRII_{2009} = 0.88$. According to these results, it is clear that as the solar activity increased, the ionization decreased as expected.

Additionally, different dynamics were observed between solar cycles 23 and 24, due to the difference in solar activity during these two solar cycles which is indicated in Table 1. Concerning the different FLs, it can be concluded that the higher the FL, the higher the CRII and the radiation exposure of aircrews and frequent flyers, since the provided shielding of the atmosphere was reduced in higher atmospheric altitudes. Comparing the CRII and dH*(10)/dt calculations for the four different rigidities/latitudes (0.1 GV, 3.1 GV, 8.5 GV and 14.9 GV), for all three FLs during the entire period 1996–2019, it was noted that the correlation was positive, with the correlation coefficient $R^2 = 0.97$.

From the above analysis, we conclude that both tools gave significant results and can be used in order to study the effect of the ionization and radiation induced by cosmic rays on the environment, space weather, climate change [62,63] and human health [15,22].

Specifically, advances in technology during the last few decades have made air traveling more accessible to everyone. This has led to an increase in the number of flights as well as an increase in flight altitude, since commercial aircraft are obliged to travel at higher altitudes due to elevated air traffic. The tools mentioned above are of great importance for the assessment of the health effects of the occupational exposure of aviation crews to radiation due to the permanent galactic radiation background. They are also useful for assessing the health effects of potential additional exposure due to sporadic events which cause elevated radiation (such as SEPs and GLEs) [24,64] and radiation clouds (which are regional radiation enhancements possibly due to photons, GCR and outer-belt relativistic electrons), where the ambient dose equivalent rates are significantly increased [65].

Furthermore, all the extracted results have a great impact on ensuring properly shielded avionic electronic systems, which depends on the levels of ionization and radiation. High ionization levels may cause severe malfunctions in semiconductor parts, decreasing the performance and the reliability of the electronic systems. An accurate estimation of such levels would help prevent hardware failures and software errors.

A detailed study of extreme events may contribute to the updating of safety measures and regulations, as well as to the updating of air traffic flow and capacity management, by taking into consideration the respective occupational exposure conditions. An extension of this work is planned in order to include more scenarios, i.e., different input parameters regarding the spectrum of incoming particles based on experimental data (such as the ones provided in [5,6]), more FLs, actual flight plans and extreme events such as SEPs and GLEs.

Supplementary Materials: The following supporting information can be downloaded at: https://www.mdpi.com/article/10.3390/app12115297/s1. Table S1. CRII and dH*(10)/dt values for cut-off rigidities 0.1GV, 3.1GV, 8.5GV and 14.9GV over the years 1996–2019.

Author Contributions: Conceptualization, P.M. and A.T.; data curation, P.M., A.T. and A.N.S.; formal analysis, A.N.S.; investigation, P.M. and A.T.; methodology, M.G.; resources, P.M., A.T. and A.N.S.; software, P.P. and I.G.U.; supervision, H.M.; project administration, P.M. and A.T.; validation, H.M. and P.K.; writing—original draft preparation, P.M., A.T and A.N.S.; writing—review and editing, H.M., N.C., M.D. and A.G.G. All authors have read and agreed to the published version of the manuscript.

Funding: This research received no external funding.

Institutional Review Board Statement: Not applicable.

Informed Consent Statement: Not applicable.

Data Availability Statement: The datasets generated and/or analyzed during the current study are available from the corresponding author on reasonable request.

Acknowledgments: This work is supported by the ESA Space Safety Programme's network of space weather service development and pre-operational activities and supported under ESA Contract 4000134036/21/D/MRP, in the context of the Space Radiation Expert Service Centre. The European Neutron Monitor Services research is funded by the ESA SSA SN IV-3 Tender: RFQ/3-13556/12/D/MRP. A.Ne.Mo.S is supported by the Special Research Account of Athens University (70/4/5803). I.G.U. acknowledges partial support from the Academy of Finland (projects ESPERA No. 321882). Thanks are due to the Special Research Account of the University of Athens for supporting the Cosmic Ray research. Thanks are also due to the Oulu Cosmic ray colleagues for kindly providing cosmic ray data as well as the cosmic-ray-induced ionization model.

Conflicts of Interest: The authors declare no conflict of interest.

References

1. Vainio, R.; Desorgher, L.; Heynderickx, D.; Storini, M.; Flückiger, E.; Horne, R.B.; Kovaltsov, G.A.; Kudela, K.; Laurenza, M.; McKenna-Lawlor, S.; et al. Dynamics of the Earth's Particle Radiation Environment. *Space Sci. Rev.* **2009**, *147*, 187–231. [CrossRef]
2. Dorman, L. *Cosmic Rays in the Earth's Atmosphere and Underground*; Kluwer Academic Publishers: Dordrecht, The Netherlands, 2004.
3. Harrison, R.G.; Tammet, H. Ions in the terrestrial atmosphere and other solar system atmospheres. *Space Sci. Rev.* **2008**, *137*, 107–118. [CrossRef]

4. Mironova, I.A.; Aplin, K.L.; Arnold, F.; Bazilevskaya, G.A.; Harrison, R.G.; Krivolutsky, A.A.; Nicoll, K.A.; Rozanov, E.V.; Turunen, E.; Usoskin, I.G. Energetic Particle Influence on the Earth's Atmosphere. *Space Sci. Rev.* **2015**, *194*, 1–96. [CrossRef]
5. Adriani, O.; Ambriola, M.; Barbarino, G.; Barbier, L.M.; Bartalucci, S.; Bazilevskaja, G.; Bellotti, R.; Bertazzoni, S.; Bidoli, V.; Boezio, M.; et al. The PAMELA experiment on satellite and its capability in cosmic rays measurements. *Nucl. Instrum. Methods Phys. Res. Sect. A* **2002**, *478*, 114–118. [CrossRef]
6. Bruno, A.; Bazilevskaya, G.A.; Boezio, M.; Christian, E.R.; de Nolfo, G.A.; Martucci, M.; Merge, M.; Mikhailov, V.V.; Munini, R.; Richardson, I.G.; et al. Solar Energetic Particle Events Observed by the PAMELA Mission. *Astrophys. J. Lett.* **2018**, *862*, 97. [CrossRef]
7. Semeniuk, K.; Fomichev, V.I.; McConnell, J.C.; Fu, C.; Melo, S.M.L.; Usoskin, I.G. Middle atmosphere response to the solar cycle in irradiance and ionizing particle precipitation. *Atmos. Chem. Phys.* **2011**, *11*, 5045–5077. [CrossRef]
8. Velinov, P.I.Y.; Mateev, L. Analytical approach for cosmic ray proton ionization in the lower ionosphere and middle atmosphere. *C. R. Acad. Bulg. Sci.* **2005**, *58*, 511–516.
9. Velinov, P.I.Y.; Mateev, L. Improved cosmic ray ionization model for the system ionosphere-atmosphere. Calculation of electron production rate profiles. *J. Atmos. Solar-Terr. Phys.* **2007**, *70*, 574–582. [CrossRef]
10. Desorgher, L.; Flückiger, E.O.; Gurtner, M.; Moser, M.R.; Bütikofer, R. ATMOCOSMICS: A GEANT4 code for computing the interaction of cosmic rays with the Earth's atmosphere. *Int. J. Mod. Phys. A* **2005**, *20*, 6802–6804. [CrossRef]
11. Scherer, K.; Fichtner, H.; Borrmann, T.; Beer, J.; Desorgher, L.; Flükiger, E.O.; Fahr, H.J. Interstellar-terrestrial relations: Variable cosmic environments, the dynamic heliosphere, and their imprints on terrestrial archives and climate. *Space Sci. Rev.* **2007**, *127*, 327–465. [CrossRef]
12. Usoskin, I.G.; Kovaltsov, G.A. Cosmic ray induced ionization in the atmosphere: Full modeling and practical applications. *J. Geophys. Res.* **2006**, *111*, D21206. [CrossRef]
13. Usoskin, I.G.; Kovaltsov, G.A.; Mironova, I.A. Cosmic ray induced ionization model CRAC: CRII: An extension to the upper atmosphere. *J. Geophys. Res.* **2010**, *115*, D10302. [CrossRef]
14. Usoskin, I.G.; Desorgher, L.; Velinov, P.; Storini, M.; Flueckiger, E.O.; Buetikofer, R.; Kovaltsov, G.A. Ionization of the Earth's atmosphere by solar and galactic cosmic rays. *Acta Geophys.* **2009**, *57*, 88. [CrossRef]
15. Singh, A.K.; Singh, D.; Singh, R.P. Impact of galactic cosmic rays on earth's atmosphere and human health. *Atmos. Environ.* **2011**, *45*, 3806–3818. [CrossRef]
16. Miroshnichenko, L.I. *Radiation Hazard in Space*; Springer: Dordrecht, The Netherlands, 2003; ISBN 978-94-017-0301-7.
17. European Commission. *Directive 96/29/EURATOM of 13 May 1996 Laying Down Basic Safety Standards for the Protection of the Health of Workers and the General Public Against the Dangers Arising from Ionizing Radiation*; Publications Office: Luxembourg, 1996.
18. International Commission on Radiation Units and Measurements. Reference data for the validation of doses from cosmic-radiation exposure of aircraft crew. ICRU Report 84. *J. Int. Commun. Radiat. Units Meas.* **2010**, *10*, 5–6.
19. International Commission on Radiological Protection. Radiological protection from cosmic radiation in aviation. *Ann. ICRP* **2016**, *45*, 132.
20. Beck, P.; Latocha, M.; Dorman, L.; Pelliccioni, M.; Rollet, S. Measurements and simulations of the radiation exposure to aircraft crew workplaces due to cosmic radiation in the atmosphere. *Radiat. Prot. Dosim.* **2007**, *126*, 564–567. [CrossRef]
21. Meier, M.M.; Matthiä, D. A space weather index for the radiation field at aviation altitudes. *J. Space Weather Space Clim.* **2014**, *4*, A13. [CrossRef]
22. Meier, M.M.; Copeland, K.; Kloble, K.E.J.; Matthia, D.; Plettenberg, M.C.; Schennetten, K.; Wirtz, M.; Hellweg, C.E. Radiation in the atmosphere. A hazard to aviation safety? *Atmosphere* **2020**, *11*, 1358. [CrossRef]
23. Mishev, A.; Usoskin, I. Numerical model for computation of effective and ambient dose equivalent at flight altitudes. Application for dose assessment during GLEs. *J. Space Weather Space Clim.* **2015**, *5*, A10. [CrossRef]
24. Mishev, A.; Usoskin, I.; Tuohino, S.; Ibragimov, A. The upgraded GLE database includes assessment of radiation exposure at flight altitudes. *J. Phys. Conf. Ser.* **2019**, *1181*, 012061. [CrossRef]
25. Mishev, A.; Usoskin, I. Current status and possible extension of the global neutron monitor network. *J. Space Weather Space Clim.* **2020**, *10*, 17. [CrossRef]
26. Flückiger, E.; Bütikofer, R. Radiation doses along selected flight profiles during two extreme solar cosmic ray events. *ASTRA* **2011**, *7*, 105–109. [CrossRef]
27. Bütikofer, R.R.; Flückiger, E.O.; Desorgher, L.; Moser, M.; Pirard, B. The solar cosmic ray ground-level enhancements on 20 January 2005 and 13 December 2006. *Adv. Space Res.* **2009**, *43*, 499–503. [CrossRef]
28. SIEVERT. Available online: https://www.sievert-system.org/ (accessed on 11 April 2022).
29. Latocha, M.; Beck, P.; Rollet, S. AVIDOS—A software package for European accredited aviation dosimetry. *Radiat. Prot. Dosim.* **2009**, *136*, 286–290. [CrossRef]
30. Mertens, C.J.; Meier, M.M.; Brown, S.; Norman, R.B.; Xu, X. NAIRAS aircraft radiation model development, dose climatology, and initial validation. *Space Weather* **2013**, *11*, 603–635. [CrossRef]
31. Copeland, K. CARI-7A: Development and validation. *Radiat. Prot. Dos.* **2017**, *175*, 419–431. [CrossRef]
32. Berger, T.; Meier, M.; Reitz, G.; Schridde, M. Longterm dose measurements applying a human anthropomorphic phantom onboard an aircraft. *Radiat. Meas.* **2008**, *43*, 580–584. [CrossRef]
33. SPENVIS. Available online: https://www.spenvis.oma.be/ (accessed on 11 April 2022).

34. Edwards, R.; Dyer, C.; Normand, E. Technical standard for atmospheric radiation single event effects, (SEE) on avionics electronics. In Proceedings of the IEEE Radiation Effects Data Workshop 2004 (IEEE Cat. No.04TH8774), Atlanta, GA, USA, 22–22 July 2004; pp. 1–5. [CrossRef]
35. Leray, J.L. Effects of atmospheric neutrons on devices, at sea level and in avionics embedded systems. *Microelectron. Reliab.* **2007**, *47*, 1827–1835. [CrossRef]
36. Brunetti, G.; McKenzie, I.; Dell'Olio, F.; Armenise, M.N.; Ciminelli, C. Measured radiation effects on InGaAsP/InP ring resonators for space applications. *Opt. Express* **2019**, *27*, 24434–24444. [CrossRef]
37. Boscherini, M.; Adriani, O.; Bongi, M.; Bonechi, L.; Castellini, G.; D'Alessandro, R.; Gabbanini, A.; Grandi, M.; Menn, W.; Papini, P.; et al. Radiation damage of electronic components in space environment. *Nucl. Instrum. Methods Phys. Res. Sect. A* **2003**, *514*, 112–116. [CrossRef]
38. Gill, K.; Cervelli, G.; Grabit, R.; Jensen, F.; Vasey, F. Radiation damage and annealing in 1310 nm InGaAsP/InP lasers for the CMS tracker. *Proc. SPIE* **2000**, *4134*, 176–184. [CrossRef]
39. Paschalis, P.; Mavromichalaki, H.; Dorman, L.I.; Plainaki, C.; Tsirigkas, D. Geant4 software application for the simulation of cosmic ray showers in the Earth's atmosphere. *New Astron.* **2014**, *33*, 26–37. [CrossRef]
40. Tezari, A.; Paschalis, P.; Mavromichalaki, H.; Karaiskos, P.; Crosby, N.; Dierckxsens, M. Assessing Radiation Exposure Inside The Earth's Atmosphere. *Radiat. Prot. Dos.* **2020**, *190*, 427–436. [CrossRef]
41. Heck, D.; Knapp, J.; Capdevielle, J.N.; Schatz, G.; Thouw, T. *CORSIKA: A Monte Carlo Code to Simulate Extensive Air Showers*; FZKA 6019; Forsch: Karlsruhe, Germany, 1998.
42. Fassò, A.; Ferrari, A.; Sala, P.R. Electron-Photon Transport in FLUKA: Status, Advanced Monte Carlo for Radiation Physics. In *Particle Transport Simulation and Applications, Proceedings of the Monte Carlo 2000 Conference, Lisbon, Portugal, 23–26 October 2000*; Springer: Berlin/Heidelberg, Germany, 2000; pp. 159–164. [CrossRef]
43. Usoskin, I.G.; Alanko-Huotari, K.; Kovaltsov, G.A.; Mursula, K. Heliospheric modulation of cosmic rays: Monthly reconstruction for 1951–2004. *J. Geophys. Res.* **2005**, *110*, A12108. [CrossRef]
44. Usoskin, I.G.; Bazilevskaya, G.A.; Kovaltsov, G.A. Solar modulation parameter for cosmic rays since 1936 reconstructed from ground-based neutron monitors and ionization chambers. *J. Geophys. Res.* **2011**, *116*, A02104. [CrossRef]
45. Burger, R.A.; Potgieter, M.S.; Heber, B. Rigidity dependence of cosmic ray proton latitudinal gradients measured by the Ulysses spacecraft: Implication for the diffusion tensor. *J. Geophys. Res.* **2000**, *105*, 447–455. [CrossRef]
46. Agostinelli, S.; Allison, J.; Amako, K.A.; Apostolakis, J.; Araujo, H.; Arce, P.; Asai, M.; Axen, D.; Banerjee, S.; Barrand, G.; et al. Geant4—A simulation toolkit. *Nucl. Instrum. Methods A* **2003**, *506*, 250–303. [CrossRef]
47. Allison, J.; Amako, K.; Apostolakis, J.; Araujo, H.; Dubois, P.A.; Asai, M.; Barrand, G.; Capra, R.; Chauvie, S.; Chytracek, R.; et al. Geant4 developments and applications. *IEEE Trans. Nucl. Sci.* **2006**, *53*, 270–278. [CrossRef]
48. Allison, J.; Amako, K.; Apostolakis, J.; Arce, P.; Asai, M.; Aso, T.; Bagli, E.; Bagulya, A.; Banerjee, S.; Barrand, G.; et al. Recent developments in Geant4. *Nucl. Instrum. Methods A* **2016**, *835*, 186–225. [CrossRef]
49. International Commission on Radiological Protection. The Recommendations of the International Commission on Radiological Protection. *Ann. ICRP* **2007**, *37*, 103.
50. ESA. *ESA SSA P3 SWE-III Acceptance Test Report, R.137 Dynamic Atmospheric Tracking Interactive Model Application (DYASTIMA)*; ESA: Paris, France, 2019.
51. *ISO 2533:1975ISO*; Standard Atmosphere. International Organization for Standardization: Geneva, Switzerland, 2007.
52. *ISO 15390:2004ISO*; Space Environment (Natural and Artificial)—Galactic Cosmic Ray Model. International Organization for Standardization: Geneva, Switzerland, 2004.
53. Smart, D.F.; Shea, M.A. World grid of calculated cosmic ray vertical cutoff rigidities for epoch 1995.0. In Proceedings of the 30th International Cosmic Ray Conference, Yucatán, Mexico, 3–11 July 2007.
54. Smart, D.F.; Shea, M.A. World grid of calculated cosmic ray vertical cutoff rigidities for epoch 2000.0. In Proceedings of the 30th International Cosmic Ray Conference, Yucatán, Mexico, 3–11 July 2007.
55. Smart, D.F.; Shea, M.A. Vertical Geomagnetic Cutoff Rigidities for Epoch 2015. In Proceedings of the 36th International Cosmic Ray Conference, Madison, WI, USA, 24 July–1 August 2019.
56. Gerontidou, M.; Katzourakis, N.; Mavromichalaki, H.; Yanke, V.; Eroshenko, E. World grid of cosmic ray vertical cut-off rigidity for the last decade. *Adv. Space Res.* **2021**, *67*, 2231–2240. [CrossRef]
57. Forbush, S.E. World-wide cosmic ray variations, 1937–1952. *J. Geophys. Res.* **1954**, *54*, 525. [CrossRef]
58. Makrantoni, P.; Mavromichalaki, H.; Usoskin, I.G.; Papaioannou, A. Calculation of the cosmic ray induced ionization for the region of Athens. *J. Phys. Conf. Ser.* **2013**, *409*, 2232. [CrossRef]
59. Makrantoni, P.; Mavromichalaki, H.; Paschalis, P. Solar cycle variation of the ionization by cosmic rays in the atmosphere at the mid-latitude region of Athens. *Astrophys. Space Sci.* **2021**, *366*, 70. [CrossRef]
60. Tezari, A.; Paschalis, P.; Stassinakis, A.; Mavromichalaki, H.; Karaiskos, P.; Gerontidou, M.; Alexandridis, D.; Kanellakopoulos, A.; Crosby, N.; Dierckxsens, M. Radiation Exposure in the Lower Atmosphere during Different Periods of Solar Activity. *Atmosphere* **2022**, *13*, 166. [CrossRef]
61. Mavromichalaki, H.; Marmatsouri, L.; Vassilaki, A. On Reproduction of Long term Cosmic-ray modulation as seen by Neutron Monitor Stations. *Astrophys. Space Sci.* **1995**, *232*, 315–326. [CrossRef]

62. Dorman, L.I. Space Weather and Cosmic Ray Effects, Chapter 30. In *Climate Change*; Elsevier: Amsterdam, The Netherlands, 2016; pp. 513–544. [CrossRef]
63. Todd, M.C.; Kniveton, D.R. Changes in cloud cover associated with Forbush decreases of galactic cosmic rays. *J. Geophys. Res.* **2001**, *106*, 32031–32042. [CrossRef]
64. Usoskin, I.G.; Kovaltsov, G.A.; Mironova, I.A.; Tylka, A.J.; Dietrich, W.F. Ionization effect of solar particle GLE events in low and middle atmosphere. *Atmos. Chem. Phys.* **2011**, *11*, 1979. [CrossRef]
65. Tobiska, W.K.; Bouwer, D.; Smart, D.; Shea, M.; Bailey, J.; Didkovsky, L.; Judge, K.; Garret, H.; Atwell, W.; Gersey, B.; et al. Global real-time dose measurements using the Automated Radiation Measurements for Aerospace Safety (ARMAS) system. *Space Weather* **2016**, *14*, 1053–1080. [CrossRef]

Communication

Natural and Anthropogenic Radioactivity Content and Radiation Hazard Assessment of Baby Food Consumption in Italy

Francesco Caridi [1,*], Giuseppe Paladini [1,*], Valentina Venuti [1,*], Sebastiano Ettore Spoto [1], Vincenza Crupi [1], Giovanna Belmusto [2] and Domenico Majolino [1]

[1] Dipartimento di Scienze Matematiche e Informatiche, Scienze Fisiche e Scienze della Terra, Università degli Studi di Messina, Viale Ferdinando Stagno D'Alcontres 31, 98166 Messina, Italy; sebastianoettore@gmail.com (S.E.S.); vcrupi@unime.it (V.C.); dmajolino@unime.it (D.M.)

[2] Dipartimento di Reggio Calabria, Agenzia Regionale per la Protezione dell'Ambiente della Calabria (ARPACal), Via Troncovito SNC, 89135 Reggio Calabria, Italy; gbelmusto@arpacal.it

* Correspondence: fcaridi@unime.it (F.C.); gpaladini@unime.it (G.P.); vvenuti@unime.it (V.V.)

Abstract: The natural (^{40}K) and anthropogenic (^{137}Cs) radioactivity concentration in four different typologies of early childhood (up to two years old) foods, i.e., *homogenized fruit*, *homogenized meat*, *childhood biscuits* and *baby pasta*, produced in Italy and sold in Italian large retailers, was investigated through High Purity Germanium (HPGe) gamma spectrometry. The present study is carried out with the aim to: (i) evaluate the background levels of the investigated radionuclides in the analyzed early childhood foods, (ii) identify whether the twenty analyzed samples were appropriate for infant consumption and (iii) contribute to construct a database on the radioactivity of early childhood foods sold in Italy.

Keywords: baby food; radioactivity; gamma spectrometry; activity concentration; radiological hazard

---

Citation: Caridi, F.; Paladini, G.; Venuti, V.; Spoto, S.E.; Crupi, V.; Belmusto, G.; Majolino, D. Natural and Anthropogenic Radioactivity Content and Radiation Hazard Assessment of Baby Food Consumption in Italy. *Appl. Sci.* **2022**, *12*, 5244. https://doi.org/10.3390/app12105244

Academic Editor: Marco Anni

Received: 2 May 2022
Accepted: 20 May 2022
Published: 22 May 2022

Publisher's Note: MDPI stays neutral with regard to jurisdictional claims in published maps and institutional affiliations.

Copyright: © 2022 by the authors. Licensee MDPI, Basel, Switzerland. This article is an open access article distributed under the terms and conditions of the Creative Commons Attribution (CC BY) license (https://creativecommons.org/licenses/by/4.0/).

1. Introduction

The main source of exposure to ionizing radiations for individuals of the population is natural radioactivity [1–4]. In particular, with reference to internal exposure, it is worth noting that radionuclides can enter the human body by the inhalation of gas in the air, by feed ingestion or through the skin (transcutaneous absorption) [5,6]. As widely reported in the literature, the major contribution to the average worldwide annual effective dose per capita (2.4 mSv) [7] is from the ingestion of food and water [8–10].

In light of this, it can be easily understood that the consumption of food that contains radionuclides can constitute a serious health threat for human beings [11,12] and, in particular, for infants, since they are at a high risk for foodborne illness and related health complications because they are under developing immune systems and cannot fight off infections such as adults [13].

Thus, in order to fill the knowledge gap related to the radioactivity content of baby food produced in Italy and sold in the Italian large retailers, four different typologies of early childhood (up to two years old) foods, i.e., *homogenized fruit*, *homogenized meat*, *childhood biscuits* and *baby pasta*, were analyzed in the present study in terms of natural (^{40}K) and anthropogenic (^{137}Cs) radioactivity concentration. In particular, regarding the first, we investigated only ^{40}K since natural radioactivity in food mainly comes from this radioisotope [14–17]. Potassium assumes a fundamental role in regulating many body functions [18,19]. Natural potassium contains 0.012% by weight of ^{40}K, and its content in the body is therefore also constant. Typically, adults and children receive annual doses of 165 µSv and 185 µSv, respectively, from ^{40}K naturally present in their bodies [1]. The higher dose received by children is due to a higher potassium concentration in their diet in relation to body mass [20].

The assessment of the ingestion dose levels was also performed in order to identify whether the twenty analyzed early childhood foods were appropriate for infant consumption, by comparing them with the internationally recommended level [16].

2. Materials and Methods

2.1. Sample Description

The investigated samples, collected during the year 2020, were divided into four groups (G#, # = 1, 2, 3, 4), according to what is reported in Table 1. The five samples in each group belong to Italian brands and different batches.

Table 1. Group identification code (ID), typology and number of samples for each group.

Group ID	Typology	Number of Samples
G1	Homogenized fruit	5
G2	Homogenized meat	5
G3	Childhood biscuits	5
G4	Baby pasta	5

Homogenized fruit and *meat* are early childhood foods with a mixed consistency between solid and liquid, frequently used for infant weaning. They do not require chewing, and therefore they are very useful in the case of an incomplete dental structure and represent transition foods between the liquid feeding of the infant and the solid one of the weaned infant [21]. The nutritional composition of homogenized foods varies significantly depending on their typology. In theory, they should be produced from raw materials and water alone, without adding anything else; however, several simple sugars are added to various fruit ones [22]. Those based on meat, on the other hand, are rich in proteins with a high biological value.

As for the non-energetic nutrients, the homogenized foods fully satisfy the needs of mineral salts and vitamins. In addition, they also show low levels of cholesterol and saturated fat, and provide a few grams of dietary fiber [23].

Childhood biscuits, commonly used for weaning children under one year of life, are not much different from a common dry biscuit in terms of nutritional composition, neither in sugar content nor in saturated fat content. They are a source of complex carbohydrates, which provide slow-release energy that can therefore be used over time, and of simple carbohydrates, which immediately enter into the circulation and are burned [24]. They are also enriched with protein, both of animal and vegetable origin, which are fundamental elements for the growth of the cells and tissues of the child's body [25]. Childhood biscuits are also integrated with vitamins, i.e., those of group B, essential for calcium absorption and cell renewal, and vitamin C, which stimulates the body's natural defenses and promotes iron absorption. In addition, they also contain minerals, such as calcium and phosphorus (for the development of the skeletal system and teeth), copper (for the nervous system), iron (for the formation of red blood cells) and zinc (to strengthen bones and muscles in addition to the immune system) [26].

Baby pasta should be given to the children at the beginning of weaning, taking into account that it has very specific characteristics [27]. First of all, it is gluten-free, so it can be given even before six months of age. Then, it is prepared with soft wheat, more digestible and easily chewable than that used for pasta commonly consumed by adults. Finally, it is obtained with diastased flour, which is subjected to a specific procedure following which the starch is broken down into simpler elements making it easier for the early children to digest, while still maintaining the right nutritional values [28]. After one year of age, durum wheat pasta in a larger format can be given to children, even combined with legumes in order to constitute a complete meal from the point of view of protein [29].

2.2. Radioactivity Measurements

For High Purity Germanium (HPGe) gamma spectrometry measurements, early childhood food samples were inserted in Marinelli containers of 1 L capacity and counted for 70,000 s [30]. The obtained spectra were then analyzed with the aim to assess the ^{137}Cs and ^{40}K specific activity [30].

A positive biased Ortec HPGe detector (GEM) was employed for the analysis [31]. In order to perform efficiency and energy calibrations, a Eckert and Ziegler Nuclitec GmbH traceable multinuclide radioactive standard (AK-5901), energy range 59.54 keV–1836 keV, reproducing the exact samples geometries in a water-equivalent epoxy resin matrix, was employed [31].

The specific activity (Bq kg^{-1}) of the investigated radionuclides was calculated as follows, by using the Gamma Vision (Ortec) software [32,33]:

$$C = \frac{N_E}{\varepsilon_E t \gamma_d M} \quad (1)$$

where N_E accounts for the net area of a peak at energy E; ε_E and γ_d indicate the efficiency and yield of the photopeak at energy E, respectively; M is the mass sample (kg); and t is the live time (s).

The quality of the results was certified by the Italian Accreditation Body (ACCREDIA) [34,35].

2.3. Evaluation of the Radiological Hazard

The radiological health risk was estimated as follows [36]:

$$D_{ing} \left(Sv\ y^{-1} \right) = h_{ing, K-40} \times J_{ing,\ K-40} \quad (2)$$

where $h_{ing,K-40}$ accounts for the coefficient of effective dose for insertion unit for ingestion of ^{40}K (5.2 × 10^{-8} Sv Bq^{-1} and 4.2 × 10^{-8} Sv Bq^{-1} for the age categories of 0–1 and 1–2 years old, respectively), as reported in [1], while $J_{ing,K-40}$ is the annual intake of ^{40}K (Bq year^{-1}), calculated by multiplying the early childhood food consumption (kg) for the specific activity of the investigated radionuclide (Bq kg^{-1}).

3. Results and Discussion

3.1. Activity Concentration

Table 2 reports the massic activities of ^{40}K and ^{137}Cs for all the analyzed early childhood food samples. For each group, the mean value (±standard deviation) is also reported.

First of all, a good agreement between the results shown in Table 2 and those reported in the food radioactivity database of the "Italian Institute for the Environmental Protection and Research" (ISPRA) [37] was found.

In the case of the ^{137}Cs specific activity, the obtained results revealed no residual contamination from artificial radioactivity, with the radiocaesium activity concentration being lower than the minimum detectable activity in all cases.

Finally, the activity concentration of ^{40}K, measured for each sample, does not allow a proper assessment of the radiological hazard for early children, and hence, to evaluate it, additional factors have to be taken into account [38], as reported in the following section.

Table 2. Massic activities (Bq kg^{-1}) of ^{40}K and ^{137}Cs in the analyzed early childhood food samples.

Group ID	Specific Activity	
	^{40}K (Bq kg^{-1})	^{137}Cs (Bq kg^{-1})
G1	111 ± 13	<0.11
	95 ± 11	<0.12
	68 ± 9	<0.10
	160 ± 19	<0.09
	51 ± 6	<0.11
Mean value	97 ± 12	<0.11
G2	171 ± 19	<0.09
	202 ± 23	<0.11
	182 ± 19	<0.12
	188 ± 20	<0.08
	142 ± 16	<0.13
Mean value	177 ± 19	<0.10
G3	120 ± 14	<0.11
	72 ± 9	<0.12
	130 ± 14	<0.10
	75 ± 9	<0.13
	55 ± 7	<0.09
Mean value	90 ± 11	<0.11
G4	106 ± 12	<0.19
	83 ± 9	<0.18
	96 ± 11	<0.13
	79 ± 9	<0.14
	78 ± 9	<0.17
Mean value	88 ± 7	<0.10

3.2. The Annual Effective Dose for Early Childhood Food Ingestion

The dose estimation due to the ingestion of radionuclides through food consumption was performed for infants up to two years old. In order to evaluate the radiological health risks for early children, we estimated the annual effective dose due to the ingestion, D_{ing}. Table 3 reports the obtained results, which take into account the annual average consumption of *homogenized fruit* (three 80 g jars per day), *homogenized meat* (one 80 g jar per day), *childhood biscuits* (four per day) and *baby pasta* (about 100 g per day), per infant in Italy [39,40].

Table 3. The annual effective dose for early childhood food ingestion.

Group ID	Effective Dose for Ingestion, D_{ing} (mSv y^{-1})	
	0–1 Year Old	1–2 Years Old
G1	0.23	0.19
G2	0.27	0.22
G3	0.02	0.01
G4	0.17	0.13

The ingestion dose for the selected age categories, due to the intake of ^{40}K, thus ranges from 0.02 mSv y^{-1} (for G3) to 0.27 mSv y^{-1} (for G2) for the age category of 0–1 year old, and from 0.01 mSv y^{-1} (for G3) to 0.22 mSv y^{-1} (for G2) for the age category of 1–2 years old, respectively. Noteworthily, the obtained values were found to be always lower than the ICRP recommended limit of 1 mSv y^{-1} for all ages [16]. Moreover, such dose values account for 0.8–11.2% (age category of 0–1 year old) and 0.4–9.1% (age category of 1–2 years old) of the average annual effective dose to the world population (2.4 mSv y^{-1}) [41].

These results show the importance of determining the radioactivity level in early childhood foods in order to ensure their safety and suitability, considering that they are typically consumed during a vulnerable period of human life.

4. Conclusions

In this work, the activity concentration of natural and anthropogenic radionuclides (^{40}K and ^{137}Cs, respectively) was evaluated for early childhood food samples of four different typologies (*homogenized fruit*, *homogenized meat*, *childhood biscuits* and *baby pasta*), produced in Italy and collected from Italian large retailers.

The HPGe gamma spectrometry results indicate that the ^{137}Cs specific activity was lower than the minimum detectable activity in all cases, thus excluding anthropogenic radioactive contamination. Moreover, the ^{40}K activity concentration was employed in order to evaluate the radiological health risk for the selected age category, by assessing the effective dose for food ingestion. The calculated values turned out to be lower than the ICRP recommended limit for all ages. They were also compared with the total natural radioactivity value for humans, resulting to be equal to the 0.8–11.2% (age category of 0–1 year old) and 0.4–9.1% (age category of 1–2 years old) of the average annual effective dose.

Finally, the results reported in this article can be used to develop a database on the radioactivity in early childhood foods sold in Italy.

Author Contributions: Conceptualization, F.C. and V.V.; methodology, F.C. and V.C.; validation, D.M.; formal analysis, G.B.; investigation, F.C., S.E.S., G.P. and V.V.; resources, F.C., V.C. and D.M.; data curation, F.C.; writing—original draft preparation, F.C.; supervision, D.M. and V.V. All authors have read and agreed to the published version of the manuscript.

Funding: This research received no external funding.

Institutional Review Board Statement: Not applicable.

Informed Consent Statement: Not applicable.

Data Availability Statement: Not applicable.

Conflicts of Interest: The authors declare no conflict of interest.

References

1. United Nations Scientific Committee on the Effects of Atomic Radiation. *Sources and Effects of Ionizing Radiation: Report to the General Assembly, with Scientific Annexes*; United Nations: New York, NY, USA, 2000; Volume 1, ISBN 92-1-142238-8.
2. Nugraha, E.D.; Hosoda, M.; Kusdiana; Untara; Mellawati, J.; Nurokhim; Tamakuma, Y.; Ikram, A.; Syaifudin, M.; Yamada, R.; et al. Comprehensive exposure assessments from the viewpoint of health in a unique high natural background radiation area, Mamuju, Indonesia. *Sci. Rep.* **2021**, *11*, 14578. [CrossRef] [PubMed]
3. Nishad, S.; Chauhan, P.K.; Sowdhamini, R.; Ghosh, A. Chronic exposure of humans to high level natural background radiation leads to robust expression of protective stress response proteins. *Sci. Rep.* **2021**, *11*, 1777. [CrossRef] [PubMed]
4. Torrisi, L.; Caridi, F.; Giuffrida, L. Protons and ion acceleration from thick targets at 1010 W/cm^2 laser pulse intensity. *Laser Part. Beams* **2011**, *29*, 29–37. [CrossRef]
5. Tsubokura, M.; Gilmour, S.; Takahashi, K.; Oikawa, T.; Kanazawa, Y. Internal Radiation Exposure after the Fukushima Nuclear Power Plant Disaster. *JAMA* **2012**, *308*, 669–670. [CrossRef] [PubMed]
6. Kovalchuk, O.; Arkhipov, A.; Barylyak, I.; Karachov, I.; Titov, V.; Hohn, B.; Kovalchuk, I. Plants experiencing chronic internal exposure to ionizing radiation exhibit higher frequency of homologous recombination than acutely irradiated plants. *Mutat. Res. Mol. Mech. Mutagen.* **2000**, *449*, 47–56. [CrossRef]
7. Bari, A.; Khan, A.J.; Semkow, T.M.; Syed, U.-F.; Roselan, A.; Haines, D.K.; Roth, G.; West, L.; Arndt, M. Rapid screening of radioactivity in food for emergency response. *Appl. Radiat. Isot.* **2011**, *69*, 834–843. [CrossRef]
8. Caridi, F.; D'Agostino, M.; Belvedere, A.; Marguccio, S.; Belmusto, G. Radon radioactivity in groundwater from the Calabria region, south of Italy. *J. Instrum.* **2016**, *11*, P05012. [CrossRef]
9. Caridi, F.; Messina, M.; D'Agostino, M. An investigation about natural radioactivity, hydrochemistry, and metal pollution in groundwater from Calabrian selected areas, southern Italy. *Environ. Earth Sci.* **2017**, *76*, 668. [CrossRef]
10. Caridi, F.; Messina, M.; Belvedere, A.; D'Agostino, M.; Marguccio, S.; Settineri, L.; Belmusto, G. Food salt characterization in terms of radioactivity and metals contamination. *Appl. Sci.* **2019**, *9*, 2882. [CrossRef]
11. Cooper, E.L.; Zeiller, E.; Ghods-Esphahani, A.; Makarewicz, M.; Schelenz, R.; Frindik, O.; Heilgeist, M.; Kalus, W. Radioactivity in food and total diet samples collected in selected settlements in the USSR. *J. Environ. Radioact.* **1992**, *17*, 147–157. [CrossRef]

12. Andric, V.; Gajic-Kvascev, M. The radioactivity parameters in the food chain—Legislation, control and critical points. *IOP Conf. Ser. Earth Environ. Sci.* **2021**, *854*, 12003. [CrossRef]
13. Pietschnig, B.; Haschke, F.; Karg, V.; Vanura, H.; Schuster, E. Radioactivity in infant food in Austria after the Chernobyl accident—A six-year follow-up. *Pediatr. Res.* **1994**, *35*, 283. [CrossRef]
14. Caridi, F.; Marguccio, S.; Belvedere, A.; D'Agostino, M.; Belmusto, G. The Natural Radioactivity in Food: A Comparison between Different Feeding Regimes. *Curr. Nutr. Food Sci.* **2019**, *15*, 493–499. [CrossRef]
15. Ramachandran, T.V.; Mishra, U.C. Measurement of natural radioactivity levels in Indian foodstuffs by gamma spectrometry. *Int. J. Radiat. Appl. Instrum. Part* **1989**, *40*, 723–726. [CrossRef]
16. International Commission on Radiological Protection. Conversion Coefficients for use in Radiological Protection against External Radiation. *Ann. ICRP* **1996**, *26*, 3–4. [CrossRef]
17. Lux, D.; Kammerer, L.; Ruehm, W.; Wirth, E. Cycling of Pu, Sr, Cs, and other longliving radionuclides in forest ecosystems of the 30-km zone around Chernobyl. *Sci. Total Environ.* **1995**, *173*, 375–384. [CrossRef]
18. Weaver, C.M. Potassium and health. *Adv. Nutr.* **2013**, *4*, 368S–377S. [CrossRef]
19. Stone, M.S.; Martyn, L.; Weaver, C.M. Potassium Intake, Bioavailability, Hypertension, and Glucose Control. *Nutrients* **2016**, *8*, 444. [CrossRef]
20. Richmond, C.R. ICRP report of the task group on reference man. *Int. J. Nucl. Med. Biol.* **1985**, *12*, 251. [CrossRef]
21. Mazur, M.; Salejda, A.M.; Pilarska, K.M.; Krasnowska, G.; Nawirska-Olszańska, A.; Kolniak-Ostek, J.; Bąbelewski, P. The Influence of Viburnum opulus Fruits Addition on Some Quality Properties of Homogenized Meat Products. *Appl. Sci.* **2021**, *11*, 3141. [CrossRef]
22. Liu, J.; Wang, R.; Wang, X.; Yang, L.; Shan, Y.; Zhang, Q.; Ding, S. Effects of High-Pressure Homogenization on the Structural, Physical, and Rheological Properties of Lily Pulp. *Foods* **2019**, *8*, 472. [CrossRef] [PubMed]
23. Khoury, C.K.; Bjorkman, A.D.; Dempewolf, H.; Ramirez-Villegas, J.; Guarino, L.; Jarvis, A.; Rieseberg, L.H.; Struik, P.C. Increasing homogeneity in global food supplies and the implications for food security. *Proc. Natl. Acad. Sci. USA* **2014**, *111*, 4001–4006. [CrossRef] [PubMed]
24. Fathonah, S.; Rosidah, R.; Septianarta, S. Yellow Corn Biscuits for Early Childhood: High Energy and Beta-carotene. *J. Bahan Alam Terbarukan* **2017**, *7*, 77–82. [CrossRef]
25. Kanwal, S.; Raza, S.; Naseem, K.; Amjad, M.; Bibi, N.; Gillani, M. Development, Physico-Chemical and Sensory Properties of Biscuits Supplemented with Pumpkin Seeds to Combat Childhood Malnutrition in Pakistan. *Pakistan J. Agric. Res.* **2015**, *28*, 400–405.
26. Nazni, P.; Pradheepa, S.; Hasan, A. Effects of weaning biscuits on the nutritional profile and the cognitive development in preschool children. *Ital. J. Pediatr.* **2010**, *36*, 18. [CrossRef]
27. Bugera, J.; Lengyel, C.; Utioh, A.; Arntfield, S. Baby boomers' acceptability of a tomato lentil pasta sauce. *Food Res. Int.* **2013**, *52*, 542–546. [CrossRef]
28. Torres Vargas, O.L.; Lema González, M.; Galeano Loaiza, Y.V. Optimization study of pasta extruded with quinoa flour (*Chenopodium quinoa* willd). *CyTA J. Food* **2021**, *19*, 220–227. [CrossRef]
29. Carletti, C.; Pani, P.; Monasta, L.; Knowles, A.; Cattaneo, A. Introduction of Complementary Foods in a Cohort of Infants in Northeast Italy: Do Parents Comply with WHO Recommendations? *Nutrients* **2017**, *9*, 34. [CrossRef]
30. Caridi, F.; D'Agostino, M.; Belvedere, A.; Marguccio, S.; Belmusto, G.; Gatto, M.F. Diagnostics techniques and dosimetric evaluations for environmental radioactivity investigations. *J. Instrum.* **2016**, *11*, C10012. [CrossRef]
31. Caridi, F.; D'Agostino, M.; Messina, M.; Marcianò, G.; Grioli, L.; Belvedere, A.; Marguccio, S.; Belmusto, G. Lichens as environmental risk detectors. *Eur. Phys. J. Plus* **2017**, *132*, 189. [CrossRef]
32. Caridi, F.; Acri, G.; Belvedere, A.; Crupi, V.; D'Agostino, M.; Marguccio, S.; Messina, M.; Paladini, G.; Venuti, V.; Majolino, D. Evaluation of the radiological and chemical risk for public health from flour sample investigation. *Appl. Sci.* **2021**, *11*, 3646. [CrossRef]
33. Caridi, F.; Marguccio, S.; Durante, G.; Trozzo, R.; Fullone, F.; Belvedere, A.; D'Agostino, M.; Belmusto, G. Natural radioactivity measurements and dosimetric evaluations in soil samples with a high content of NORM. *Eur. Phys. J. Plus* **2017**, *132*, 56. [CrossRef]
34. ACCREDIA. Available online: https://www.accredia.it/ (accessed on 20 April 2022).
35. Caridi, F.; Paladini, G.; Venuti, V.; Crupi, V.; Procopio, S.; Belvedere, A.; D'Agostino, M.; Faggio, G.; Grillo, R.; Marguccio, S.; et al. Radioactivity, Metals Pollution and Mineralogy Assessment of a Beach Stretch from the Ionian Coast of Calabria (Southern Italy). *Int. J. Environ. Res. Public Health* **2021**, *18*, 12147. [CrossRef] [PubMed]
36. Chen, J. Doses to children from intakes by ingestion. *Radiat. Prot. Dosimetry* **2010**, *142*, 46–50. [CrossRef] [PubMed]
37. Ispra. Available online: https://www.isprambiente.gov.it/it (accessed on 20 April 2022).
38. Onosohwo, B.; Olatunji, M.; Khandaker, M.; Amin, Y.; Bradley, D.; Alkhorayef, M.; Alzimami, K. Measurement of Natural and Artificial Radioactivity in Infant Powdered Milk and Estimation of the Corresponding Annual Effective Dose. *Environ. Eng. Sci.* **2015**, *32*, 10. [CrossRef]
39. Santonicola, S.; Albrizio, S.; Murru, N.; Ferrante, M.C.; Mercogliano, R. Study on the occurrence of polycyclic aromatic hydrocarbons in milk and meat/fish based baby food available in Italy. *Chemosphere* **2017**, *184*, 467–472. [CrossRef]

40. Juan, C.; Mañes, J.; Raiola, A.; Ritieni, A. Evaluation of beauvericin and enniatins in Italian cereal products and multicereal food by liquid chromatography coupled to triple quadrupole mass spectrometry. *Food Chem.* **2013**, *140*, 755–762. [CrossRef]
41. Hendry, J.H.; Simon, S.L.; Wojcik, A.; Sohrabi, M.; Burkart, W.; Cardis, E.; Laurier, D.; Tirmarche, M.; Hayata, I. Human exposure to high natural background radiation: What can it teach us about radiation risks? *J. Radiol. Prot.* **2009**, *29*, A29–A42. [CrossRef]

Communication

A New Methodological Approach for the Assessment of the ^{238}U Content in Drinking Water

Francesco Caridi [1,*], Giuseppe Paladini [1,*], Valentina Venuti [1,*], Vincenza Crupi [1], Sebastiano Ettore Spoto [1], Santina Marguccio [2], Maurizio D'Agostino [2], Alberto Belvedere [2] and Domenico Majolino [1]

[1] Dipartimento di Scienze Matematiche e Informatiche, Scienze Fisiche e Scienze della Terra, Università degli Studi di Messina, Viale Ferdinando Stagno D'Alcontres 31, 98166 Messina, Italy; vcrupi@unime.it (V.C.); sebastianoettore@gmail.com (S.E.S.); dmajolino@unime.it (D.M.)

[2] Agenzia Regionale per la Protezione dell'Ambiente della Calabria (ARPACal)—Dipartimento di Reggio Calabria, Via Troncovito SNC, 89135 Reggio Calabria, Italy; s.marguccio@arpacal.it (S.M.); m.dagostino@arpacal.it (M.D.); a.belvedere@arpacal.it (A.B.)

* Correspondence: fcaridi@unime.it (F.C.); gpaladini@unime.it (G.P.); vvenuti@unime.it (V.V.)

Abstract: The radiological quality of drinking water is directly associated with the health of the population. Indeed, it is well known that the presence of radionuclides in drinking water constitutes a health risk for humans because the consumption of such water increases the likelihood of incurring cancer. For this reason, all the studies aimed at developing new methodologies for the qualitative and quantitative analysis of the radioisotopic composition of drinking water are absolutely desired by the international scientific community, as well as by the institutes that deal with the protection of public health. In this paper, a new methodological approach was developed for the evaluation of the ^{238}U content in drinking water. A sample coming from Paola, Calabria region, southern Italy, was taken as a case study. The assessment was performed by using High Purity Germanium (HPGe) gamma-ray spectrometry, with the aim of quantifying the specific activity of the ^{234m}Pa radioisotope after a preconcentration procedure, and thus to assess the activity concentration of ^{238}U, in the hypothesis of the secular radioactive equilibrium between it and its daughter. The obtained results were validated through the comparison with the ^{238}U (µg/L) concentration as measured with Inductively Coupled Plasma-Mass Spectrometry (ICP-MS).

Keywords: drinking water; radioactivity; uranium; High Purity Germanium (HPGe) gamma-ray spectrometry; Inductively Coupled Plasma-Mass Spectrometry (ICP-MS)

1. Introduction

As is well known, the study of natural radioactivity, due to the presence of primordial radionuclides in the Earth's crust and to cosmogenics [1,2], provides information on the radiological risk for the population and on the variations in background radiation due to nuclear activities, industries, power plants, etc. [3,4]. In this context, environmental monitoring of natural radionuclides and their progeny has received considerable attention around the world [5,6]. Although the environmental aspects of natural radioactivity have been discussed in numerous scientific publications [7–10], the presence of natural radioisotopes in drinking water as a hazard factor for the public has not yet been addressed in sufficient detail [11,12]. It is well known that water is very important for our life, since it constitutes from 50% to 60% of the weight of our body, playing an active role in all its vital processes [13]. For this reason, water must be free from pollutants that could pose a risk to human health [14]. Water quality assurance is therefore one of the most important issues in environmental programs to protect public health [15,16]. The Italian Legislative Decree 28/2016 constitutes the current national legislative reference for the quality of water intended for human consumption as regards radioactivity. It regulates the modalities of control of radionuclides by means of indicator parameters [17]. Among the natural radioisotopes to be controlled, ^{238}U is certainly one of the most significant, given the predominant role assumed in the determination of the gross alpha activity concentration, and therefore of the total Indicative Dose (ID) [18].

As a matter of fact, the concentration of uranium in water depends on many factors, including the type of rock of the host aquifer, the presence of oxygen and complexing agents, the chemicals present in the aquifer, the chemical reactions with the ions in solution and the natural contact between uranium ores and water [19]. For example, if the bedrock consists mainly of uranium-rich granitoids and granites and contains soft and slightly alkaline bicarbonate waters, uranium is highly soluble under oxidizing conditions over a wide pH range [20]. Generally, the uranium content of natural water can range from trace levels to 600 µg/L or more [21].

This article reports a new methodological approach, developed in order to evaluate the ^{238}U content in a drinking water sample from Paola, Calabria region, southern Italy, taken as a case study. The evaluation was carried out through High Purity Germanium (HPGe) gamma-ray spectrometry measurements, with the aim of quantifying the specific activity of the natural radionuclide ^{234m}Pa after preconcentration and therefore of evaluating the activity concentration of ^{238}U, in secular radioactive equilibrium with its daughter. Generally, such a condition occurs when the half-life of the child radionuclide is much shorter than that of the parent radionuclide. In our case, as the half-life of ^{234m}Pa (child) and ^{238}U (parent) are equal to 69.5 s and 141×10^{15} s, respectively, their secular radioactive equilibrium can be reasonably hypothesized [22,23]. Although the ^{238}U is a pure alpha-emitter radionuclide, the choice of using HPGe gamma spectrometry with respect to other alpha-based techniques, i.e., alpha spectrometry or liquid scintillation, is due to a more simplified overall analytical activity. The obtained results were then validated by a comparison with the concentration of ^{238}U (µg/L) determined by Inductively Coupled Plasma-Mass Spectrometry (ICP-MS) analysis.

2. Materials and Methods

2.1. Geological Notes, Sampling and Treatment

A representative sample of drinking water was collected, in three different aliquots, in a water tank at Paola, a selected location of the Calabria region, southern Italy. The GPS coordinates of the sampling point, indicated in the map reported in Figure 1, are 39.351132 (latitude) and 16.038091 (longitude).

The geology of the area around Paola (Figure 2) is mainly composed of heterogeneous crystalline–metamorphic rocks and their related weathering products [24]. Crystalline–metamorphic rocks are indeed affected by weathering processes, which are responsible for their chemical and mechanical transformation when interacting with the atmosphere, the hydrosphere and the biosphere [25].

As reported in the published cartography [24] and several research studies [24,25], marble, phyllarenites, muscovite-biotite gneiss, garnet and epidote micaschists, foliated and laminated granites, conglomerates, arenites and alluvial sediments crop out in the area surrounding the city of Paola. The high uranium concentration in the local drinking water can be explained according to the mineralogical composition of the surrounding area. In particular, with biotite having a relevant role in the sorption of radionuclides in granitic rocks, the high content of biotite can cause uranium enrichment [26]. Moreover, epidote minerals, with their structure composed of endless chains of edge-sharing octahedra that are crosslinked by isolated SiO_4 tetrahedra and Si_2O_7 groups, can incorporate significant amounts of geochemically important trace elements such as uranium [27].

Figure 1. The map of the Calabria region, southern Italy, with the sampling point indicated.

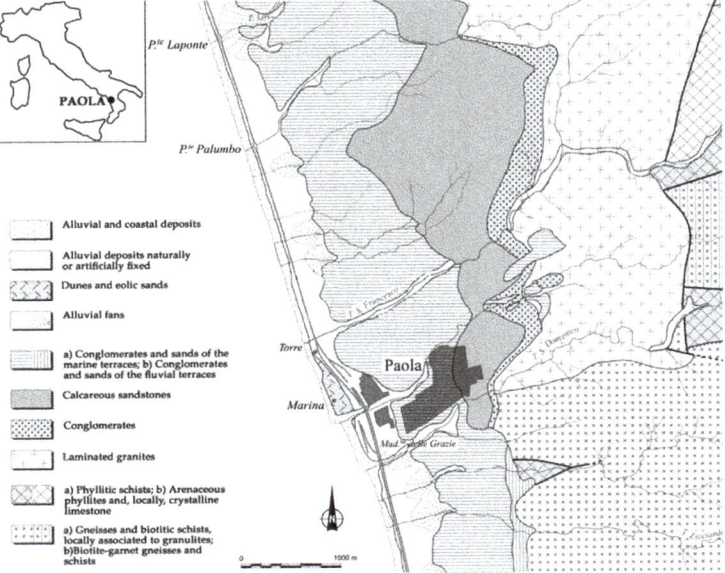

Figure 2. The geological map of the area around Paola, Calabria region, southern Italy.

Each aliquot of drinking water was collected into a 750 mL acidified polyethylene bin, in order to avoid radionuclide precipitation and adsorption on the container walls, and then stored in the laboratory for the sample preparation and analysis. Before use, each beaker was first soaked with diluted nitric acid, then washed, rinsed with distilled water and finally left to dry in the oven to prevent contamination [28]. In the laboratory, the first aliquot was taken as it was, while the other two were evaporated on a plate in order to reach: (i) a final volume of 250 mL, i.e., factor of preconcentration equal to 3, for the second aliquot and (ii) a final volume of 20 mL, i.e., factor of preconcentration equal to 37.5, for the third aliquot. The volumes of 250 mL and 20 mL correspond to the two sample holder geometries available for the gamma spectrometry analyses [29].

2.2. Diagnostics Techniques and Samples Measurements

2.2.1. High Purity Germanium (HPGe) Gamma-Ray Spectrometry

For the gamma spectrometry analysis, the first aliquot, as it was, and the second one, preconcentrated, were inserted in a Marinelli container with a volume of 250 mL, while the third one, preconcentrated, was stored in a 20 mL vial. After that, they were counted for 70,000 s and spectra were analyzed in order to obtain the activity concentration of ^{238}U by means of that of its daughter ^{234m}Pa, with which uranium is in secular equilibrium. The 1001.03 keV gamma-ray line was used to determine ^{234m}Pa specific activity.

The experimental set-up was composed of a positive biased Ortec HPGe detector (GMX), whose operating parameters are reported in Table 1.

Table 1. The HPGe GMX operating parameters.

HPGe GMX Detector	
Parameter	Value
Full Width at Half Maximum	1.94 keV
Peak to Compton ratio	65:1
Relative efficiency	37.5% (at the 1.33 MeV ^{60}Co γ-line)
Bias voltage	−4800 V
Energy range	5 keV–2 MeV

It was placed inside lead wells to shield the background radiation environment. It is worth noting that, for the sample holder geometry of 250 mL, efficiency and energy calibrations were performed using a multipeak Marinelli geometry gamma source (BC-4464) of 250 mL capacity, covering the energy range 60–1836 keV, customized to reproduce the exact geometries of samples in a water-equivalent epoxy resin matrix. Moreover, the ANGLE 4 code was employed for the efficiency transfer factors calculations to the 20 mL vial sample holder geometry [30]. The Gamma Vision (Ortec) software was used for data acquisition and analysis [31].

The activity concentration of the investigated radioisotope was calculated using the following formula [32,33]

$$C = \frac{N_E}{\varepsilon_E t \gamma_d V} \quad (1)$$

where N_E indicates the net area of the radioisotope photopeak, ε_E and γ_d are the efficiency and yield of the photopeak, respectively, V is the volume of the sample (L) and t is the live time (s).

The measurement result uncertainty, coverage factor k = 2, was calculated taking into account the following components: uncertainty of the counting estimation, of the calibration source, of the efficiency calibration, of the background subtraction and of the γ-branching ratio [34].

The quality of the gamma spectrometry experimental results was certified by the Italian Accreditation Body (ACCREDIA) [35].

2.2.2. Inductively Coupled Plasma-Mass Spectrometry (ICP-MS)

The concentration of ^{238}U was obtained through ICP-MS analysis with a Thermo Scientific iCAP Qc ICP-MS. The sample introduction system consisted of a Peltier cooled (3 °C), baffled cyclonic spray chamber, PFA nebulizer and quartz torch with a 2.5 mm i.d. removable quartz injector. The instrument operated in a single collision cell mode, with kinetic energy discrimination (KED), using pure He as collision gas. All samples were presented for analysis using a Cetac ASX-520. The iCAP Qc ICP-MS operated in a single KED mode using the parameters reported in Table 2 [36]. For the "direct analysis" of analytes in drinking water where sample turbidity is <1 NTU, the sample was prepared by the appropriate addition of nitric acid (1%).

Table 2. The iCAP Qc ICP-MS operating parameters.

iCAP Qc Detector	
Parameter	Value
Nebulizer gas	0.98 L/min
Auxiliary gas	0.8 L/min
Collision cell gas He	4.5 mL/min
Point per peak	One
Forward power	1550 W
Cool gas flow	14.0 L/min
Optimized dwell time for analyte	0.01 s
Repeat per sample	Three
Sample uptake/wash time	45 s each

Sample material in solution was introduced by pneumatic nebulization into a radiofrequency plasma where energy transfer processes cause desolvation, atomization and ionization. Ions were extracted from the plasma through a differentially pumped vacuum interface and separated on the basis of their mass-to-charge ratio by a quadrupole mass spectrometer having a minimum resolution capability of 1 amu peak width at 5% peak height. Ions transmitted through the quadrupole were detected by an electron multiplier or Faraday detector and the ion information processed by a data handling system. Interferences relating to the technique had to be identified and corrected. Such corrections included compensation for isobaric elemental interferences and interferences from polyatomic ions derived from the plasma gas, reagents or sample matrix. Instrumental drift as well as suppressions or enhancements of instrument response caused by the sample matrix were corrected for using internal standards [36].

The quality of the ICP-MS results was certified by the Italian Accreditation Body (ACCREDIA) [35].

The massic elemental concentrations in µg/L for uranium was converted in ^{238}U activity concentration, according to the following formula [37]

$$C = \frac{\lambda N_A f}{MK} F \qquad (2)$$

where C is the measured specific activity (Bq/L) of the radionuclide under consideration, λ the decay constant of the measured isotope of element (s^{-1}), N_A the Avogadro's number, f the fractional atomic abundance in nature, M the atomic mass (kg/mol), K a constant with value of 10^6 for U and F the fraction of element in the sample.

2.3. Accuracy Assessment

In order to assess the accuracy of the experimental ^{238}U specific activity obtained by the new methodological approach here proposed, a comparison between HPGe gamma spectrometry and ICP-MS results was performed through the z-score calculation, according to [38]

$$z = \frac{x - X}{\sqrt{u_x^2 + U_x^2}} \qquad (3)$$

where x is the ^{238}U activity concentration obtained by HPGe gamma spectrometry, X the ^{238}U concentration (in µg/L) obtained by ICP-MS and then converted into specific activity through Equation (2), u_x the total uncertainty of the HPGe gamma spectrometry results (at a coverage factor k = 1) and U_x the uncertainty of the ICP-MS results (for k = 1).

For environmental radioactivity measurements the criterion of acceptability of $z \leq 2$ was used [39].

3. Results and Discussion

Figure 3 reports the HPGe gamma spectra acquired, for the investigated drinking water sample, with no preconcentration (a), factor of preconcentration equal to 3 (b) and to 37.5 (c).

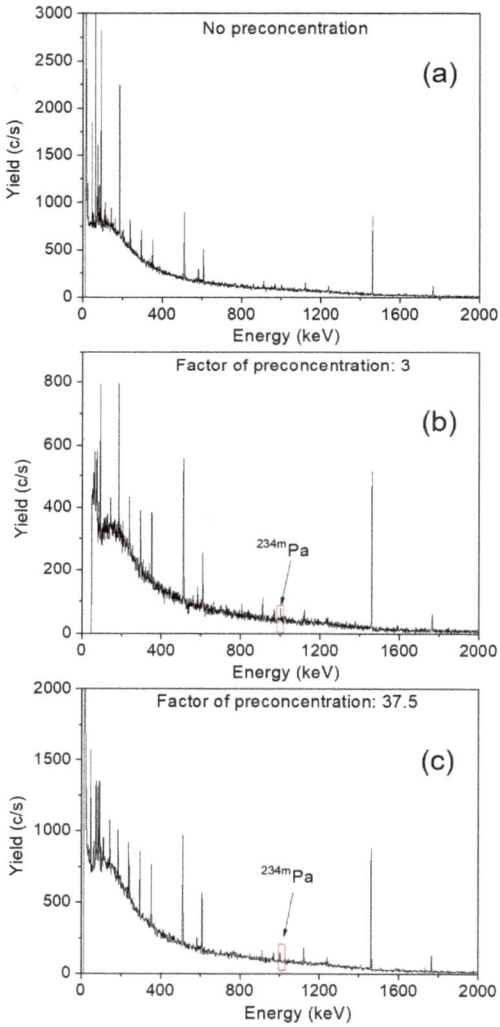

Figure 3. The HPGe gamma spectra acquired, for the investigated drinking water sample, with no preconcentration (**a**), factor of preconcentration equal to 3 (**b**) and 37.5 (**c**).

The 1001.03 keV gamma-ray line of ^{234m}Pa appears more and more evident in the spectra, as the preconcentration of the analyzed sample increases. According to Equation (1), the activity concentration of ^{238}U, in the hypothesis of the secular radioactive equilibrium between it and its daughter, was found to be not quantifiable without preconcentration, and equal to (0.76 ± 0.22) Bq/L and (0.31 ± 0.13) Bq/L for factors of preconcentration 3 and 37.5, respectively.

Moreover, these results were then compared with the concentration of ^{238}U obtained through ICP-MS measurement. The massic elemental concentration for uranium turned out to be (5.6 ± 1.1) μg/L and, according to Equation (2), it was converted in ^{238}U activity concentration, giving rise to a specific activity of (69 ± 14) mBq/L. The comparison was therefore performed by calculating the z-score parameter, as reported in Equation (3). It was found to be not quantifiable without preconcentration, and equal to 3.13 and 1.85 for factors of preconcentration 3 and 37.5, respectively.

On the basis of the obtained results, we can therefore affirm that the preconcentration of a drinking water sample with a factor equal to 37.5, followed by a gamma spectrometry analysis of the preconcentrated aliquot, allows us to quantify, with a high degree of accuracy (z-score < 2), the specific activity of ^{238}U.

As a matter of fact, it is widely reported in the literature that ^{238}U in drinking water is usually quantified by means of a gamma spectrometry, under the hypothesis of secular equilibrium with its daughter ^{234}Th, using the percolation through a mixed bed ion exchange resin as a preconcentration technique, with the reduction to a final volume of 1 L starting from 80 L (preconcentration factor 80), or 2 L starting from 300 L (preconcentration factor 150) [40,41]. In the light of this, it must be emphasized how the methodological approach reported in this article is characterized by a relatively simple preconcentration process that does not require the use of chemical procedures. In addition, it can be of great utility in commonly performed drinking water monitoring activities, in which aliquots with volumes of the order of a few liters are sampled.

Finally, from the point of view of the radiological health risk assessment, it is important to point out that the activity concentration of ^{238}U in the analyzed drinking water sample taken as a case study is much lower than the reference value of 3 Bq/L, corresponding to an Indicative Dose of 0.1 mSv/year [42]. This last parameter, calculated in the precautionary hypothesis that the water sample contains only the radioisotope in question, that the age class considered is only the one corresponding to adults, and that the water consumption is equal to 730 L/year [43], is set as a threshold by the regulatory limit [42]. Therefore, it is possible to exclude any radiological health risk for the population of the studied area, with reference to the drinking water consumption.

4. Conclusions

In the present article, a new methodological approach to evaluate the ^{238}U content in drinking water was reported. A sample from Paola, a selected location of the Calabria region, southern Italy, was taken as a case study.

HPGe gamma-ray spectrometry was employed, with the aim of quantifying the specific activity of the ^{234m}Pa radioisotope after a preconcentration procedure and thus to assess the activity concentration of ^{238}U, under the hypothesis of the secular radioactive equilibrium between it and its daughter. The accuracy of the obtained results was then evaluated through the calculation of the z-score parameter, taking into account the ^{238}U (μg/L) concentration, as measured with ICP-MS as reference value.

From the results, i.e., z-score equal to 1.85 for a factor of preconcentration equal to 37.5, the validity of the proposed methodological approach is assessed.

Moreover, with reference to the radiological health risk evaluation, the specific activity of ^{238}U in the analyzed drinking water sample was much lower than the reference value of 3 Bq/L, set as a threshold by the regulatory limit. This result thus indicates that the ingestion of drinking water might not pose any significant radiological health hazards for the population of the studied area.

Author Contributions: Conceptualization, F.C. and V.V.; methodology, F.C. and V.C.; validation, D.M.; formal analysis, A.B., S.M. and M.D.; investigation, F.C., S.E.S., G.P. and V.V.; resources, F.C.,

V.C. and D.M.; data curation, F.C.; writing-original draft preparation, F.C.; supervision, D.M. and V.V. All authors have read and agreed to the published version of the manuscript.

Funding: This research received no external funding.

Institutional Review Board Statement: Not applicable.

Informed Consent Statement: Not applicable.

Conflicts of Interest: The authors declare no conflict of interest.

References

1. Caridi, F.; D'Agostino, M.; Messina, M.; Marcianò, G.; Grioli, L.; Belvedere, A.; Marguccio, S.; Belmusto, G. Lichens as environmental risk detectors. *Eur. Phys. J. Plus* **2017**, *132*, 189. [CrossRef]
2. Omar-Nazir, L.; Shi, X.; Moller, A.; Mousseau, T.; Byun, S.; Hancock, S.; Seymour, C.; Mothersill, C. Long-term effects of ionizing radiation after the Chernobyl accident: Possible contribution of historic dose. *Environ. Res.* **2018**, *165*, 55–62. [CrossRef] [PubMed]
3. Alzubaidi, G.; Hamid, F.B.S.; Abdul Rahman, I. Assessment of Natural Radioactivity Levels and Radiation Hazards in Agricultural and Virgin Soil in the State of Kedah, North of Malaysia. *Sci. World J.* **2016**, *2016*, 6178103. [CrossRef]
4. Günoğlu, K.; Seçkiner, S. Evaluation of dose parameters and radiological hazards in gravel samples of Konyaaltı Beach, Antalya. *Arab. J. Geosci.* **2018**, *11*, 457. [CrossRef]
5. Ravisankar, R.; Chandramohan, J.; Chandrasekaran, A.; Prince Prakash Jebakumar, J.; Vijayalakshmi, I.; Vijayagopal, P.; Venkatraman, B. Assessments of radioactivity concentration of natural radionuclides and radiological hazard indices in sediment samples from the East coast of Tamilnadu, India with statistical approach. *Mar. Pollut. Bull.* **2015**, *97*, 419–430. [CrossRef]
6. Caridi, F.; D'Agostino, M.; Belvedere, A.; Marguccio, S.; Belmusto, G. Radon radioactivity in groundwater from the Calabria region, south of Italy. *J. Instrum.* **2016**, *11*, P05012. [CrossRef]
7. Ramasamy, V.; Suresh, G.; Meenakshisundaram, V.; Ponnusamy, V. Horizontal and vertical characterization of radionuclides and minerals in river sediments. *Appl. Radiat. Isot.* **2011**, *69*, 184–195. [CrossRef]
8. Caridi, F.; D'Agostino, M.; Belvedere, A.; Marguccio, S.; Belmusto, G.; Gatto, M.F. Diagnostics techniques and dosimetric evaluations for environmental radioactivity investigations. *J. Instrum.* **2016**, *11*, C10012. [CrossRef]
9. Laraia, M. Radioactive contamination and other environmental impacts of waste from nuclear and conventional power plants, medical and other industrial sources. In *Environmental Remediation and Restoration of Contaminated Nuclear and Norm Sites*; Woodhead Publishing Series in Energy; Elsevier: Amsterdam, The Netherlands, 2015; pp. 35–56. [CrossRef]
10. Khaled, A.; Hessein, A.; Abdel-Halim, A.M.; Morsy, F.M. Distribution of heavy metals in seaweeds collected along marsa-matrouh beaches, Egyptian mediterranean sea. *Egypt. J. Aquat. Res.* **2014**, *40*, 363–371. [CrossRef]
11. Caridi, F.; Belmusto, G. Assessment of the public effective dose due to the 222Rn radioactivity in drinking water: Results from the Calabria region, southern Italy. *J. Instrum.* **2021**, *16*, P02033. [CrossRef]
12. Håkanson, L. An Ecological Risk Index for Aquatic Pollution Control—A Sedimentological Approach. *Water Res.* **1980**, *14*, 975–1001. [CrossRef]
13. Eckerman, K.; Harrison, J.; Menzel, H.G.; Clement, C.H. ICRP publication 119: Compendium of dose coefficients based on ICRP publication 60. *Ann. ICRP* **2012**, *41*, 1–130. [CrossRef] [PubMed]
14. Caridi, F.; Messina, M.; D'Agostino, M. An investigation about natural radioactivity, hydrochemistry, and metal pollution in groundwater from Calabrian selected areas, southern Italy. *Environ. Earth Sci.* **2017**, *76*, 668. [CrossRef]
15. Briffa, J.; Sinagra, E.; Blundell, R. Heavy metal pollution in the environment and their toxicological effects on humans. *Heliyon* **2020**, *6*, e04691. [CrossRef]
16. Zheng, L.-G.; Liu, G.-J.; Kang, Y.; Yang, R.-K. Some potential hazardous trace elements contamination and their ecological risk in sediments of western Chaohu Lake, China. *Environ. Monit. Assess.* **2010**, *166*, 379–386. [CrossRef]
17. Caridi, F.; Belmusto, G. Overview of the technologies for assessment of natural radioactivity in drinking water. *J. Instrum.* **2019**, *14*, T02002. [CrossRef]
18. Caridi, F.; Belmusto, G. Gross Alpha and Beta Radioactivity Evaluation in Drinking Water: Results from the Calabria Region, Southern Italy. *Int. J. Environ. Res.* **2021**, *15*, 695–700. [CrossRef]
19. Andò, S. Gravimetric separation of heavy minerals in sediments and rocks. *Minerals* **2020**, *10*, 273. [CrossRef]
20. Hassan, N.M.; Rasmussen, P.E.; Dabek-Zlotorzynska, E.; Celo, V.; Chen, H. Analysis of Environmental Samples Using Microwave-Assisted Acid Digestion and Inductively Coupled Plasma Mass Spectrometry: Maximizing Total Element Recoveries. *Water Air Soil Pollut.* **2007**, *178*, 323–334. [CrossRef]
21. Turekian, K.K.; Wedepohl, K.H. Distribution of the elements in some major units of the earth's crust. *Geol. Soc. Am. Bull.* **1961**, *72*, 175–192. [CrossRef]
22. Kraemer, T.F.; Genereux, D.P. Chapter 20—Applications of Uranium- and Thorium-Series Radionuclides in Catchment Hydrology Studies. In *Isotope Tracers in Catchment Hydrology*; Kendall, C., McDonnell, J., Eds.; Elsevier: Amsterdam, The Netherlands, 1998; pp. 679–722. ISBN 978-0-444-81546-0.
23. Northern Agency Tronox Mines, Appendix D, Uranium Equilibrium Report. Response, Assessment, and Evaluation Services (RAES). In *Tetra Tech, Ed.*; Tetra Tech: Pasadena, CA, USA, 2019.

24. Lanzafame, G.; Zuffa, G.G. Geologia e petrografia del Foglio Bisignano (Bacino del Crati, Calabria). *Geol. Rom.* **1976**, *15*, 223–270.
25. Calcaterra, D.; Parise, M. Weathering in the crystalline rocks of Calabria, Italy, and relationships to landslides. In *Weathering as a Predisposing Factor to Slope Movements*; Geological Society, London, Engineering Geology Special Publications: London, UK, 2010; pp. 105–130. [CrossRef]
26. Idemitsu, K.; Obata, K.; Furuya, H.; Inagaki, Y. Sorption Behavior of Uranium(VI) on a Biotite Mineral. *MRS Online Proc. Libr.* **1994**, *353*, 981–988. [CrossRef]
27. Frei, D.; Liebscher, A.; Franz, G.; Dulsk, P. Trace Element Geochemistry of Epidote Minerals. *Rev. Mineral. Geochem.* **2004**, *56*, 553–606. [CrossRef]
28. Caridi, F.; D'Agostino, M. Evaluation of drinking water radioactivity content and radiological risk assessment: A new methodological approach. *J. Instrum.* **2020**, *15*, P10016. [CrossRef]
29. Babu, S.H.; Kumar, K.S.; Suvardhan, K.; Kiran, K.; Rekha, D.; Krishnaiah, L.; Janardhanam, K.; Chiranjeevi, P. Preconcentration technique for the determination of trace elements in natural water samples by ICP-AES. *Environ. Monit. Assess.* **2007**, *128*, 241–249. [CrossRef]
30. Ortec Angle 4 Software User Manual. 2016. Available online: https://www.ortec-online.com/-/media/ametekortec/manuals/a/angle-mnl.pdf?la=en&revision=a81e1418-e874-4693-be48-0c2b47f38166 (accessed on 3 March 2022).
31. Caridi, F.; Di Bella, M.; Sabatino, G.; Belmusto, G.; Fede, M.R.; Romano, D.; Italiano, F.; Mottese, A. Assessment of natural radioactivity and radiological risks in river sediments from calabria (Southern Italy). *Appl. Sci.* **2021**, *11*, 1729. [CrossRef]
32. Caridi, F.; Acri, G.; Belvedere, A.; Crupi, V.; D'Agostino, M.; Marguccio, S.; Messina, M.; Paladini, G.; Venuti, V.; Majolino, D. Evaluation of the radiological and chemical risk for public health from flour sample investigation. *Appl. Sci.* **2021**, *11*, 3646. [CrossRef]
33. Huang, Y.; Lu, X.; Ding, X.; Feng, T. Natural radioactivity level in beach sand along the coast of Xiamen Island, China. *Mar. Pollut. Bull.* **2015**, *91*, 357–361. [CrossRef]
34. Caridi, F.; Paladini, G.; Venuti, V.; Crupi, V.; Procopio, S.; Belvedere, A.; D'agostino, M.; Faggio, G.; Grillo, R.; Marguccio, S.; et al. Radioactivity, metals pollution and mineralogy assessment of a beach stretch from the ionian coast of calabria (Southern italy). *Int. J. Environ. Res. Public Health* **2021**, *18*, 12147. [CrossRef]
35. ACCREDIA. Available online: https://www.accredia.it/ (accessed on 17 January 2022).
36. *Thermo Fisher iCAP Q Operating Manual*; Thermo Fisher: Waltham, MA, USA, 2012.
37. Dragović, S.; Janković, L.; Onjia, A.; Bačić, G. Distribution of primordial radionuclides in surface soils from Serbia and Montenegro. *Radiat. Meas.* **2006**, *41*, 611–616. [CrossRef]
38. Berengolts, A.; Lindenbaum, M. On the distribution of z-score. *Iran. J. Sci. Technol. Trans. A Sci.* **2008**, *32*, A1. [CrossRef]
39. *UNI CEI EN ISO/IEC 17025*; General Requirements for the Competence of Testing and Calibration Laboratories. UNI: Milan, Italy, 2018.
40. Forte, M.; Bertolo, A.; D'Alberti, F.; De Felice, P.; Desideri, D.; Esposito, M.; Fresca Fantoni, R.; Lorenzelli, R.; Luciani, A.; Magnoni, M.; et al. Standardized methods for measuring radionuclides in drinking water. *J. Radioanal. Nucl. Chem.* **2006**, *269*, 397–401. [CrossRef]
41. Forte, M.; Rusconi, R.; Cazzaniga, M.; Sgorbati, G. The measurement of radioactivity in drinking water. *Microchem. J.* **2007**, *105*, 98–102. [CrossRef]
42. *Italian Legislation D. Lgs. n. 28/2016*; FAO, FAOLEX: Rome, Italy, 2016; pp. 1–4.
43. Kamiya, K.; Ozasa, K.; Akiba, S.; Niwa, O.; Kodama, K.; Takamura, N.; Zaharieva, E.K.; Kimura, Y.; Wakeford, R. Long-term effects of radiation exposure on health. *Lancet* **2015**, *386*, 469–478. [CrossRef]

Article

Monte Carlo Simulation-Based Calculations of Complex DNA Damage for Incidents of Environmental Ionizing Radiation Exposure

Spyridon A. Kalospyros [1,†], Violeta Gika [1,†], Zacharenia Nikitaki [1], Antigoni Kalamara [1], Ioanna Kyriakou [2], Dimitris Emfietzoglou [2], Michael Kokkoris [1] and Alexandros G. Georgakilas [1,*]

[1] Physics Department, School of Applied Mathematical and Physical Sciences, National Technical University of Athens (NTUA), 15780 Zografou, Greece; spkals@central.ntua.gr (S.A.K.); guika@mail.ntua.gr (V.G.); znikitaki@mail.ntua.gr (Z.N.); antigonikalamara@gmail.com (A.K.); kokkoris@central.ntua.gr (M.K.)

[2] Medical Physics Laboratory, Department of Medicine, University of Ioannina, 45110 Ioannina, Greece; ikyriak@uoi.gr (I.K.); demfietz@uoi.gr (D.E.)

* Correspondence: alexg@mail.ntua.gr; Tel.: +30-210-772-4453

† Equal contribution for these authors.

Abstract: In this paper, we present a useful Monte Carlo (MC)-based methodology that can be utilized to calculate the absorbed dose and the initial levels of complex DNA damage (such as double strand breaks-DSBs) in the case of an environmental ionizing radiation (IR) exposure incident (REI) i.e., a nuclear accident. Our objective is to assess the doses and complex DNA damage by isolating only one component of the total radiation released in the environment after a REI that will affect the health of the exposed individual. More specifically, the radiation emitted by radionuclide ^{137}Cs in the ground (under the individual's feet). We use a merging of the Monte Carlo N-Particle Transport code (MCNP) with the Monte Carlo Damage Simulation (MCDS) code. The DNA lesions have been estimated through simulations for different surface activities of a ^{137}Cs ground-based γ radiation source. The energy spectrum of the emitted secondary electrons and the absorbed dose in typical mammalian cells have been calculated using the MCNP code, and then these data are used as an input in the MCDS code for the estimation of critical DNA damage levels and types. As a realistic application, the calculated dose is also used to assess the Excess Lifetime Cancer Risk (ELCR) for eight hypothetical individuals, living in different zones around the Chernobyl Nuclear Power Plant, exposed to different time periods at the days of the accident in 1986. We conclude that any exposition of an individual in the near zone of Chernobyl increases the risk of cancer at a moderate to high grade, connected also with the induction of complex DNA damage by radiation. Generally, our methodology has proven to be useful for assessing γ rays-induced complex DNA damage levels of the exposed population, in the case of a REI and for better understanding the long-term health effects of exposure of the population to IR.

Keywords: Monte Carlo simulation; complex DNA damage; double strand breaks; ionizing radiation; radiological incident; radionuclide; absorbed dose; 137-caesium; surface activity

1. Introduction

Large-scale exposure to IR, in terms of both the amount of radiation and the number of people exposed occurs rarely due to international safeguards that are currently in force. All the nuclear accidents that have taken place have provided us with valuable information and experience about the health consequences of the leaked radioactivity to the public and the appropriate health management of such incidents. The nuclear accident of Chernobyl in April 1986, as the first large-scale REI, has been a great challenge to the scientific community that deals with the radiation protection, to revise much of its knowledge until that time and to improve the relevant nuclear safeguard rules. The value of the experience gained from that nuclear accident found application [1] to other accidents that followed of a smaller scale, such as in Brazil (the Goiânia ^{137}Cs accident in 1987) and the two accidents that took place in Tokaimura of Japan on 11 March 1997 and 30 September 1999 [2,3], as well as of a larger scale, as with the accident that too place in Fukushima Daiichi on 11 March 2011 [4]. It is of note that environmental pollution due to man-made radionuclides began in the period 1946–1980, during the process of nuclear materials testing, when approximately 400 nuclear tests were performed in the northern hemisphere [5].

Radionuclides released in the air from a radioactive source may be in a gaseous, particulate, or multi-phase (i.e., simultaneously gaseous and particle) form [6]. These particles are generally transported through the air by adhesion to aerosols, construction particles or soil particles, as well as weather conditions such as the wind, rain and snow, which play a crucial role in transporting particles from the place of their release to the surrounding areas. Concerning the radionuclide spreading mechanism following an REI (i.e., a nuclear power plant accident, a nuclear weapon detonation, a radiological dispersal device, a transportation incident, sabotage or an improvised nuclear device), it is suggested that part of these radioparticles are deposited on the surface soil, while others are transported to the underground layers with rain, snow and watering, or they are transferred to surrounding geographic areas by re-floating [7]. The migration of radionuclides across the ground surface depends on the particle and surface characteristics. The transport of contaminants may vary depending on their physiochemical characteristics; for example, ^{137}Cs is characterized as highly mobile because of its high-water solubility [8].

Two main pathways leading to radiation exposure of the general public due to a nuclear 'fallout' are the external exposure from radionuclides deposited on the ground, and the internal exposure through contaminated air inhalation, ingestion of contaminated food or water from the affected areas [9]. Radionuclide analysis of environmental samples is very practical for the evaluation of the current environmental radioactivity level. However, in the case of a nuclear accident, it is highly important to evaluate the environmental contamination, as well as the external and internal exposure risks for radiation protection and public health purposes. In the latter case, the risks of an internal exposure are extremely low because of the corresponding international regulations which demand restrictions in food and water intake (http://www.mhlw.go.jp/english/topics/2011eq/index.html (accessed on 29 July 2021)). On the other hand, the risks of external exposure for the public are enforced for safety reasons.

The Chernobyl Nuclear Power Plant (CNPP) accident, classified as Level 7 ('major accident') on the International Nuclear and Radiological Event Scale of the International Atomic Energy Agency (IAEA) [10], resulted in a massive release of radionuclides into the atmosphere and caused an extensive contamination of the environment. Ten-day major releases from the Unit 4 of the CNPP injected about 14 EBq of radioactive substances into the atmosphere, including radioactive gases, condensed aerosols, and a large amount of fuel particles. The total release of radioactive substances included the radionuclides: ^{132}Te, ^{134}Cs, ^{137}Cs, ^{99}Mo, ^{103}Ru, ^{106}Ru, ^{140}Ba, ^{95}Zr, ^{141}Ce, ^{144}Ce, ^{89}Sr, and ^{90}Sr. The noble gases contributed about 50% of the total release [11]. A terrestrial surface of more than 200,000 square kilometres in Europe received ^{137}Cs with levels above 37 kBq m^{-2} [12]. Over 70% of the contaminated area comprised Belarus, Russia and Ukraine of the former USSR [13]. The radiation exposure of the population to these biologically dangerous releases was classified into two main phases: the earlier phase included exposure to rapidly decaying radionuclides, whose doses were delivered over a short period (no more than three months after the accident), while the later one comprised of an exposure to radionuclides of a long life that were deposited on the ground [14]. Most of the strontium and plutonium isotopes were deposited within 100 km of the destroyed reactor due to their larger particle sizes, while other important radionuclides decayed away. In the early months after the accident, the radionuclide levels of agricultural plants and plant-consuming animals were dominated by surface deposits [15]. The deposition of $^{131}_{53}$I caused the most immediate concern, but the problem was confined to the first two-three months after the accident because of its decay. The radioiodine was rapidly absorbed into milk, leading to significant thyroid doses in people consuming milk products, especially children in Belarus, Russia and Ukraine. Increased levels of ^{131}I in milk products were also detected in some southern areas of Europe, while dairy animals were being fed outdoors [16]. Radioisotopes of Caesium (^{137}Cs and ^{134}Cs) were the nuclides which led to the largest problems. The Cs hazard may be attributed to its incorporation into the human body from food consumption (especially dairy products) and via γ-irradiation from the ground. It is characterized by a relatively slow accumulation of doses, compared to radioiodine, but also by a whole-body irradiation [17]. ^{131}I also concentrates inside the human body through dairy products and has a gamma-component, resulting in a significant whole-body dose. Once inside the body, this radionuclide is absorbed mainly by the thyroid gland, potentially increasing the risk for thyroid cancer, since this gland uses iodine to produce its hormones and cannot distinguish between the radioactive particles and its stable natural form. As ^{131}I builds up in the thyroid gland, its emitted radiation can induce DNA damage, removing normal limits to cell growth and division and, thus, causing unchecked growth of thyroid tissue [18]. Additionally, the radionuclide ^{90}Sr (half-life: ~28.79 years), due to its chemical similarity to calcium, accumulates in bones and irradiates the bone marrow, and therefore can also cause problems for human health. The latter was concentrated in a more restricted area around the reactor, as its larger particle size and its deposition levels at large distances were not radiologically significant. It is of note that gamma emitter nuclides (such as caesium and iodine isotopes) have been studied more extensively than the beta emitter strontium, since it is much simpler to measure gamma than beta emitters [19]. Therefore, ^{137}Cs was chosen in our study for the mapping of the deposition because of its radiological importance and its easiness for measurements.

Increased contamination levels remained within the atmosphere for years after the accident, while radionuclide deposition values, depending on meteorological and environmental conditions, as well as the particle size, showed a substantial reduction in their transfer to vegetation and animals in agricultural systems during the first few years. The ^{137}Cs activity concentrations still remain high in the surrounding areas of Chernobyl (in Ukraine, Belarus and Russia), especially in natural ecosystems (forests, rivers and lakes), while the surface contamination and the air dose rate have been reduced significantly due to radioactive decay, rain, wind and human activities [20]. Caesium-137 levels are still present, even in the southern areas of Europe, as monitored through plants such as lichens and mushrooms [21], which have a high retention capacity of such radionuclides; through the lichen Stereocaulon vasuvianum, Savino et al. [22] have accurately determined the effective half-life of ^{137}Cs.

In general, many significant radionuclides released by the CNPP accident have already decayed away. Radioactive iodine isotopes caused great concern within the first few months after the accident since they are short-lived. In the future, ^{137}Cs will continue to be of greater importance, with less attention paid to ^{90}Sr. Over the longer term (hundreds of years), the plutonium isotopes and ^{241}Am will remain radioactive, although at levels that are relatively low [9].

One recent "major" (according to IAEA 2008 criteria) nuclear accident occurred in Fukushima Daiichi Nuclear Power Plant (FDNPP) in Japan, on 11 March 2011, as a result of a tsunami (caused by a strong earthquake) that struck the east coast of the island. The radioactive releases from this nuclear accident were not as large as those from Chernobyl but were still considered substantial [23]. A radioactive plume derived from the Units 1, 2, 3 and 4 of the FDNPP was dispersed in the atmosphere, causing significant radioactive pollution (mainly due to ^{134}Cs, ^{137}Cs and ^{131}I release) of the environment within a radius of 40 km from the damaged reactors. Immediately after the accident, the prevalent dose-forming radionuclides collected from soil samples from the nearby areas around the reactors were ^{131}I, ^{134}Cs, ^{137}Cs, ^{129m}Te, ^{95}Nb and ^{136}Cs, while, after several months, the corresponding ones were ^{134}Cs, ^{137}Cs and ^{129m}Te. It was also estimated (some months after the accident) that the amount of radioactive materials released into the environment at that time was approximately 10% (1.6×10^{17} Bq for ^{131}I and 1.5×10^{16} Bq for ^{137}Cs) that of the Chernobyl accident [24].

Up until now, a large area of a few thousand square kilometres around CNPP (the 'Chernobyl Exclusion Zone') remains evacuated, with restricted human access. ^{131}I (half-life: 8 days) has long decayed, and ^{134}Cs (half-life: 2 years) has already been considered depleted, therefore, the main existing problem is the radioactive hazard from contamination by ^{137}Cs (half-life: 30.17 years), although half of the initial release has now decayed. The whole restricted zone gives the opportunity for the study of radiation transmission to the animals of this area, since wildlife is flourishing in the absence of human activities [25]. In Fukushima, there are confined areas within a radius of 40 km around the FDNPP, where the annual effective dose exceeds 20 mSv (the effective dose limit established by the Japanese Government for the lifting of the human exclusion order) and other areas where the corresponding value is up to 50 mSv. Although remediation measures through the years have been taken for the maximum possible decrease in the radioactive nuclides of the terrestrial area, the radio-contamination levels do not permit the return of evacuees to their land. Gamma-radiation from the deposited ^{137}Cs still remains a big problem for authorities [26]. As referred to above, the ^{137}Cs content in these areas is also investigated through lichens and other plants [27]. As also occurred in Chernobyl, ^{90}Sr dispersion over the Fukushima territory was limited and the biggest part of this released radionuclide was deposited in the proximity of the FDNPP [19].

One of the main pathways leading to human exposure after such a REI is the external exposure from radionuclides deposited on the ground [28]. Gamma-radiation from these radionuclides has been a major contributor to the external exposure of the public due to a nuclear accident [29]. In our study, we focus on the ^{137}Cs as the most prominent radionuclide for ground contamination due to its substantial contribution to the lifetime effective dose to humans, its long radioactive half-life, and its ease of measurement.

Exposure to IR induces a range of DNA lesions to living cells. IR photons especially can target the nuclear DNA molecule in two ways: either by directly striking it, with the induction of secondary electrons, causing breaks in the phosphodiester bond connecting adjacent nucleotides on the same side of the DNA helix, or by water radiolysis, which can result in the formation of reactive oxidative species (ROS) and additional oxidative DNA damage. All the above can result in the formation of simple or complex lesions [30,31]. In such a DNA lesion, a single nucleotide is characterized by an abnormal chemical alteration, i.e., a missing or damaged base or a strand break. These lesions may comprise base damage (BD), single-strand breaks (SSBs, i.e., a cluster of lesions that contains at least one strand break and which has no other additional break within 10 bp on the opposed strand), double-strand breaks (DSBs, i.e., this is a lesion that consists of two SSBs, which are located on opposite strands within 10 bp of each other) and complex DNA damage (groups of several lesions within 1 or 2 helical turns of the DNA molecule) [32]. Among them, DSBs and non-DSB clustered damage (i.e., two or more lesions within one or two helical turns of DNA induced by the passage of a single radiation track) [33] are considered to be the primary cause of radiation-induced cell killing, mutagenesis and neoplastic transformation. Through the process of breaking and re-joining, DSBs are converted into small- or large-scale chromosomal exchanges with the ability to induce phenotypic tumor lesions and, finally, cell death. Other types of non-DSB lesions, such as clustered oxidized bases, are considered to be resistant to the repair process and more susceptible to DSB formation through their repair processing [34].

Throughout the last decade, Monte Carlo (MC) codes have proved to be a useful tool for assessing DNA lesions in a cell exposed to IR, since they have been constructed to simulate damage induction at the DNA scale [35,36]. Radiation risks for an individual exposed to IR depend on different factors. One factor of great importance is the overall dose of radiation absorbed by the human body, while another equally important one is the dose distribution within it.

In our study, we have used a serial combination of two MC codes with different roles in order to estimate the number of induced lesions (SSBs and DSBs) per cell of a person exposed to IR from a radioactive source (^{137}Cs) placed in the ground, as a remnant from a hypothetical nuclear accident. These lesions were assessed for different values of surface activities and exposure times of the radioactive material to make conclusions about the health risk in such exposures. We have developed an efficient computational method with the combination of a small-scale MC biophysical model (MCDS), with a larger-scale and general-purpose MC transport code (MCNP) to reproduce the results induced in the cell environment after such an exposure. Specifically, we have used the general-purpose MC N-particle (MCNP) radiation transport code to estimate the absorbed dose and secondary electron spectra of ^{137}Cs irradiation in cell DNA. Subsequently, we combined the estimates of the secondary electron spectrum and the absorbed dose acquired from MCNP with MCDS simulations in order to calculate the initial DNA Damage.

In synopsis, we have developed a computational method to study the potential biological effects on cell DNA after IR exposures. It is crucial to know the absorbed dose after the radiation exposure because, based on the recording of this magnitude and the analysis of the effects of radiation in living organisms (DNA damage), we can estimate the severity of each exposure. Ultimately, this information may help medical personnel to respond appropriately to such cases with individuals exposed to IR after a radiological incident.

2. Materials and Methods

2.1. Monte Carlo (MC) Codes: MCNP and MCDS

Our calculations have been based on the Model Carlo simulation technique. MC codes have been widely used to simulate damage induction to a cell exposed to any type of the IR spectrum [37]. Theoretical studies, together with MC Track Structure codes (MCTS), have contributed remarkably to the understanding of the DNA damage dynamics and to the simulation of particle tracks in biological matter, leading scientific research to the estimation of the radiation effect parameters and, therefore, providing important information applied in radiation protection and radiotherapy [35,36]. In this way, MCTS simulations have proved to be the most sophisticated tool for studying and understanding the interactions of IR with biological matter and for determining the damage induced by it to the major target of the cell: its DNA macromolecule [31].

In our study, we have used two different MC codes for obtaining our calculations. The first one, MCNP, being one of the most accurate in its category, is a multipurpose code used widely in nuclear and medical applications, utilizing a large spectrum of particles. The simulation of particle interactions with living matter are based on databases that are embedded in the software and include internationally recognized libraries of cross sections [38]. The MCNP6.1 version of the code used by us, especially, has the ability to accurately describe the electron transport down to 10 eV [39]. Via this code, we have estimated the absorbed dose by our target and the spectrum of secondary electrons produced in it. As aforementioned, one part of the damage induced to a cell is due to secondary electrons ejected as a result of the ionizations in the medium.

The second MC code used in our study, in combination with MCNP, is the Monte Carlo damage simulation (MCDS) algorithm, which has been selected among the other MC codes of the bibliography because of its simplicity and its results production swiftness. It does not have the accuracy of other codes in its category, but it can yield major trends in the spectrum of DNA damage predicted by other detailed MCTS simulations. This code has been developed in order to predict the initial yield and types of DNA damage formed by IR and is much faster compared to conventional track structure simulations (it can give results within seconds to minutes), in addition to its easy-to-use algorithm [34]. MCDS algorithm is characterized as a quasi-phenomenological model, which can predict the full spectrum of DNA damage induced by electrons, protons, α-particles and ions up to ^{56}Fe. Although this code does not possess the ability to directly simulate the damage in irradiated cells for photons or other neutral particles, secondary electron spectra for ^{137}Cs in a monolayer cell geometry were used to produce DNA damage yields [40]. The estimates of the code parameters are based on the interpolated damage yields, derived mainly from the track structure simulations of Nikjoo et al. [41–44] and Friedland et al. [45,46]. MCDS [47] uses only four adjustable parameters, three of which are the same for electrons, protons and α-particles. In brief, simulations are performed in two steps: (1) random distribution of the expected number of lesions produced in a cell per Gy of radiation in a DNA segment and (2) subdivision of the lesions in the former segment into clusters [34].

2.2. MCNP Setting for the Simulations of Our Study

Estimation of the absorbed dose to tissues of the human body, from radiations emitted by an arbitrary distribution of a radionuclide in an environmental medium is an extremely difficult computational task. By using the MCNP code, we create the geometry of the experimental setup. In this case, we base our simulations on a "human phantom" (filled with water as content), which appears as a cylinder with a radius of 25 cm and 180 cm in height, simulating an average man standing on the soil at the air–ground interface. This phantom is separated into layers of 10 μm thickness, which represents the typical average size of a eukaryotic mammalian cell (Figure 1).

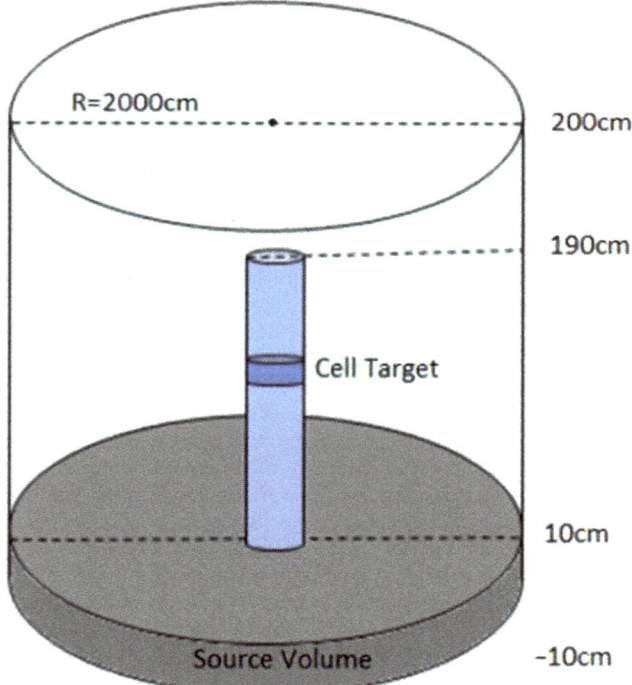

Figure 1. MC geometry model of the MCNP6.1 simulation including the source, the phantom and all the patterns used in it. The whole setting is as follows: the human phantom (depicted as a blue thin cylinder of 1.80 m height and 25 cm radius) stands in the middle of the outer azure cylinder (radius 20 m) which is filled with air (surrounding environment). The grey base cylinder (radius 20 m) represents the source volume on which the "human" stands (i.e., the surrounding ground, composed of soil and contaminated with the radionuclide ^{137}Cs in different surface activity values) There is no proportionality in the depicted dimensions of the patterns for the sake of simplicity.

Additionally, an isotropically distributed cylindrical source of ^{137}Cs has been placed in the ground, at a depth of 20 cm; the latter value represents a mean typical depth of radiocasium deposition in soil after its release as a consequence of a nuclear accident [48]. We have chosen to use this specific value for the deposition depth of ^{137}Cs in all our measurements, since many fundamental studies about the vertical distribution of this key artificial radionuclide in the environment show its biggest concentrations in the topsoil layers, especially above the depth of 20 cm [5,49,50]. The content of this radionuclide in soil is influenced by vertical migration due to the physical processes of diffusion, convection transfer with the soil moisture, and migration through the roots of plants. Generally, the concentration of radiocaesium is decreased exponentially with depth, depending on the landscape and mainly the soil type; the latter includes factors such as the mineral and physical composition of the soil, its organic composition, cation exchange capacity, acidity, and the presence of certain kinds of vegetation (e.g., coniferous trees and mosses which play the role of a filter, engulfing radionuclides for long periods after the initial fallout)[51–55]. In our study, we have considered an isotropic cylindrical source (the base cylinder in Figure 1) and, therefore, in our simulations we have planned its surface area (base of the cylinder) to be 1256 m^2 (radius 20 m). Of course, a larger source area would result in a higher effective dose to our phantom, but based on the results of a similar study by Han et al., 2010 [56] where the effective dose proves to increase <2% when the source area increases by 78%, we have assumed in all our simulations that a source area with the aforementioned value is a reasonable one, representable of a contaminated area beneath the ground. In our study, the material which is mixed with the source of gamma rays (^{137}Cs) includes all those elements contained in soil in the respective proportions (mass percentage) (i.e., Si: 27.1183%, Fe: 5.6283%, Mg: 1.3303%, K: 1.4327%, Ca: 5.1167%, O: 51.3713%, Na: 0.614%, Al: 6.8563%, Ti: 0.4605% and Mn: 0.0716%), considering a typical value of dry density ~1.52 g/cm^3 [57]. The entire assembly is surrounded by air (i.e., the external cylinder in which the human phantom stands). Varying the perpendicular distance of the DNA cell that we study from the source (keeping its position stable in the other two axes), we scanned the surface of the human body, i.e., the height between 5 cm and 180 cm from the ground level and estimated the absorbed dose (in MeV/g per particle) and the spectrum of secondary electrons produced in the DNA target for each different case. We applied a series of simulations by MCNP6.1 for the various distances mentioned above, having chosen various values of source activities of ^{137}Cs for different specific values of surface exposure (i.e., 37, 555, 1480 and 3700 kBq/m^2—these specific values are defined as the limit ones discerning areas of a different grade of ^{137}Cs surface ground deposition, according to UNSCEAR 2000 Report [58]), in order to simulate the conditions of a nuclear accident. It is worth mentioning that the value of 37 kBq/m^2 was taken as the lower limit defining the boundaries of contaminated zones, while the value of 555 kBq/m^2 designate an area of strict control [58,59]. Likewise, for the exposure time we have chosen the typical time periods of one day, one week and one month.

In order to get the results from the MCNP code (through the output file), we completed a corresponding input file providing certain information about the geometry of our experiment, the definitions of the surfaces included, the materials contained (in the appropriate proportions), the choice of the particles emitted by the radioactive source and its dimensions. For each value of surface exposure and exposure time we have run the code for 10^{10} histories ('NPS') in order to get better results by reducing the error in the doses received to less than 5%. For the absorbed dose calculation, the energy pulse-height tally (energy balance tally *F8: P, E) was exported. Notably, this code extended electron transport down to 10 eV, adopting this value as the electron tracking and production threshold [60].

As one may notice, in our calculations via this code, we refer only to the secondary electron's spectrum produced by γ radiation. This does not mean that we omitted the β radiation emitted by ^{137}Cs [61], which is known to have a short range, a fact that could play a crucial role in our final results. For this reason, before performing all our calculations through MCNP6.1, we ran the same input files for the same geometry model in the MCNP-CP code [62], which has the ability to calculate the corresponding beta decay spectrum. Through the latter calculation, we inferred that the range of the electrons emitted by ^{137}Cs during β decay in the soil towards the human phantom is only some μm; this happens because we use an extended source (source diameter: 40 m) in comparison to the dimensions of the phantom, and in a long distance from the standing "human", in comparison to the range of beta-radiation. In this way, we may neglect the β radiation emitted from our source.

2.3. MCDS-Based Estimates of DNA Damage

The MCDS provides a simple algorithm that calculates the DNA damage yields for a given absorbed dose of a chosen particle, and for a set of parameters such as cell size, nucleus size, type of radiation, and other parameters related to cell environment (e.g., oxygen and water cell concentration). As a whole, MCDS calculates complex DNA damage (DSBs, SSBs, non-DSB oxidative lesions) that are induced through both the direct ionization and excitation of the DNA and the indirect action of hydroxyl, or other radicals formed in close proximity to DNA. DNA damage by the bystander effect is neglected in this code. The MCDS code "reads" data from particles and other necessary information for the simulation from an input file (in which we set the calculated value of the absorbed dose by MCNP, as well as the energy spectrum of the secondary electrons down to 10 eV) and yields its results through an output file [63]. In our calculations, we have considered cells irradiated under normoxic conditions (O$_2$ concentration: 10% for tissues). Our simulations have been based on the default parameter values: σSb = 217 Gy^{-1} Gbp^{-1}, f = 3 and nmin = 9 bp, where σSb is the number of individual strand breaks per unit dose per amount of DNA in the cell, f is the ratio of base damage to strand breaks and nmin the minimum length (in bp) of undamaged DNA between neighboring elementary damages, such that these elementary damages are considered to belong to two different lesions [63]. We also assumed that the DNA of each diploid cell has a length equal to 6.4 Gbp, which is the average value for a diploid human cell with 46 chromosomes, as well as the diameter of the cell nucleus is 5 μm, and the cell diameter is 10 μm. All the simulations in our study have been performed through the MCDS Version 3.10A [64].

3. Results

The results of this study comprise, firstly, the calculation of the absorbed dose through the MCNP6 code for the radionuclide ^{137}Cs. In particular, the absorbed dose has been estimated as a function of height (distance from the ground) of a typical man (5–180 cm) for the surface activity values of 37, 555, 1480 and 3700 kBq/m^2, respectively and for the exposure time of a week. These results are depicted in Figure 2.

As can be seen, when the height (distance from the source) is increased, an exponential decrease in absorbed dose occurs. In addition, an initial sharp decrease in the slope of the curve is observed at small heights on the water phantom; this happens because an increase in the distance from the source is equivalent to the reduction in the number of photons which penetrate a surface along the direction of the radiation. On the other hand, the dose becomes quite constant after the first 80 cm from the ground, with surface activity of 3700 kBq/m^2, and after the first 30 cm for the corresponding values of 555 and 1480 kBq/m^2, while it is constantly near zero for the value of 37 kBq/m^2; this was expected, since the aforementioned values of distance are within the range of gamma rays in the air [65]. It is of note that the estimated doses for the deposition density of 37 kBq/m^2, as the limit of the high radiation control safe zone according to the UNSCEAR 2000 Report [58] for the Chernobyl nuclear accident, are in the range of 1.1×10^{-4}–1.99×10^{-2}—mGy and are considered as "low absorbed doses".

Next, we present our results of the MCDS for the calculation of the DSB and SSB damage (number of lesions per cell) (Figure 3a,b) for the same values of deposition densities of ^{137}Cs and for the exposure time of one week.

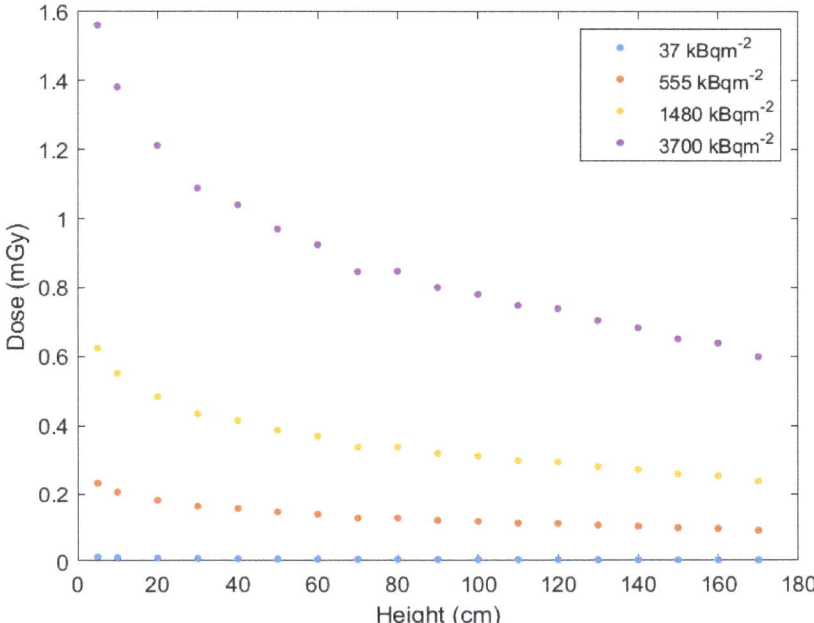

Figure 2. Absorbed dose to the cell (target) as a function of height (on the water phantom used in our simulations) induced by different ^{137}Cs surface activities for the exposure time of one week, using MCNP6.1 code.

The first thing to note is that the analogy between SSBs and DSBs seems to be in the range reported in irradiated typical mammalian cells [66]. It can also be noted that, for the higher value of surface activity, an exponential decrease is observed in both the numbers of the expected DNA lesions (DSBs and SSBs per cell) of the cell target as a function of distance (height) from the source of ^{137}Cs. For the value of 1480 kBq·m^{-2} the corresponding numbers show a small decrease at the first 30 cm, while for the other two (and lesser) values of deposition density, the number of the lesions is quite stable as the distance from the source is increased. This means that for the highest value of surface activity, i.e., for a man standing on the ground, exposed to ^{137}Cs radiation in the near zone (<100 km from the place of the nuclear accident), the number of induced SSBs and DSBs in the cells of his genitals and the rest of his body organs are quite the half of those induced to the cells of his feet. For places in the far zone (100 km to approximately 2000 km), the number of the same lesions is low and quite stable throughout his whole body. It is of note that as the distance from the source increases (and consequently the absorbed dose is reduced), the number of the expected SSBs per cell for the deposition density of 3700 kBq·m^{-2} decreases by a factor of 2.5, reducing, in this way the biological effects of radiation; the corresponding decrease in DSBs with distance is lesser, since this kind of lesion is more complex than SSBs and occurs more scarcely. All our MCDS simulations have been performed with a standard error of the mean better than 0.2%.

DSBs are considered to be the most biologically deleterious lesions, since one single unrepaired DSB can lead a cell death or can cause chromosomal aberrations with subsequent genomic instability, and possible malignant transformation [67]. Therefore, this kind of damage was chosen to be analysed mainly in association with the aforementioned results. As reported previously, the MCDS code does not involve the process of repair in its results and thus, we take into account the existing literature in order to translate the numbers of lesions shown in the above diagrams into cancer risk information.

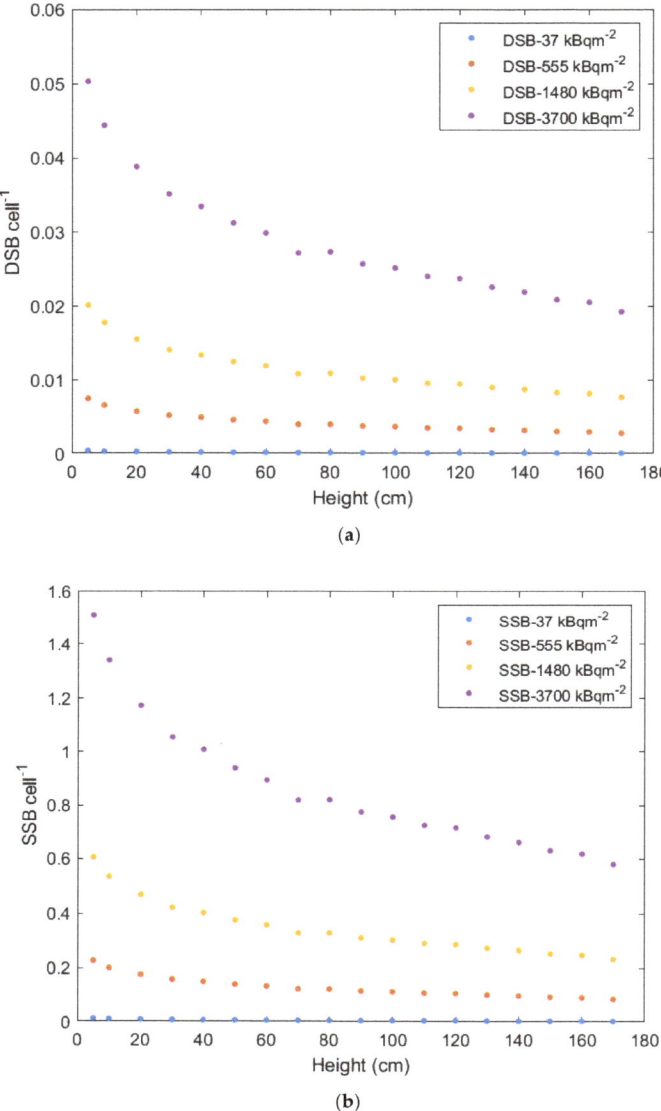

Figure 3. Estimation of the number of (**a**) DSBs and (**b**) SSBs per cell, respectively, induced by different levels of ^{137}Cs contamination in the ground, for the exposure time of one week, according to our MCDS simulations.

In the dose range related to a REI, as in our study, the associated cancer risk cannot be deduced from epidemiological data, due to a lack of sensitivity. Such estimates for persons exposed to an environmental IR incident have been based on a linear extrapolation of high-dose data obtained from the study of atomic bomb survivors of Hiroshima and Nagasaki through the years; the linear-no-threshold (LNT) model assumes that the DNA damage is proportional to the dose and that the response of the irradiated cell functions equal efficiently from high to low doses [68]. However, the validity of such an extrapolation is questioned by phenomena such as the low-dose hypersensitivity, the adaptive and hormetic response, the bystander effects, and the threshold hypothesis [69–72]. In attempting to associate a low dose irradiation with cancer risk, it is important to make the distinction between acute exposures over a very short period of time and protracted ones [73]. Clearly, the atomic bomb survivor risks represent the average of all those exposed to an REI population. Considering the existing data, the fact that individuals are at lower or greater risk than the average, depends on genetic status, age, age of exposure and other factors [74].

Deep sequencing studies have confirmed that biomarkers (such as the micronucleus assay and scoring of chromosome aberrations) are important tools for the detection of the early stages of radiation-induced carcinogenesis. These validated techniques, however, do not have the sensitivity to study the effects of IR on cells at doses below 100 mGy [75,76]. For this reason, phosphorylated histone H2AX (γ-H2AX) foci immunodetection has become the internationally accepted quantitative biomarker of human low-level IR exposure [77]. DSBs activate histone H2AX right after their induction by phosphorylating a highly conserved serine (Ser-139). The phosphorylated γ-H2AX forms foci in the cell nucleus. In this way, a γ-H2AX focus represents a DSB [77,78].

Focused on the range of low doses (i.e., doses <0.05 Gy [79]), as this very low ($\leq$1 mGy, see Figure 2) in our study, Rothkamm and Löbrich have shown that in non-dividing primary human fibroblasts cultured in vitro, irradiated by doses ~ 1 mGy of IR, the induced DSBs remain unrepaired for many days and the cells with unrepaired DSBs are eventually eliminated [80]. Similar results were observed by Osipov et al. in a study conducted on human MSCs, isolated from oral mucosa, where for the lower doses, after the initial rise in γH2AX foci number, there was no decrease observed [81]. It appears that, in cellular responses at low compared to high doses, different pathways may be activated, and non-linear responses prevail that are not compatible with the LNT model.

Unrepaired or mis-repaired DSBs may give rise to chromosomal aberrations and alterations, micronuclei formation, gene amplification, sister chromatid exchange and other genetic instability hallmarks. In vitro observations show the induction of unstable chromosomal aberrations in cells irradiated in G1 phase and chromatid-type aberrations in the ones exposed to IR at the G2 phase of the cell cycle [82]. Aberrations, such as a dicentric chromosome, or a ring with an acentric fragment, or a reciprocal translocation, permit the continuation of cell proliferation with the over expression of truncated oncogene which leads to oncogenic transformation. For example, rearrangements of the RET (rearranged during transfection) gene are observed in papillary thyroid carcinoma. Studies conducted after the CNPP accident show a sharp increase in the incidence of pediatric thyroid papillary cancer [83].

Examining the human breast tissue after its irradiation with very low doses (a few mGy) of IR, one may detect, except for induced DSBs, changes in the transcription level of genes [84]. Female breast tissue is proved to be very sensitive to radiation due to the presence of reproductive hormones, including estrogens; the latter may function as carcinogens since they energize the estrogen receptor-mediated cell proliferation [85]. Depuydt et al. investigated the irradiation of glandular epithelial cells of breast tissue in the dose range representative for mammography screening, with results indicating the existence of a hypersensitive response for DSB induction [86]. In a previous study, they showed that the number of mammography-induced DSBs resulted in chromosomal aberrations, which are a hallmark for cancer [87]. Other studies demonstrated that for very low doses of IR, the γH2AX foci induction is much higher than at higher doses [88–90].

Another effect which plays a key role in the IR-induced carcinogenesis is the bystander effect; this is more relevant to low-dose radiation [91]. At low doses of IR, the response to radiation becomes important in regard to how dominant and extended the bystander effect is in the vicinity of the irradiated cell, and the consequences this will have. Thus, the IR-induced genomic instability and the consequences of the bystander effects indicate a non-linear behavior in the low-dose area. The evidence arising from the published data indicate that the cellular response to low-dose IR is a complex interaction of various modulating factors [92].

Shimure and Kojima recently attempted to identify the lowest IR dose causing molecular changes in the human body [93]. They concluded that, although the extent of DSBs formation differed depending on the irradiated cell species that were investigated, the lowest limit at which these DNA lesions are formed is approximately 1 mGy. Halm et al. indicated that blood doses ranging between 0.22 and 1.22 mGy may induce somatic DNA lesions, one hour after C.T. examination [94]. Additionally, Vandervoorde et al. [95] showed that a very low blood dose 0.15 mGy caused DSBs five minutes after the C.T. examination. An increase in leukemia risk is suggested in children under five years old who were exposed to radioactive fallout from nuclear weapons testing (estimated fallout marrow dose: 1.5 mGy) [96].

According to all the aforementioned data, exposure of an individual to the dose of the underground caesium-137 in areas of such values of surface activity for a period not more than a week, seems to be of very low risk for any future health problems. It would be interesting to investigate the same cases but in a more extended exposure time to IR.

In order to study the absorbed dose as a function of the exposure time, we have calculated its values for the deposition density of 3700 kBq·m^{-2} (in the near zone of the nuclear accident) at the exposure times of one day, one week and one month through MCNP code (Figure 4).

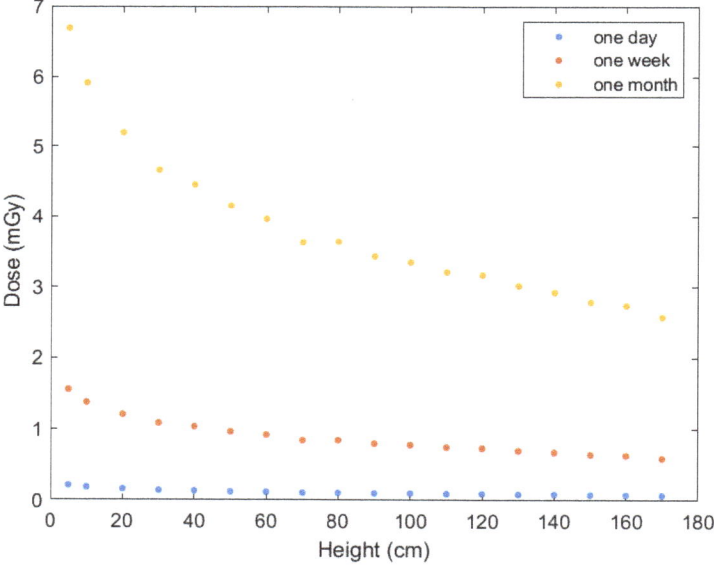

Figure 4. Cell–target absorbed dose of the water phantom at various values of height from the ground surface, induced by the ^{137}Cs ionizing radiation of 3700 kBq/m^2 for the exposure time of one day, one week and a month, using MCNP6.1 simulations.

It is of note that there is an exponential decrease (for the exposure time of one month) in the absorbed dose with the increase in height from the ground (source), while in shorter time periods the curve is converted to a nearly stable line and, simultaneously, a linear increase in this dose with the increase in exposure time. As can be seen in Figure 5, the same trends have the estimated DSBs and SSBs per cell as a function of height and exposure time, correspondingly. This linear trend also holds for the relationship between the absorbed dose and the number of inducted DSBs and SSBs. This trend could support, in part, the LNT model. On the other hand, the estimated absorbed dose for the exposure time of one month (see Figure 4) takes an average value ~3 mGy for the vital organs of a 1.80 m tall man; this fact may pose a risk for the induction of unrepairable DSBs and unstable chromosomal formations, which in turn, may enter an organ of the exposed organism to early potential stages of carcinogenesis. This would also mean that a man standing on the radioactive ground of such an area for the time period of one month (in practice, this means that the individual is exposed to a daily eight-hour-irradiation from such a source in the ground for three consecutive months) has a real risk of being a cancer patient in the future.

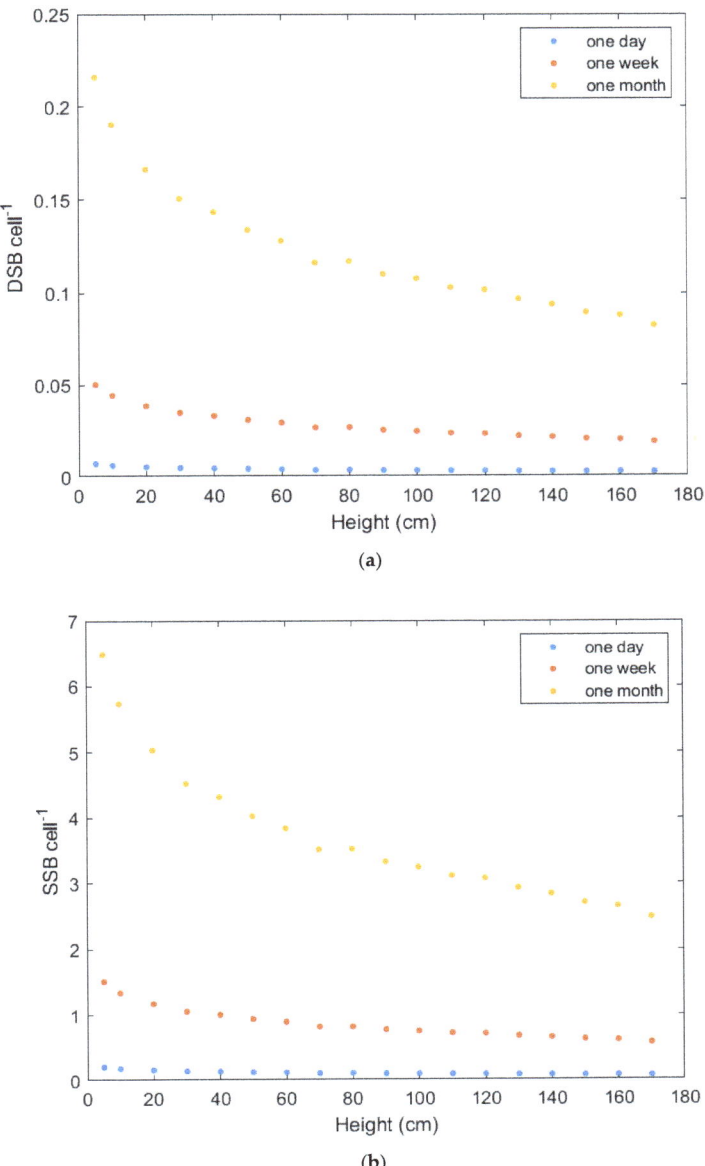

Figure 5. Estimation of the number of (**a**) DSBs and (**b**) SSBs per cell, formed by dose induced by a ^{137}Cs ionizing radiation of surface activity 3700 kBq·m^{-2} for an exposure time of a day, one week and a month, using MCDS simulations.

Since the exact details of the microscopic association between radiation and carcinogenesis is not yet known, it would be interesting to explain how the aforementioned calculated numbers are connected with the risk of carcinogenesis in the organs of an exposed individual in a relatively macroscopic scale. For this reason, we have used the National Cancer Institute NCI (USA) Radiation Risk Assessment Tool—Lifetime Cancer Risk from Ionizing Radiation: https://radiationcalculators.cancer.gov/radrat/model/inputs/ (accessed on 29 July 2021).

With this tool, we evaluated the risk for various organs of different characteristic adults exposed to such doses. In our following estimates, thyroid cancer has been excluded since it is by far attributed to the intake of ^{131}I; this radionuclide is the main contributor to the thyroid doses received mainly through internal body irradiation (via milk consumption) [97]. On the other hand, ^{137}Cs is considered the main contributor to doses of the body organs and tissues, other than the thyroid gland, from external and internal irradiation. For this reason, we have considered presumably eight different individuals (two males and six females) with different ages and different exposures to the nuclear accident of Chernobyl in 1986. Through this online risk calculator, by filling the age (at the year of the accident) of each individual (all considered about 1.80 m high) and the absorbed dose (in mGy) as calculated before (see Figs 1 and 4), in which they were exposed for a certain single exposure time (in days) and rate (acute or chronic), we estimate their Excess Lifetime Cancer Risk (ELCR) for different body organs in a certain height from the ground. In fact, the real exposure time of an individual is a longer one, since this person does not keep standing on the ground for the total time of exposure, as referred above. Based on these data, the possibility of a certain organ cancer development (chances expressed as cases per 100,000) is evaluated. By the ELCR, we refer to the average probability of cancer development to a certain organ of an individual exposed to IR higher than their unexposed peers. Our selection of the specific organs for the evaluation of their ELCR was based on the sensitivity of the human tissues to radiation [98], the availability of these organs in the quoted list of the NCI tool, and the volume that they occupy in the human body; in the latter criterion we selected such organs so that they are not extended (such as the bowel) and correspond to a certain height from the ground (for the use of a certain value of dose, according to Figures 2 and 4).

More analytically (see Table 1), the first calculation is about an adolescent, 16 years old at the year of the Chernobyl nuclear accident, exposed to a 30-day irradiation because his family—for various reasons—delayed to evacuate their homestead in the near zone of 3700 kBq·m^{-2}: assessing a total dose of 3.44 mGy for all those days of exposure, we evaluate an ELCR for his prostate gland equal to 3.91×10^{-5}, which is considered high according to the World Health Organization [99], the Canadian Council of Ministers of the Environment [100] and the New Zealand Ministry for the Environment [101]. In the same way, the next examined case is that of a 60-year-old woman, living in the aforementioned zone, who refused to evacuate her home; considering a chronic exposure of 3.02 mGy for a period of 30 days, we assess an ELCR for her breast equal to 2.15×10^{-5}, which is also considered high (according to the aforementioned criteria). The third case is that of a 16-year-old lady, who received only an acute dose of 0.1 mGy for only 1 day of exposure in the near zone before evacuating the contaminated area with her family; this dose yields an ELCR equal to 0.58×10^{-5} for her breast, which is considered as moderate. If, for the same young lady, we assess the ELCR for all her organs (in this case we considered an average height of 130 cm from the ground for her vital organs), we calculate a value of 2.4×10^{-5} which is considered high, while the corresponding value for leukemia is 0.08×10^{-5}, considered low. Our next case is that of a 50-year-old cattleman who lived in the same area and promptly evacuated his ranch under the first governmental recommendations for the general public, but after some weeks returned to live again in his area at his own risk. This man, exposed to a 30-day-irradiation after the first days of his reinstallation of 3.20 mGy from the radiation under his feet, has an ELCR value for his pancreas equal to 0.66×10^{-5}, which is considered as a moderate one. We then consider a 16-year–old lady, living in an area of the outer contaminated zone of 37 kBq m^{-2}, exposed to a 7-day-external irradiation of 8 mGy (due to a delay in her family's evacuation of their home) for whom we assess an ELCR for her ovaries equal to 0.005×10^{-5}; this value is a low one. Our last case is that of a 30-year-old woman living those days in the contaminated zone of 555 kBq·m^{-2}, who, for a 7-day-delay of evacuation, has been exposed to an external dose of 0.068 mGy, equivalent to a low ELCR value for her brain equal to 0.004×10^{-5}.

Table 1. Data of hypothetical individuals exposed to the radiation from Chernobyl nuclear accident [sex (male, female), birth year, exposure year, exposed organ, surface activity (kBq/m^2), total exposure time (days), exposure rate, dose (mGy)] for the assessment of ELCR and risk grade (High, Medium and Low).

Sex	BirthYear	Exp. Year	Organ	S. Activ. (kBq/m^2)	Tot. Exp. Time (Days)	Exp. Rate	Dose (mGy)	Elcr	Risk Grade
M	1970	1986	Prostate	3700	30	chronic	3.44	3.91×10^{-5}	H
F	1926	1986	Breast	3700	30	chronic	3.02	2.15×10^{-5}	H
F	1970	1986	Breast	3700	1	acute	0.1	0.58×10^{-5}	M
F	1970	1986	all organs	3700	1	acute	0.1	2.4×10^{-5}	H
F	1970	1986	leukemia	3700	1	acute	0.1	0.08×10^{-5}	L
M	1936	1986	pancreas	3700	30	chronic	3.20	0.66×10^{-5}	M
F	1970	1986	ovaries	37	7	acute	0.008	0.005×10^{-5}	L
F	1956	1986	brain	555	7	acute	0.068	0.004×10^{-5}	L

As a conclusion to all the previous calculations, it may be noticed that any exposition of an individual in the near zone of 3700 kBq·m^{-2} increases the risk of cancer at a moderate to high grade (only in the case of leukemia there is a low-risk grade estimation for exposed individuals in this zone, and this happens due to the selected short time of exposure, i.e., 1 day).

The objective of this study is the calculation of the absorbed dose and the estimation of a critical marker for biological damage i.e. the one induced at the DNA of an individual exposed to the radiation emitted by the ^{137}Cs in the ground. In this way, we have isolated only one component of the total radiation that can affect the health of a human exposed to it after a nuclear accident and could lead to carcinogenesis. The latter, as we know, is a multistage and multifactorial process and in order to assess any risk estimate with the most accurate approach possible for cancer, one has to investigate at the same time all the factors associated with this disease. For example, in the case of radiation-induced leukemia, one should know not only the absorbed dose and the time of exposure, but also diverse factors connected to genetic susceptibility to the disease. We should also know other environmental factors and dietary habits referred to the specific agricultural cohort of this area around the Chernobyl Nuclear Power Plant. Noshchenko et al. [102] estimated the radiation-induced risk of acute leukemia that occurred from 1987–1997 among residents 0–5 years of age at the time of the Chernobyl accident, who lived in the most radioactively contaminated territories of the Ukraine; this risk was significantly increased among those who were exposed to doses higher than 10 mGy. If we compare our results (Figure 4: lower doses in shorter exposure periods) to those above then we will have to extend the exposure time to much longer periods (e.g., more than 2 months) in order to reach similar doses. Some reports about an increase in infant leukemia due to the prenatal irradiation after the Chernobyl accident in more remote countries, such as Greece [103] and

Germany [104], quote an average of ~2 mSv and 0.49 mSv correspondingly, (for radiation protection purposes, absorbed dose and effective dose are used, including a radiation-dependent weighting factor: for X-rays and γ-rays, 1mSv = 1 mGy) for the added radiation exposure during the first year after the accident, while others in neigboring countries such as Belarus [105] quote multiple values of doses.

4. Discussion

Simulating the biological DNA damage effects in the human body in the case of REI, utilizing MC methodologies, has proved to be a useful methodology to better understand the effects of environmental radiation exposure. MC methods are computational algorithms of high predictive accuracy and useful for modelling phenomena with significant uncertainty inputs. Thus, this is a powerful approach for confirming that, given the characteristics of the living matter and the medium, such as density, distance from the radiation source, radiation energy and geometry, as well as the kind of particles, effectively affect the photon transport path. The associated expected DNA damage levels (DSBs, SSBs) are usually accompanied by 5–10 times more non-DSB lesions, increasing the mutational potential even at low levels of radiation dose [31,106].

As expected, our results show that, for a given exposure time and ^{137}Cs surface activity, the absorbed dose decreases exponentially as a function of the height from the ground surface of the gamma-ray source. In the same way, the number of initial complex damage levels per cell decreased exponentially when the height increased and depended on the duration of the exposure and the source activity. It is obvious that a higher surface activity of ^{137}Cs can induce a greater number of DSBs and SSBs. It is worth noting that according to in vitro experiments on normal mammalian cells, 10–35 DSBs/cell and 200–1000 SSBs/cell are expected to occur with doses of 0.2–1 Gy, respectively [80,107]. This means that if an individual has received such a dose, they would have a 1–3% increased risk of cancer as well [108]. Additionally, if the number of DSBs per cell is greater than 35 in any irradiated cell, this cell will have a dramatic risk increase of mutations, probably leading to apoptosis or cell death [109].

Although we know that many of the DSB lesions induced to a cell after IR exposure can be repaired by endogenous mechanisms within 24 h, some of these lesions are difficult to repair, leading possibly to mutation or cell death [110]. What we really need in order to evaluate the damage induced to an individual after an IR exposure caused by a REI is a correlation between the absorbed dose and the DNA damage.

This study has several limitations. In particular, in order to obtain a reliable cancer risk estimate for a specific cohort of people affected by a REI, there are more factors that have to be taken into consideration i.e., chemical factors (smoking, alcohol drinking, heterocyclic amine intake by overcooked meat, occupational contact with pesticides, herbicides and fertilizers), biological factors (medical history of hepatitis B, C and D) and genetic ones (hereditary abnormalities in DNA repair and cell cycle genes), together with the IR relevant magnitudes measured in the affected area [111]. Another issue is the fact that it is difficult to isolate only one physical component of the total radiation relevant to a REI that affects a certain geographic area, since there no specific non variable irradiation limits in time and space, and the radionuclides released by such incidents affect public health both individually and as a whole. The latter issue has been overcome in part, via the use of MC techniques, which are useful tools utilized for modelling phenomena with uncertainty inputs.

5. Conclusions

Using Monte Carlo simulations, we have calculated the absorbed dose and estimated the induced complex DNA damage types in the cells of a hypothetical individual exposed to IR after a nuclear accident, in order to show the association between this type of radiation and the resulting damage yields. Specifically, in order to assess the potential biological consequences of ^{137}Cs source activity more efficiently, we have used the MCNP radiation transport code for an accurate estimation of the secondary electron spectrum, produced by emitted photons in cells by using an irradiation geometry, similar to the conditions under which a possible radiological incident may occur. We have combined the aforementioned MCNP estimation with DNA damage yields assessed via the MCDS code. Based on the great need for biodosimetry combined with physical dosimetry, our methodology can be considered as an intermediate step between these, providing a useful estimate of the DNA damage that has been induced in cells after radiation exposure; these damage levels and types could be used by the scientific community for a better assessment of the long-term health effects of IR. All these, in conjunction with simple experimental measurements of the DSB lesions in the blood of exposed individuals in specific time periods after exposure, by using, for example, the γ-H2AX assay [112,113], can provide a reliable basis for calculating the level of initial DNA damage with very good approximation, and the expected radiation exposure levels.

Author Contributions: Conceptualization, A.G.G. and M.K.; methodology, S.A.K., V.G., A.K. and M.K.; formal analysis, S.A.K. and V.G.; data curation, D.E., I.K., Z.N. and M.K.; writing—original draft preparation, S.A.K. and V.G.; writing—review and editing, all authors; supervision, A.G.G. All authors have read and agreed to the published version of the manuscript.

Funding: This research received no external funding.

Data Availability Statement: Any logical additional data requests may be sent to A.G.G.

Acknowledgments: We sincerely thank Rob D. Stewart (University of Washington) for his helpful comments regarding DNA damage simulations using the Monte Carlo code MCDS.

Conflicts of Interest: The authors declare no conflict of interest.

References

1. Balonov, M. The Chernobyl accident as a source of new radiological knowledge: Implications for Fukushima rehabilitation and research programmes. *J. Radiol. Prot.* **2013**, *33*, 27–40. [CrossRef]
2. Steinhauser, G.; Brandl, A.; Johnson, T.E. Comparison of the Chernobyl and Fukushima nuclear accidents: A review of the environmental impacts. *Sci. Total Environ.* **2014**, *470*, 800–817. [CrossRef] [PubMed]
3. United Nations Scientific Committee on the Effects of Atomic Radiation. *Sources and Effects of Ionizing Radiation, United Nations Scientific Committee on the Effects of Atomic Radiation (UNSCEAR) 2008 Report*; United Nations Scientific Committee on the Effects of Atomic Radiation: New York, NY, USA, 2011; Volume II. [CrossRef]
4. Aliyu, A.S.; Evangeliou, N.; Mousseau, T.A.; Wu, J.; Ramli, A.T. An overview of current knowledge concerning the health and environmental consequences of the Fukushima Daiichi Nuclear Power Plant (FDNPP) accident. *Environ. Int.* **2015**, *85*, 213–228. [CrossRef] [PubMed]
5. Ladygienė, R.; Orentienė, A.; Žukauskienė, L. Investigation into 137Cs found in the soil profile within Vilnius region and estimation of inhabitants exposed to 137Cs transfered through the food chain. *J. Environ. Eng. Landsc. Manag.* **2012**, *20*, 213–220. [CrossRef]
6. Salbu, B.; Lind, O.C.; Skipperud, L. Radionuclide speciation and its relevance in environmental impact assessments. *J. Environ. Radioact.* **2004**, *74*, 233–242. [CrossRef] [PubMed]
7. Karam, P.A. Radiological Terrorism. *Hum. Ecol. Risk Assess. Int. J.* **2005**, *11*, 501–523. [CrossRef]
8. Andersson, K.G.; Roed, J.; Fogh, C.L. Weathering of radiocaesium contamination on urban streets, walls and roofs. *J. Environ. Radioact.* **2002**, *62*, 49–60. [CrossRef]
9. Christodouleas, J.P.; Forrest, R.D.; Ainsley, C.G.; Tochner, Z.; Hahn, S.M.; Glatstein, E. Short-term and long-term health risks of nuclear-power-plant accidents. *N. Engl. J. Med.* **2011**, *364*, 2334–2341. [CrossRef]
10. IAEA. *INES: The International Nuclear and Radiological Event Scale User's Manual*; International Atomic Energy Agency (IAEA): Vienna, Austria, 2008.
11. Kashparov, V.A.; Lundin, S.M.; Zvarych, S.I.; Yoshchenko, V.I.; Levchuk, S.E.; Khomutinin, Y.V.; Maloshtan, I.M.; Protsak, V.P. Territory contamination with the radionuclides representing the fuel component of Chernobyl fallout. *Sci. Total Environ.* **2003**, *317*, 105–119. [CrossRef]
12. Publications Office of the EU. Atlas of Caesium Deposition on Europe after the Chernobyl Accident. Available online: https://op.europa.eu/el/publication-detail/-/publication/110b15f7-4df8-49a0-856f-be8f681ae9fd (accessed on 29 July 2021).
13. Balonov, M.I. On protecting the inexperienced reader from Chernobyl myths. *J. Radiol. Prot.* **2012**, *32*, 181–189. [CrossRef]
14. Ilyin, L.A.; Balonov, M.I.; Buldakov, L.A. Radiocontamination patterns and possible health consequences of the accident at the Chernobyl nuclear power station. *J. Radiol. Prot.* **1990**, *10*, 3–29. [CrossRef]
15. Aarkrog, A. Past and recent trends in radioecology. *Environ. Int.* **1994**, *20*, 633–643. [CrossRef]

16. Ostroumova, E.; Rozhko, A.; Hatch, M.; Furukawa, K.; Polyanskaya, O.; McConnell, R.J.; Nadyrov, E.; Petrenko, S.; Romanov, G.; Yauseyenka, V.; et al. Measures of thyroid function among Belarusian children and adolescents exposed to iodine-131 from the accident at the Chernobyl nuclear plant. *Environ. Health Perspect.* **2013**, *121*, 865–871. [CrossRef] [PubMed]
17. Il'in, L.A. *The Chernobyl Experience in the Context of Contemporary Radiation Protection Problems*; International Atomic Energy Agency (IAEA): Vienna, Austria, 1988; pp. 47–63.
18. Braverman, E.R.; Blum, K.; Loeffke, B.; Baker, R.; Kreuk, F.; Yang, S.P.; Hurley, J.R. Managing terrorism or accidental nuclear errors, preparing for iodine-131 emergencies: A comprehensive review. *Int. J. Environ. Res. Public Health* **2014**, *11*, 4158–4200. [CrossRef] [PubMed]
19. Sahoo, S.K.; Kavasi, N.; Sorimachi, A.; Arae, H.; Tokonami, S.; Mietelski, J.W.; Łokas, E.; Yoshida, S. Strontium-90 activity concentration in soil samples from the exclusion zone of the Fukushima daiichi nuclear power plant. *Sci. Rep.* **2016**, *6*, 23925. [CrossRef] [PubMed]
20. International Atomic Energy Agency, V. *Chernobyl's Legacy: Health, Environmental and Socio-Economic Impacts and Recommendations to the Governments of Belarus, the Russian Federation and Ukraine The Chernobyl Forum*; International Atomic Energy Agency (IAEA): Vienna, Austria, 2005; p. 52.
21. Chiaravalle, A.E.; Mangiacotti, M.; Marchesani, G.; Bortone, N.; Tomaiuolo, M.; Trotta, G. A ten-year survey of radiocontamination of edible Balkan mushrooms: Cs-137 activity levels and assessed dose to the population. *Food Control* **2018**, *94*, 263–267. [CrossRef]
22. Savino, F.; Pugliese, M.; Quarto, M.; Adamo, P.; Loffredo, F.; De Cicco, F.; Roca, V. Thirty years after Chernobyl: Long-term determination of (137)Cs effective half-life in the lichen Stereocaulon vesuvianum. *J. Environ. Radioact* **2017**, *172*, 201–206. [CrossRef]
23. UNSCEAR. *Levels and Effects of Radiation Exposure Due to the Nuclear Accident after the 2011 Great East-Japan Earthquake and Tsunami*; United Nations Scientific Committee on the Effects of Atomic Radiation: New York, NY, USA, 2013.
24. Taira, Y.; Hayashida, N.; Yamashita, S.; Kudo, T.; Matsuda, N.; Takahashi, J.; Gutevitc, A.; Kazlovsky, A.; Takamura, N. Environmental contamination and external radiation dose rates from radionuclides released from the Fukushima Nuclear Power Plant. *Radiat. Prot. Dosim.* **2012**, *151*, 537–545. [CrossRef]
25. Bondarkov, M.D.; Zheltonozhsky, V.A.; Zheltonozhskaya, M.V.; Kulich, N.V.; Maksimenko, A.M.; Farfan, E.B.; Jannik, G.T.; Marra, J.C. Vertical migration of radionuclides in the vicinity of the chernobyl confinement shelter. *Health Phys.* **2011**, *101*, 362–367. [CrossRef]
26. IAEA. *The Fukushima Daiichi Accident*; International Atomic Energy Agency (IAEA): Vienna, Austria, 2015.
27. Dohi, T.; Ohmura, Y.; Yoshimura, K.; Sasaki, T.; Fujiwara, K.; Kanaizuka, S.; Nakama, S.; Iijima, K. Radiocaesium accumulation capacity of epiphytic lichens and adjacent barks collected at the perimeter boundary site of the Fukushima Dai-ichi Nuclear Power Station. *PLoS ONE* **2021**, *16*, e0251828. [CrossRef]
28. IAEA. *Environmental Consequences of the Chernobyl Accident and their Remediation: Twenty Years of Experience*; International Atomic Energy Agency (IAEA): Vienna, Austria, 2006.
29. UNSCEAR. *Sources and Effects of Ionizing Radiation*; United Nations Scientific Committee on the Effects of Atomic Radiation: New York, NY, USA, 2008.
30. Santivasi, W.L.; Xia, F. Ionizing radiation-induced DNA damage, response, and repair. *Antioxid. Redox Signal.* **2014**, *21*, 251–259. [CrossRef]
31. Mavragani, I.V.; Nikitaki, Z.; Kalospyros, S.A.; Georgakilas, A.G. Ionizing Radiation and Complex DNA Damage: From Prediction to Detection Challenges and Biological Significance. *Cancers* **2019**, *11*, 1789. [CrossRef]
32. Liang, Y.; Yang, G.; Liu, F.; Wang, Y. Monte Carlo simulation of ionizing radiation induced DNA strand breaks utilizing coarse grained high-order chromatin structures. *Phys. Med. Biol.* **2016**, *61*, 445–460. [CrossRef] [PubMed]
33. Eccles, L.J.; O'Neill, P.; Lomax, M.E. Delayed repair of radiation induced clustered DNA damage: Friend or foe? *Mutat. Res.* **2011**, *711*, 134–141. [CrossRef] [PubMed]
34. Semenenko, V.A.; Stewart, R.D. A fast Monte Carlo algorithm to simulate the spectrum of DNA damages formed by ionizing radiation. *Radiat. Res.* **2004**, *161*, 451–457. [CrossRef] [PubMed]
35. Chatzipapas, K.P.; Papadimitroulas, P.; Emfietzoglou, D.; Kalospyros, S.A.; Hada, M.; Georgakilas, A.G.; Kagadis, G.C. Ionizing Radiation and Complex DNA Damage: Quantifying the Radiobiological Damage Using Monte Carlo Simulations. *Cancers* **2020**, *12*, 799. [CrossRef]
36. Nikjoo, H.; Emfietzoglou, D.; Liamsuwan, T.; Taleei, R.; Liljequist, D.; Uehara, S. Radiation track, DNA damage and response—A review. *Rep. Prog. Phys.* **2016**, *79*, 116601. [CrossRef]
37. Nikjoo, H.; Uehara, S.; Emfietzoglou, D.; Cucinotta, F.A. Track-structure codes in radiation research. *Radiat. Meas.* **2006**, *41*, 1052–1074. [CrossRef]
38. Hendricks, J.S.; Adam, K.J.; Booth, T.E.; Briesmeister, J.F.; Carter, L.L.; Cox, L.J.; Favorite, J.A.; Forster, R.A.; McKinney, G.W.; Prael, R.E. Present and future capabilities of MCNP. *Appl. Radiat. Isot.* **2000**, *53*, 857–861. [CrossRef]
39. Goorley, J.T. *Initial MCNP6 Release Overview—MCNP6 Version 1.0*; Los Alamos National Lab.(LANL): Los Alamos, NM, USA, 2013.
40. Hsiao, Y.; Stewart, R.D. Monte Carlo simulation of DNA damage induction by X-rays and selected radioisotopes. *Phys. Med. Biol.* **2008**, *53*, 233–244. [CrossRef]
41. Nikjoo, H.; O'Neill, P.; Terrissol, M.; Goodhead, D.T. Modelling of radiation-induced DNA damage: The early physical and chemical event. *Int. J. Radiat. Biol.* **1994**, *66*, 453–457. [CrossRef] [PubMed]

42. Nikjoo, H.; O'Neill, P.; Goodhead, D.T.; Terrissol, M. Computational modelling of low-energy electron-induced DNA damage by early physical and chemical events. *Int. J. Radiat. Biol.* **1997**, *71*, 467–483. [CrossRef] [PubMed]
43. Nikjoo, H.; O'Neill, P.; Wilson, W.E.; Goodhead, D.T. Computational approach for determining the spectrum of DNA damage induced by ionizing radiation. *Radiat. Res.* **2001**, *156*, 577–583. [CrossRef]
44. Nikjoo, H.; Bolton, C.E.; Watanabe, R.; Terrissol, M.; O'Neill, P.; Goodhead, D.T. Modelling of DNA damage induced by energetic electrons (100 eV to 100 keV). *Radiat. Prot. Dosim.* **2002**, *99*, 77–80. [CrossRef]
45. Friedland, W.; Jacob, P.; Bernhardt, P.; Paretzke, H.G.; Dingfelder, M. Simulation of DNA damage after proton irradiation. *Radiat. Res.* **2003**, *159*, 401–410. [CrossRef]
46. Friedland, W.; Dingfelder, M.; Jacob, P.; Paretzke, H.G. Calculated DNA double-strand break and fragmentation yields after irradiation with He ions. *Radiat. Phys. Chem. (1993)* **2005**, *72*, 279–286. [CrossRef]
47. Semenenko, V.A.; Stewart, R.D. Fast Monte Carlo simulation of DNA damage formed by electrons and light ions. *Phys. Med. Biol.* **2006**, *51*, 1693–1706. [CrossRef]
48. Butkus, D.; Konstantinova, M. Modelling vertical migration of 137Cs in Lithuanian soils. *J. Environ. Eng. Landsc. Manag.* **2008**, *16*, 23–29. [CrossRef]
49. Vukašinović, I.; Todorović, D.; Životić, L.; Kaluđerović, L.; Đorđević, A. An analysis of naturally occurring radionuclides and 137Cs in the soils of urban areas using gamma-ray spectrometry. *Int. J. Environ. Sci. Technol.* **2018**, *15*, 1049–1060. [CrossRef]
50. Liu, W.; Li, Y.; Yu, H.; Saggar, S.; Gong, D.; Zhang, Q. Distribution of 137Cs and 60Co in plough layer of farmland: Evidenced from a lysimeter experiment using undisturbed soil columns. *Pedosphere* **2021**, *31*, 180–190. [CrossRef]
51. Hrabovskyy, V.; Dzendzelyuk, O.; Katerynchuk, I.; Furgala, Y. Monitoring of radionuclides contamination of soils in Shatsk National Natural Park (Volyn region, Ukraine) during 1994–2001. *J. Environ. Radioact* **2004**, *72*, 25–33. [CrossRef]
52. Keum, D.-K.; Kim, B.-H.; Lim, K.-M.; Choi, Y.-H. Radiation exposure to Marine biota around the Fukushima Daiichi NPP. *Environ. Monit. Assess.* **2014**, *186*, 2949–2956. [CrossRef]
53. Kiss, E.; Volford, P. Depth and Areal Distribution of Cs-137 in the Soil of a Small Water Catchment in the Sopron Mountains. *Acta Silv. Lignaria Hung.* **2014**, *9*, 147–159. [CrossRef]
54. Evangeliou, N.; Hamburger, T.; Talerko, N.; Zibtsev, S.; Bondar, Y.; Stohl, A.; Balkanski, Y.; Mousseau, T.A.; Møller, A.P. Reconstructing the Chernobyl Nuclear Power Plant (CNPP) accident 30 years after. A unique database of air concentration and deposition measurements over Europe. *Environ. Pollut.* **2016**, *216*, 408–418. [CrossRef] [PubMed]
55. IAEA. *Present and Future Environmental Impact of the Chernobyl Accident*; International Atomic Energy Agency (IAEA): Vienna, Austria, 2001.
56. Han, B.; Zhang, J.; Na, Y.H.; Caracappa, P.F.; Xu, X.G. Modelling and Monte Carlo organ dose calculations for workers walking on ground contaminated with Cs-137 and Co-60 gamma sources. *Radiat. Prot. Dosim.* **2010**, *141*, 299–304. [CrossRef] [PubMed]
57. Bunzl, K.; Schimmack, W.; Zelles, L.; Albers, B.P. Spatial variability of the vertical migration of fallout 137Cs in the soil of a pasture, and consequences for long-term predictions. *Radiat. Environ. Biophys.* **2000**, *39*, 197–205. [CrossRef] [PubMed]
58. UNSCEAR. *Sources and Effects of Ionizing Radiation*; United Nations Scientific Committee on the Effects of Atomic Radiation: New York, NY, USA, 2000.
59. Gerasimova, N.V.; Marchenko, T.A.; Shoigu, S.K. *Twenty Years of the Chernobyl Accident: Results and Problems in Eliminating Its Consequences in Russia 1986–2006 Russian National Report*; International Atomic Energy Agency (IAEA): Vienna, Austria, 2006; p. 86.
60. Hughes, I.; Grady, H. *Quick-Start Guide to Low-Energy Photon/Electron Transport in MCNP6*; Los Alamos National Lab.(LANL): Los Alamos, NM, USA, 2013.
61. Delacroix, D.; Guerre, J.P.; Leblanc, P.; Hickman, C. Radionuclide and radiation protection data handbook 2nd edition (2002). *Radiat. Prot. Dosim.* **2002**, *98*, 9–168. [CrossRef] [PubMed]
62. Berlizov, A. MCNP-CP: A correlated particle radiation source extension of a general purpose monte carlo N-particle transport code. *ACS Symp. Ser.* **2006**, *945*, 183–194.
63. Stewart, R.D.; Streitmatter, S.W.; Argento, D.C.; Kirkby, C.; Goorley, J.T.; Moffitt, G.; Jevremovic, T.; Sandison, G.A. Rapid MCNP simulation of DNA double strand break (DSB) relative biological effectiveness (RBE) for photons, neutrons, and light ions. *Phys. Med. Biol.* **2015**, *60*, 8249–8274. [CrossRef] [PubMed]
64. Stewart, R.D.; Yu, V.K.; Georgakilas, A.G.; Koumenis, C.; Park, J.H.; Carlson, D.J. Effects of radiation quality and oxygen on clustered DNA lesions and cell death. *Radiat. Res.* **2011**, *176*, 587–602. [CrossRef]
65. Endo, S.; Fujii, K.; Kajimoto, T.; Tanaka, K.; Stepanenko, V.; Kolyzhenkov, T.; Petukhov, A.; Akhmedova, U.; Bogacheva, V. Comparison of calculated beta- and gamma-ray doses after the Fukushima accident with data from single-grain luminescence retrospective dosimetry of quartz inclusions in a brick sample. *J. Radiat. Res.* **2018**, *59*, 286–290. [CrossRef]
66. Ward, J.F. DNA damage produced by ionizing radiation in mammalian cells: Identities, mechanisms of formation, and reparability. *Prog. Nucleic Acid Res. Mol. Biol.* **1988**, *35*, 95–125. [CrossRef] [PubMed]
67. Polo, S.E.; Jackson, S.P. Dynamics of DNA damage response proteins at DNA breaks: A focus on protein modifications. *Genes Dev.* **2011**, *25*, 409–433. [CrossRef] [PubMed]
68. Breckow, J. Linear-no-threshold is a radiation-protection standard rather than a mechanistic effect model. *Radiat. Environ. Biophys.* **2006**, *44*, 257–260. [CrossRef]

69. Löbrich, M.; Rief, N.; Kühne, M.; Heckmann, M.; Fleckenstein, J.; Rübe, C.; Uder, M. In vivo formation and repair of DNA double-strand breaks after computed tomography examinations. *Proc. Natl. Acad. Sci. USA* **2005**, *102*, 8984–8989. [CrossRef] [PubMed]
70. Brenner, D.J.; Doll, R.; Goodhead, D.T.; Hall, E.J.; Land, C.E.; Little, J.B.; Lubin, J.H.; Preston, D.L.; Preston, R.J.; Puskin, J.S.; et al. Cancer risks attributable to low doses of ionizing radiation: Assessing what we really know. *Proc. Natl. Acad. Sci. USA* **2003**, *100*, 13761–13766. [CrossRef] [PubMed]
71. Averbeck, D. Does scientific evidence support a change from the LNT model for low-dose radiation risk extrapolation? *Health Phys.* **2009**, *97*, 493–504. [CrossRef]
72. Averbeck, D. Non-targeted effects as a paradigm breaking evidence. *Mutat. Res.* **2010**, *687*, 7–12. [CrossRef]
73. Howard, A. *Influence of Dose and Its Distribution in Time on Dose-Response Relationships for Low-LET Radiations*; National Council on Radiation Protection and Measurements: Bethesda, MD, USA, 1981; Volume 39, p. 233. [CrossRef]
74. Herold, D.M.; Hanlon, A.L.; Hanks, G.E. Diabetes mellitus: A predictor for late radiation morbidity. *Int. J. Radiat. Oncol. Biol. Phys.* **1999**, *43*, 475–479. [CrossRef]
75. Bauchinger, M. Quantification of low-level radiation exposure by conventional chromosome aberration analysis. *Mutat. Res.* **1995**, *339*, 177–189. [CrossRef]
76. Chaudhry, M.A. Biomarkers for human radiation exposure. *J. Biomed. Sci.* **2008**, *15*, 557–563. [CrossRef]
77. Fernandez-Capetillo, O.; Lee, A.; Nussenzweig, M.; Nussenzweig, A. H2AX: The histone guardian of the genome. *DNA Repair* **2004**, *3*, 959–967. [CrossRef] [PubMed]
78. Sedelnikova, O.A.; Rogakou, E.P.; Panyutin, I.G.; Bonner, W.M. Quantitative detection of (125)IdU-induced DNA double-strand breaks with gamma-H2AX antibody. *Radiat. Res.* **2002**, *158*, 486–492. [CrossRef]
79. Kadhim, M.; Salomaa, S.; Wright, E.; Hildebrandt, G.; Belyakov, O.V.; Prise, K.M.; Little, M.P. Non-targeted effects of ionising radiation–implications for low dose risk. *Mutat. Res.* **2013**, *752*, 84–98. [CrossRef]
80. Rothkamm, K.; Löbrich, M. Evidence for a lack of DNA double-strand break repair in human cells exposed to very low X-ray doses. *Proc. Natl. Acad. Sci. USA* **2003**, *100*, 5057–5062. [CrossRef] [PubMed]
81. Osipov, A.N.; Pustovalova, M.; Grekhova, A.; Eremin, P.; Vorobyova, N.; Pulin, A.; Zhavoronkov, A.; Roumiantsev, S.; Klokov, D.Y.; Eremin, I. Low doses of X-rays induce prolonged and ATM-independent persistence of γH2AX foci in human gingival mesenchymal stem cells. *Oncotarget* **2015**, *6*, 27275–27287. [CrossRef] [PubMed]
82. Natarajan, A.T.; Obe, G.; van Zeeland, A.A.; Palitti, F.; Meijers, M.; Verdegaal-Immerzeel, E.A. Molecular mechanisms involved in the production of chromosomal aberrations. II. Utilization of Neurospora endonuclease for the study of aberration production by X-rays in G1 and G2 stages of the cell cycle. *Mutat. Res.* **1980**, *69*, 293–305. [CrossRef]
83. Nikiforov, Y.E.; Rowland, J.M.; Bove, K.E.; Monforte-Munoz, H.; Fagin, J.A. Distinct pattern of ret oncogene rearrangements in morphological variants of radiation-induced and sporadic thyroid papillary carcinomas in children. *Cancer Res.* **1997**, *57*, 1690–1694.
84. Franco, N.; Lamartine, J.; Frouin, V.; Le Minter, P.; Petat, C.; Leplat, J.-J.; Libert, F.; Gidrol, X.; Martin, M.T. Low-Dose Exposure to γ Rays Induces Specific Gene Regulations in Normal Human Keratinocytes. *Radiat. Res.* **2005**, *163*, 623–635. [CrossRef] [PubMed]
85. Shao, C.; Folkard, M.; Held, K.D.; Prise, K.M. Estrogen enhanced cell-cell signalling in breast cancer cells exposed to targeted irradiation. *BMC Cancer* **2008**, *8*, 184. [CrossRef]
86. Depuydt, J.; Viaene, T.; Blondeel, P.; Roche, N.; Van den Broecke, R.; Thierens, H.; Vral, A. DNA double strand breaks induced by low dose mammography X-rays in breast tissue: A pilot study. *Oncol. Lett.* **2018**, *16*, 3394–3400. [CrossRef]
87. Depuydt, J.; Baert, A.; Vandersickel, V.; Thierens, H.; Vral, A. Relative biological effectiveness of mammography X-rays at the level of DNA and chromosomes in lymphocytes. *Int. J. Radiat. Biol.* **2013**, *89*, 532–538. [CrossRef] [PubMed]
88. Beels, L.; Bacher, K.; De Wolf, D.; Werbrouck, J.; Thierens, H. gamma-H2AX foci as a biomarker for patient X-ray exposure in pediatric cardiac catheterization: Are we underestimating radiation risks? *Circulation* **2009**, *120*, 1903–1909. [CrossRef] [PubMed]
89. Beels, L.; Werbrouck, J.; Thierens, H. Dose response and repair kinetics of gamma-H2AX foci induced by in vitro irradiation of whole blood and T-lymphocytes with X- and gamma-radiation. *Int. J. Radiat. Biol.* **2010**, *86*, 760–768. [CrossRef] [PubMed]
90. Groesser, T.; Cooper, B.; Rydberg, B. Lack of bystander effects from high-LET radiation for early cytogenetic end points. *Radiat. Res.* **2008**, *170*, 794–802. [CrossRef] [PubMed]
91. Prise, K.M.; Folkard, M.; Michael, B.D. A review of the bystander effect and its implications for low-dose exposure. *Radiat. Prot. Dosim.* **2003**, *104*, 347–355. [CrossRef] [PubMed]
92. Hei, T.K.; Zhou, H.; Chai, Y.; Ponnaiya, B.; Ivanov, V.N. Radiation induced non-targeted response: Mechanism and potential clinical implications. *Curr. Mol. Pharm.* **2011**, *4*, 96–105. [CrossRef]
93. Shimura, N.; Kojima, S.J.D.-R. The Lowest Radiation Dose Having Molecular Changes in the Living Body. *Dose Response* **2018**, *16*. [CrossRef]
94. Halm, B.M.; Franke, A.A.; Lai, J.F.; Turner, H.C.; Brenner, D.J.; Zohrabian, V.M.; DiMauro, R. γ-H2AX foci are increased in lymphocytes in vivo in young children 1 h after very low-dose X-irradiation: A pilot study. *Pediatr. Radiol.* **2014**, *44*, 1310–1317. [CrossRef]
95. Vandevoorde, C.; Franck, C.; Bacher, K.; Breysem, L.; Smet, M.H.; Ernst, C.; De Backer, A.; Van De Moortele, K.; Smeets, P.; Thierens, H. γ-H2AX foci as in vivo effect biomarker in children emphasize the importance to minimize X-ray doses in paediatric CT imaging. *Eur. Radiol.* **2015**, *25*, 800–811. [CrossRef]

96. Darby, S.C.; Olsen, J.H.; Doll, R.; Thakrar, B.; Brown, P.D.; Storm, H.H.; Barlow, L.; Langmark, F.; Teppo, L.; Tulinius, H. Trends in childhood leukaemia in the Nordic countries in relation to fallout from atmospheric nuclear weapons testing. *BMJ* **1992**, *304*, 1005–1009. [CrossRef]
97. Likhtarev, I.A.; Sobolev, B.G.; Kairo, I.A.; Tronko, N.D.; Bogdanova, T.I.; Oleinic, V.A.; Epshtein, E.V.; Beral, V. Thyroid cancer in the Ukraine. *Nature* **1995**, *375*, 365. [CrossRef]
98. Grundmann, O.; Mitchell, G.C.; Limesand, K.H. Sensitivity of salivary glands to radiation: From animal models to therapies. *J. Dent. Res.* **2009**, *88*, 894–903. [CrossRef]
99. Joint FAO/WHO Expert Committee on Food Additives; World Health Organization. *Evaluation of certain food contaminants: Sixty-fourth report of the Joint FAO/WHO Expert Committee on Food Additives*; WHO Technical Report Series 930; World Health Organization: Geneva, Switzerland, 2006; Volume 930, pp. 1–99.
100. Canadian Council of Ministers of the Environment. *A Protocol for the Derivation of Environmental and Human Health Soil Quality Guidelines*; Canadian Council of Ministers of the Environment: Winnipeg, MB, Canada, 2006.
101. Ministry for the Environment. *Toxicological Intake Values for Priority Contaminants in Soil*; Ministry for the Environment: Wellington, New Zealand, 2011.
102. Noshchenko, A.G.; Bondar, O.Y.; Drozdova, V.D. Radiation-induced leukemia among children aged 0–5 years at the time of the Chernobyl accident. *Int. J. Cancer* **2010**, *127*, 412–426. [CrossRef]
103. Petridou, E.; Trichopoulos, D.; Dessypris, N.; Flytzani, V.; Haidas, S.; Kalmanti, M.; Koliouskas, D.; Kosmidis, H.; Piperopoulou, F.; Tzortzatou, F. Infant leukaemia after in utero exposure to radiation from Chernobyl. *Nature* **1996**, *382*, 352–353. [CrossRef]
104. Michaelis, J.; Kaletsch, U.; Burkart, W.; Grosche, B. Infant leukaemia after the Chernobyl accident. *Nature* **1997**, *387*, 246. [CrossRef]
105. Ivanov, E.P.; Tolochko, G.V.; Shuvaeva, L.P.; Ivanov, V.E.; Iaroshevich, R.F.; Becker, S.; Nekolla, E.; Kellerer, A.M. Infant leukemia in Belarus after the Chernobyl accident. *Radiat. Environ. Biophys.* **1998**, *37*, 53–55. [CrossRef] [PubMed]
106. Lumniczky, K.; Impens, N.; Armengol, G.; Candéias, S.; Georgakilas, A.G.; Hornhardt, S.; Martin, O.A.; Rödel, F.; Schaue, D. Low dose ionizing radiation effects on the immune system. *Environ. Int.* **2021**, *149*, 106212. [CrossRef] [PubMed]
107. Thompson, L.H. *Origin, Recognition, Signaling and Repair of DNA Double-Strand Breaks in Mammalian Cells*; Landes Bioscience: Austin, TX, USA, 2013.
108. National Research Council. *Health Risks from Exposure to Low Levels of Ionizing Radiation: BEIR VII, Phase I*; The National Academies Press: Washington, DC, USA, 2006. [CrossRef]
109. Asaithamby, A.; Chen, D.J. Cellular responses to DNA double-strand breaks after low-dose gamma-irradiation. *Nucleic Acids Res.* **2009**, *37*, 3912–3923. [CrossRef] [PubMed]
110. Löbrich, M.; Rydberg, B.; Cooper, P.K. Repair of X-ray-induced DNA double-strand breaks in specific Not I restriction fragments in human fibroblasts: Joining of correct and incorrect ends. *Proc. Natl. Acad. Sci. USA* **1995**, *92*, 12050–12054. [CrossRef] [PubMed]
111. Saeki, H.; Sugimachi, K. Carcinogenic Risk Factors. *J. Jpn. Med. Assoc.* **2001**, *125*, 297–300.
112. Ivashkevich, A.N.; Martin, O.A.; Smith, A.J.; Redon, C.E.; Bonner, W.M.; Martin, R.F.; Lobachevsky, P.N. γH2AX foci as a measure of DNA damage: A computational approach to automatic analysis. *Mutat. Res.* **2011**, *711*, 49–60. [CrossRef]
113. Bonner, W.M.; Redon, C.E.; Dickey, J.S.; Nakamura, A.J.; Sedelnikova, O.A.; Solier, S.; Pommier, Y. GammaH2AX and cancer. *Nat. Rev. Cancer* **2008**, *8*, 957–967. [CrossRef] [PubMed]

Article

Natural Radioactivity and Radon Exhalation from Building Materials in Underground Parking Lots

Dainius Jasaitis * and Milda Pečiulienė

Department of Physics, Vilnius Gediminas Technical University, Saulėtekio Ave. 11, LT-10223 Vilnius, Lithuania; milda.peciuliene@vilniustech.lt
* Correspondence: dainius.jasaitis@vilniustech.lt

Abstract: The change of natural ionizing radiation and the radon exhalation rates from typical building materials in underground parking lots are presented in the article. The activity concentration of natural radionuclides ^{232}Th, ^{226}Ra, and ^{40}K in six important types of construction materials, which are mostly used in Lithuania, were analyzed using high-resolution gamma spectroscopy. The highest values were found in concrete and ferroconcrete samples: ^{226}Ra 44 and 90 Bq kg^{-1}; ^{232}Th 29 and 34 Bq kg^{-1}; ^{40}K 581 and 603 Bq kg^{-1}. A strong positive correlation (0.88) was observed between radium activity concentration and radon concentration. The activity indexes (I_α and I_γ) and radium equivalent activity (R_{eq}) evaluating the suitability of materials for such constructions from the view of radiation safety were determined. The average values of the calculated absorbed dose rate in samples ranged from 18.24 nGy h^{-1} in the sand to 87.26 nGy h^{-1} in ferroconcrete. The calculated annual effective dose was below the limit of 1.0 mSv y^{-1}. The values of the external and internal hazards index (H_{ex} and H_{in}) were all below unity, and the values of I_γ and I_α were below the recommended levels of 0.5 and 1. Dosimetric analysis of underground parking lots was carried out. It was determined that the external equivalent dose rate caused by the ^{222}Rn progeny radiation in the underground car parking lots varies from 17 to 30% of the total equivalent dose rate.

Keywords: natural radioactivity; radon exhalation; equivalent dose rate; car parking lots

1. Introduction

Ionizing radiation is one of the factors that can have a negative impact on human health. Natural radiation such as cosmic radiation, radionuclides in the soil and construction materials, radon gas are the highest sources of human radiation exposure. Even low doses of ionizing radiation can cause chronic diseases, cancer can also lead to various negative health effects. Negative consequences can occur many years after exposure. It is impossible to avoid the impact of radiation, but it can be reduced.

^{226}Ra, ^{232}Th, and ^{40}K in construction materials is an important source of human exposure [1,2]. Gamma radiation of these natural radionuclides causes external exposure. Building materials can be radioactive for various reasons, mostly due to the raw materials with a high activity concentration of natural radionuclides that are used for their production. Therefore, it is important to control the activity concentration of radionuclides in construction materials. One of the ways to reduce the external exposure dose is to select building materials with the low-level activity of radionuclides. Calculation of doses due to radionuclides in building materials is important from the point of radiation safety. High activities of natural radionuclides in building materials may be the cause of higher dose rates indoors, especially when products from various industries are used in the production process [3].

Radon exhalation from building materials is also an important problem as this radioactive inert gas is the most important source of internal exposure. According to some studies, radon and its decay products determine about 50% of the total dose from natural radiation [4,5]. Although the main source of radon indoors is soil, in some cases, the main

sources of indoor radon can be construction materials—contribution is estimated to be up to 30% [6]. Radon is an alpha emitter; therefore, radon radiation is easily absorbed by human skin. However, radon gas can be inhaled by humans, and radon decay products (^{218}Po, ^{214}Pb, and ^{214}Bi) can cause internal exposure [7]. The main risk posed by radon and its progeny is that it can cause respiratory tract and lung cancer. Radon disperses rapidly outdoors and is not a health issue. Most radon exposure occurs indoors where radon can have high activity concentration. It has been evaluated that the equivalent dose rate caused by ionizing radiation of radon progeny ^{214}Pb and ^{214}Bi can vary from 2 to 20% of the total equivalent dose rate [8,9]. The average annual effective dose from natural sources is 2.4 mSv: 1.1 mSv of it is due to the basic background radiation, 1.3 mSv due to exposure to radon [10]. According to Lithuanian Hygiene Norms and European Union directives, the indoor radon concentration must not exceed 300 Bq m^{-3} [11,12].

The exposure of radon progeny concentration in underground parking lots is determined by the ventilation intensity and radon exhalation from the soil and building materials. To reduce the amount of radioactive inert gas in parking places, it is necessary to study and use emanation blocking means in building materials; it is also important to know and control the activity concentration of ^{226}Ra in soil and building materials, as the intensity of radon exhalation depends on it [13]. It has been evaluated that the used quantity of building material and its particular place in a building determines the exposure [14].

In order for the population to be exposed to less radiation from radionuclides in construction materials, the activity concentration of radionuclides in building materials used in the construction must not exceed predefined limit values. Indoor radon research is carried out regularly. After assessing the exposure to ionizing radiation from radionuclides in building materials and the change and formation of this exposure, it is possible to plan measures that must be taken to optimally reduce the exposure.

Although the typical duration of stay for persons in underground parking lots is from a few minutes to a few hours per day, there are exceptions. In Lithuania, car cleaning centers, car wheel services, and various small repair workshops are found in the underground shopping centers. The people who work in them and customers spend a lot of time. Additionally, there are known cases when humans set up sports and training facilities and creative workshops in underground garages under apartment buildings. Therefore, it must be taken into account that some people can spend much more time in underground parking places than others. This is important from the point of view of radiation protection.

Identification of radiation sources, determination of exposure, investigation of variation, and distribution principles of radiation doses is an important stage of radiation safety optimization; therefore, it is important to analyze the human exposure sources and to choose the most optimal protection against ionizing radiation.

2. Materials and Methods

The measurements were undertaken in typical parking lots, located one floor below dwellings or shopping centers. Samples were taken in several ways. Some samples were collected from manufacturers and suppliers. Other samples, if it was possible, were taken at underground parking lots. For the statistical evaluation of the activity concentration distribution of natural radionuclides, 20 to 50 samples of the same material were taken.

To identify gamma radionuclides ^{40}K, ^{232}Th, ^{226}Ra and measure their activity concentration the samples of the main building materials used for the construction of underground parking lots (clay, cement, sand, gravel, concrete, and ferroconcrete) were prepared for spectrometric analysis. The samples were dried at 105 °C in a laboratory oven, then crushed and homogeneously put into measuring containers of 200 mL and left for four weeks to reach secular equilibrium between ^{226}Ra and its progeny. The samples were analyzed with the gamma spectrometry system Canberra, USA, with the semiconductor Hyper Pure germanium (HPGe) detector (model GC2520). HPGe detector has an energy resolution full width at half-maximum (FWHM) of 1.9 keV at 1330 keV (^{60}Co). The detector has a high peak to Compton ratio of 58:1 and relative efficiency of 30%. The samples of building materials were measured spectrometrically for at least 90 000 s. ^{226}Ra activity concentration in the samples was defined based on its decay products ^{214}Pb (352 keV) and ^{214}Bi (609 keV), while ^{232}Th was defined based on ^{228}Ac (911 keV) and ^{208}Tl (583 keV). ^{40}K was determined directly according to the 1460 keV energy gamma-radiation peak.

The radon exhalation rate was measured by hermetically closing the sample in a container and observing the radon activity growth as a time function [3,15,16]. The samples were kept in cylindrical containers of 400 mL capacity. LR-115 track detector was used in this study. The detector is exposed to the exhaled radon from the sample and fixes α-particles resulting from the radon progeny in the volume of the container and ^{218}Po and ^{214}Po deposited on the inner walls of the container. Following the long-term exposure, the LR-115 detector was chemically etched for developing the tracks registered in the films and the concentrations of radon and its decay products were determined.

The equivalent dose rate (EDR, nSv h^{-1}) caused by natural radionuclides in underground parking lots building materials was measured. Dosimetric measurements were performed using an InSpector 1000 a high-performance digital handheld multichannel analyzer with a NaI detector (IPROS-3), energy range 50 keV to 3 MeV [17]. The analyzer has computer interface software Genie 2000. The equivalent dose results are updated once per second. The parking lot where the EDR was measured (no closer than 50 cm from the wall) was split into imaginary squares with an edge length of 2 m. The average EDR value of the five measurements was recorded at the center of each imaginary square with the detector held at a height of 1 m. The number of measurement points depends on the size of the parking lot.

At the same time, radon concentration was measured using radon and thoron measurement system SARAD RTM2200. The monitor is based on α-spectrometry forming ^{222}Rn progeny (^{218}Po and ^{214}Po) inside the high-quality silicon radiation detector chamber. Radon progeny deposit on the surface of the semiconductor detector and alpha radiation was registered. Measurement upper range of the radon concentration is 10 MBq m^{-3}, device sensitivity—3 or 7 cpm/(kBq·m^{-3}) for fast or slow mode. Radon concentrations can be registered at different time intervals.

3. Results and Discussion
3.1. Radon Exhalation Rate

Radon surface and mass exhalation rates were calculated using Equations (1) and (2), respectively [15,18].

$$E_S = \frac{CV\lambda/A}{T + (1/\lambda)(e^{-\lambda T} - 1)} \quad (1)$$

and

$$E_M = \frac{CV\lambda/M}{T + (1/\lambda)(e^{-\lambda T} - 1)} \quad (2)$$

where E_S is surface exhalation rate (Bq m^{-2} h^{-1}); E_M is mass exhalation rate (Bq kg^{-1} h^{-1}); C is integrated radon exposure (Bq m^{-3} h^{-1}); V is the volume of air (m^3); λ is radon decay constant (h^{-1}); T is the exposure time (h), A is the surface area (m^2)m and M is the mass (kg) of the sample, respectively.

Radon surface and mass exhalation rates and other parameters of the most commonly used building materials are presented in Table 1.

Table 1. Radon surface and mass exhalation rates and other parameters of studied building materials (M.V. ± σ).

Building Material	Rn Surface Exhalation Rate (mBq·m^{-2}·h^{-1})	Rn Mass Exhalation Rate (mBq·kg^{-1}·h^{-1})	Emanation Factor (%)	Porosity (%)	Bulk Density (kg·m^{-3})
Sand	10.2 ± 1.5	1.12 ± 0.16	5 ± 0.7	32 ± 3.5	1620
Clay bricks	18.3 ± 1.3	1.22 ± 0.15	3 ± 0.5	23 ± 3.2	1950
Cement	19.9 ± 1.6	1.19 ± 0.13	11 ± 1.9	12 ± 2.2	2020
Concrete	24.3 ± 1.2	2.93 ± 0.18	10 ± 1.3	16 ± 2.6	2200
Ferroconcrete	26.2 ± 1.4	2.95 ± 0.17	16 ± 2.1	18 ± 2.9	2400

Radon surface exhalation rates vary from 10.2 ± 0.5 to 26.2 ± 0.4 mBq m^{-2} h^{-1}; radon mass exhalation rates vary from 1.12 ± 0.06 to 2.95 ± 0.07 mBq m^{-2} h^{-1} (uncertainties are given with coverage factor k = 2). The maximum rate of radon exhalation was observed in the concrete and ferroconcrete samples. It is worth mentioning that the radon exhalation rate changes with the age of the concrete. Various researchers [3,19–21] estimated that the radon exhalation rate was decreased with the increasing age of concrete. Additionally, it was estimated that the radon exhalation rate of concrete is reduced by low humidity conditions. Therefore, the results show that radon exhalation from samples of concrete measurements is dependent on the humidity and age of the sample and should be standardized.

Radon surface exhalation and mass exhalation rates found for sand are the lowest values and for concrete and ferroconcrete are found to be the maximum. The emanation fraction varies from 5 to 16%. The results obtained in this work are within the values measured in other countries [18,22–25]. Correlation analysis showed a strong positive correlation (0.88) between radon concentration and radium activity concentration in various samples, which may be due to the radium content and porosity in the samples (Figure 1).

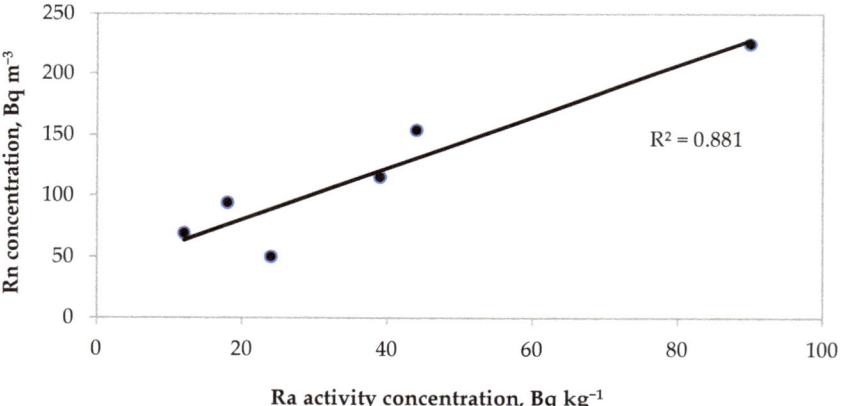

Figure 1. The correlation between radon concentration and radium activity concentration.

Research of radon activity concentrations in underground parking lots with workplaces has shown that people work in a safe environment in terms of radiation safety. The radon activity concentration varied from 22 ± 3 to 270 ± 18 Bq m^{-3} (the average value was 83 ± 7 Bq m^{-3}). Indoor radon activity concentration did not exceed the level of the Lithuanian hygiene standard [11]. However, several cases were close to the maximum level. Such results may have been due to the fact that no mechanical ventilation systems were installed that do not allow radon to accumulate on the lower floors of the building.

3.2. Estimation of Radium, Thorium, and Potassium in Various Samples

The activity concentration (C, Bq kg^{-1}) of potassium, thorium, and radium were calculated using the following Equation (3) [26]:

$$C = \frac{CPS \times 100 \times 100}{B.I. \times E_{ff} \times m} \pm \frac{SD_{CPS} \times 100 \times 100}{B.I. \times E_{ff} \times m} \quad (3)$$

where CPS is the net count rate per second, SD_{CPS} is the standard deviation of net count rate per second, $B.I.$ is the branching intensity, E_{ff} is the efficiency of the detector, and m is sample mass in kg.

Table 2 shows the average activity concentrations of the radionuclides ^{40}K, ^{232}Th, and ^{226}Ra in structural materials used for building underground parking lots, as well as the corresponding standard deviation in the materials under investigation. It has been determined a wide range of activity concentrations of natural radionuclides contained in building materials: ^{40}K—13–1217 Bq kg^{-1}, ^{226}Ra—2–124 Bq kg^{-1}, ^{232}Th—1–72 Bq kg^{-1}. The lowest activity concentrations of natural radionuclides have been found in sand, cement, and gravel, while their highest activity concentrations have been measured in ferroconcrete, clay, and concrete. The commonly used building materials samples satisfy the safety criterion of the recommended safety limit for the public [27]. Therefore, these samples do not pose any health hazard for the human.

Table 2. Activity concentrations of ^{40}K, ^{232}Th, ^{226}Ra in studied building materials and activity indexes.

Building Material	^{40}K M.V. ± σ (Range)	^{232}Th M.V. ± σ (Range)	^{226}Ra M.V. ± σ (Range)	I_γ	I_α
Clay	493 ± 16 (108–734)	8 ± 2 (2–16)	24 ± 2 (10–41)	0.28	0.12
Cement	126 ± 17 (13–362)	5 ± 1 (1–8)	39 ± 4 (7–66)	0.20	0.20
Sand	232 ± 21 (137–460)	5 ± 1 (1–19)	12 ± 1 (5–17)	0.14	0.06
Gravel	301 ± 11 (118–342)	5 ± 1 (1–9)	18 ± 1 (2–23)	0.19	0.09
Concrete	581 ± 27 (18–1217)	29 ± 3 (2–47)	44 ± 3 (3–92)	0.48	0.22
Ferroconcrete	603 ± 21 (47–1108)	34 ± 4 (1–72)	90 ± 4 (4–124)	0.67	0.45

The values of activity indexes I_γ and I_α are given in Table 2. These indexes are used for the overall evaluation of building materials from the view of radiation protection.

The gamma activity index (I_γ) is calculated using the following Equation (4):

$$I_\gamma = \frac{C_{Ra}}{300} + \frac{C_{Th}}{200} + \frac{C_K}{3000} \quad (4)$$

where C_{Ra}, C_{Th}, C_K are activity concentrations of ^{226}Ra, ^{232}Th, and ^{40}K in Bq kg^{-1}.

The gamma activity indexes of natural radionuclides in building materials varied from 0.14 to 0.67. They did not exceed the values determined by the Lithuanian Hygiene Norm [28] and regulated by the European Commission [29].

Alpha index (I_α) assesses internal hazards originating from the alpha activity of building materials. This parameter evaluates the exposure level due to radon inhalation originating from building materials. The I_α has been proposed by S. Righi [30].

The alpha index calculated using Equation (5).

$$I_\alpha = \frac{C_{Ra}}{200} \quad (5)$$

The activities of radium must not exceed a value of 200 Bq kg^{-1}, to avoid exposure to the indoor radon concentration of more than 200 Bq m^{-3}. In this work, the alpha index ranged from 0.06 to 0.45 from building materials. The highest value of I_α 0.45 was found in ferroconcrete samples as well as the highest value of I_γ 0.67.

The values of activity concentration index I_α and I_γ regulated by the European Commission radiation protection principles shall not exceed 0.5 and 1, respectively [29].

It is known that the absorbed dose rate is not directly related to radionuclide concentrations in constructions materials. Other parameters that are important for dose rate indoors are analyzed below.

3.3. Evaluation of Radiological Hazard Parameters in Building Materials

3.3.1. Radium Equivalent Activity

The natural radioactivity of construction materials is usually determined from the content of natural radionuclides ^{40}K, ^{232}Th, and ^{226}Ra. The distribution of these radionuclides in building materials samples under investigation is not uniform; therefore, a radium equivalent activity index (Ra_{eq}) was introduced. Ra_{eq} is an index used to represent the activity concentrations of ^{40}K, ^{232}Th, and ^{226}Ra by a single quantity, which takes into account the radiation hazards associated with them. Ra_{eq} is calculated according to the following Equation (6):

$$Ra_{eq} = C_{Ra} + 1.43 C_{Th} + 0.077 C_K \quad (6)$$

The calculated values of Ra_{eq} for all types of building materials ranged from 37.01 to 185.05 Bq kg^{-1}, which is less than the limit of 370 Bq kg^{-1} [17,31–33]. This value is defined by the Organization for Economic Cooperation and Development to keep the external dose below 1.5 mSv y^{-1}. The highest value of Ra_{eq} is estimated in ferroconcrete samples (Table 3).

Table 3. The average values of absorbed dose rate, annual effective dose, and hazard parameters for building materials.

Building Material	Ra_{eq} (Bq kg^{-1})	Average Absorbed Dose Rate (nGy h^{-1})	Outdoor Annual Effective Dose (mSv)	Indoor Annual Effective Dose (mSv)	H_{ex}	H_{in}
Clay	73	36	0.045	0.18	0.20	0.26
Cement	56	26	0.032	0.13	0.15	0.26
Sand	37	18	0.022	0.09	0.10	0.13
Gravel	48	24	0.029	0.12	0.13	0.18
Concrete	130	62	0.076	0.31	0.35	0.47
Ferroconcrete	185	87	0.107	0.43	0.50	0.74

The results show that Ra_{eq} of different building materials can vary significantly. This is important in choosing the appropriate materials for building constructions. Actually, Ra_{eq} of the same type of building materials can have large variations. Therefore, it is important to identify their radioactivity levels before using building materials.

3.3.2. Absorbed and Annual Effective Dose Rate

Gamma radiation hazards related to building materials can be evaluated by calculating the different radiation hazard parameters [34]. One of the parameters to estimate radiation risk to humans is absorbed dose rate (D). The absorbed dose rate can be calculated by the concentrations of ^{40}K, ^{226}Ra, and ^{232}Th by applying the conversion factors 0.0417, 0.462, and 0.604 for potassium, radium, and thorium, respectively [32]. These conversion factors were used to calculate the total absorbed gamma dose rate in the air of underground car parks at 1 m above the ground level. The absorbed dose rate has been calculated by using the Monte Carlo method [35]:

$$D = 0.0417 C_K + 0.462 C_{Ra} + 0.604 C_{Th} \tag{7}$$

where D is the absorbed dose rate (nGy h^{-1}).

To determine annual effective dose (AED) the conversion coefficient from absorbed dose to effective dose and the indoor and outdoor occupancy factor must be taken into account. The conversion coefficient from absorbed dose rate in the air to effective dose is 0.7 Sv Gy^{-1}, which is used to convert the absorbed dose rate to human effective dose equivalent with an outdoor occupancy of 20% and 80% for indoors, proposed by [32].

The annual effective doses are calculated as follows:

$$AED_{outdoor} = 0.2 \times D \times t \times F \times 10^{-6} \tag{8}$$

$$AED_{indoor} = 0.8 \times D \times t \times F \times 10^{-6} \tag{9}$$

where AED is the annual effective dose (mSv y^{-1}); D is absorbed dose rate (nGy h^{-1}); t is the duration of the exposure (8760 h); F is the conversion factor of 0.7 Sv Gy^{-1}.

Applying Equations (7)–(9), the absorbed and annual effective dose rates from the samples were calculated, as given in Table 3. The average values of the calculated absorbed dose rate in samples ranged from 18.24 nGy h^{-1} in the sand to 87.26 nGy h^{-1} in ferroconcrete. The values of AED_{indoor} were found to vary from 0.09 to 0.43 mSv y^{-1}. $AED_{outdoor}$ varied from 0.022 to 0.107 mSv y^{-1}. The annual effective dose from ferroconcrete is higher than the other samples. The lowest annual effective dose was found in sand and gravel. However, it was estimated that all these building materials samples satisfy the safety criteria for radiation safety point of view, and hence, these samples do not pose any environmental and health hazard problems. The calculated annual effective dose is below the limit of 1.0 mSv y^{-1} recommended by the International Commission on Radiological Protection for the general public.

3.3.3. External and Internal Hazard Index

The values of external (H_{ex}) and internal (H_{in}) hazards are shown in Table 3. External hazard index is calculated using Equation (10) [36,37].

$$H_{ex} = \frac{C_{Ra}}{370} + \frac{C_{Th}}{259} + \frac{C_K}{4810} \leq 1. \tag{10}$$

Internal hazard index is calculated using the following Equation (11) [36,37]:

$$H_{in} = \frac{C_{Ra}}{185} + \frac{C_{Th}}{259} + \frac{C_K}{4810} \leq 1 \tag{11}$$

The values of these indices must be lower than 1, to ensure that the radiation hazard is insignificant in the investigated area [32,38].

As can be seen, the maximum values of H_{ex} and H_{in} are found in ferroconcrete samples, 0.50 and 0.74, respectively. The values of H_{ex} and H_{in} are all below unity; therefore, the materials analyzed in this study can be safely used for the construction of buildings.

3.4. Estimation of Equivalent Dose Rate Caused by Radon

Consistently registering the records of the dosimeter, information on the equivalent dose rate of parking places was collected. The equivalent dose rate is influenced by ionizing radiation of radionuclides in the ground surface and air as well as cosmic radiation [39].

External equivalent dose rate (EDR) values caused by radiation of natural radionuclides, respectively, ^{40}K, ^{226}Ra, and ^{232}Th are presented in Figure 2. To evaluate the measured equivalent dose rate in the underground parking lots, the results were compared with the measurement results in the aboveground parking lots. Figure 2 shows the equivalent dose rate measured in artificial ventilated underground parking lots and natural ventilated aboveground parking lots.

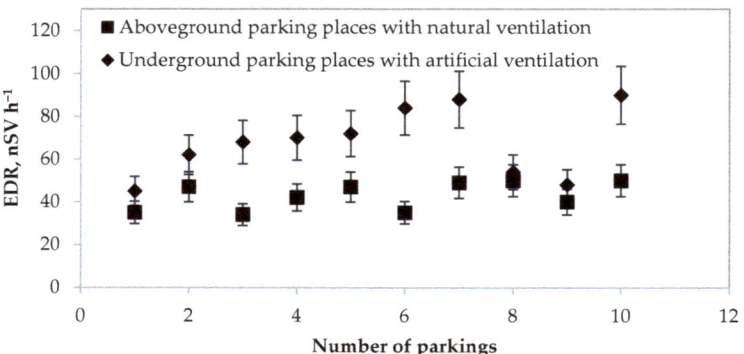

Figure 2. Equivalent dose rate (EDR) in different types of parking lots.

Experiments show that the highest values of *EDR* are measured in underground parking lots with artificial ventilation. About 2–20% of the radiation is radon progeny in these parking places, and this is explained by the fact that the biggest amount of radon is in the soil, and it tends to accumulate specifically in rooms and underground structures that are in contact with the ground [40].

Figure 3 shows a variation of the equivalent dose rate caused by radon and the total equivalent dose rate. *EDR* was measured and the ^{222}Rn activity concentration in the air was determined in the underground parking lots at the same time to estimate which part of the total *EDR* is due to the ^{222}Rn.

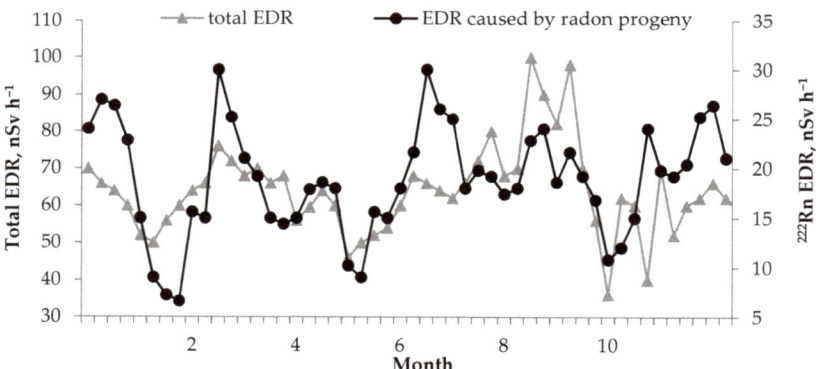

Figure 3. Variations of the equivalent dose rate caused by ^{222}Rn and total equivalent dose rate in the underground parking lots.

It was evaluated that *EDR* caused by the ^{222}Rn and its progeny varies from 17 to 30% of the total *EDR* in the underground parking lots. Radon activity concentration can be reduced by using radon exhalation from the ground and building materials blocking means: seal cracks, cover surfaces (e.g., paint), fill pores, and others. It is important to ventilate underground parking lots more frequently. Additionally, building materials with the lowest ^{226}Ra activity concentration should reduce radon and its progeny concentration.

4. Conclusions

Activity concentrations of ^{40}K, ^{232}Th, and ^{226}Ra in the building materials used for construction underground parking lots were determined. The highest values were found in concrete and ferroconcrete samples: ^{40}K 581 and 603 Bq kg^{-1}, ^{232}Th 29 and 34 Bq kg^{-1}, ^{226}Ra 44 and 90 Bq kg^{-1}, respectively. A statistically significant positive correlation (i.e., 0.88) between radium activity concentration in building materials and radon concentration in underground parking lots has been found. The highest values of radon exhalation were determined in ferroconcrete samples. The radon exhalation rates showed a good correlation with radium concentration.

It was estimated that the values of external (H_{ex}) and internal (H_{in}) hazard indexes in the studied samples were lower than the recommended limits. The calculated values of H_{ex} and H_{in}, as well as the values of gamma (I_γ) and alpha (I_α) activity indexes, were below the recommended level of 1. Therefore, it is safe to use the materials analyzed in this study for the construction of underground parking lots.

Having assessed the possible additional exposure induced by the radioactivity of the building materials contained in underground parking lots, it was established that the absorbed dose rate (D) and annual effective dose (AED) increase up to 2.5 times; however, they do not exceed the maximum permissible rates of natural exposure. The studied areas may be considered safe from a radiological point of view. The calculated radium equivalent activity (Ra_{eq}) was below the upper limit of 370 Bq kg^{-1} in all types of building materials.

The equivalent dose rate (EDR) in artificial ventilated underground and natural ventilated aboveground parking lots was experimentally determined. It was estimated that the highest values of EDR are measured in artificial ventilated underground parking lots and EDR caused by the radon, and its progeny varies from 17 to 30% of the total EDR.

Author Contributions: Conceptualization, D.J. and M.P.; methodology, D.J. and M.P.; validation, D.J. and M.P.; formal analysis, M.P.; investigation, D.J. and M.P.; resources, D.J. and M.P.; data curation, D.J. and M.P.; writing—original draft preparation, D.J. and M.P.; writing—review and editing, D.J. and M.P.; visualization, D.J.; supervision, D.J. All authors have read and agreed to the published version of the manuscript.

Funding: This research received no external funding.

Institutional Review Board Statement: Not applicable.

Informed Consent Statement: Not applicable.

Data Availability Statement: Not applicable.

Conflicts of Interest: The authors declare no conflict of interest.

References

1. Faghihi, R.; Mehdizadeh, S.; Sina, S. Natural and artificial radioactivity distribution in soil of Fars province, Iran. *Radiat. Prot. Dosim.* **2011**, *145*, 66–74. [CrossRef] [PubMed]
2. Mehra, R.; Kumar, S.; Sonkawade, R.; Singh, N.P.; Badhan, K. Analysis of terrestrial naturally occurring radionuclides in soil samples from some areas of Sirsa district of Haryana, India using gamma ray spectrometry. *Environ. Earth Sci.* **2010**, *59*, 1159–1164. [CrossRef]
3. Stoulos, S.; Manolopoulo, M.; Papastefanou, C. Assessment of natural radiation exposure and radon exhalation from building materials in Greece. *J. Environ. Radioact.* **2003**, *69*, 225–240. [CrossRef]
4. United Nations Scientific Committee on the Effects of Atomic Radiation. *Sources and Effects of Ionizing Radiation. Report to the General Assembly, with Scientific Annexes 2008*; United Nations: New York, NY, USA, 2010.
5. United Nations Scientific Committee on the Effects of Atomic Radiation. *Report of the United Nations Scientific Committee on the Effects of Atomic Radiation 2010*; United Nations: New York, NY, USA, 2011.
6. Trevisi, R.; Nuccetelli, C.; Risica, S. Screening tools to limit the use of building materials with enhanced/elevated levels of natural radioactivity: Analysis and application of index criteria. *Constr. Build. Mater.* **2013**, *49*, 448–454. [CrossRef]
7. Leung, J.K.C.; Tso, M.Y.W.; Ho, C.W.; Hung, L.C. Radon mitigation in a typical underground car park in Hong Kong. *Radiat. Protect. Dosim.* **1997**, *71*, 289–296. [CrossRef]
8. Lebedyte, M.; Butkus, D.; Morkunas, G. Variations of the ambient dose equivalent rate in the ground level air. *J. Environ. Radioact.* **2003**, *64*, 45–57. [CrossRef]

9. Chibowski, S.; Komosa, A. Radon concentration in basements of old town buildings in the Lublin region, Poland. *J. Radioanal. Nucl. Chem.* **2001**, *247*, 53–56. [CrossRef]
10. Al-Jundi, J.; Salah, W.; Bawa'aneh, M.S.; Afaneh, F. Exposure to radiation from the natural radioactivity in Jordanian building materials. *Radiat. Prot. Dosim.* **2006**, *118*, 93–96. [CrossRef]
11. Lithuanian Hygiene Norm HN 73: 2018. Basic Radiation Protection Standards. Available online: https://e-seimas.lrs.lt/portal/legalAct/lt/TAD/TAIS.159355/asr (accessed on 5 August 2021). (In Lithuanian).
12. Official Journal of the European Union. *Council Directive 2013/59/Euratom*; Official Journal of the European Union: Luxembourg, 2015.
13. Moharram, B.M.; Suliman, M.N.; Zahran, N.F.; Shennawy, S.E.; El-Sayed, A.R. External exposure doses due to gamma emitting natural radionuclides in some Egyptian building materials. *Appl. Radiat. Isot.* **2012**, *70*, 241–248. [CrossRef] [PubMed]
14. Trevisi, R.; Risica, S.; D'Alessandro, M.; Paradiso, D.; Nuccetelli, C. Natural radioactivity in building materials in the European Union: A database and an estimate of radiological significance. *J. Environ. Radioact.* **2012**, *105*, 11–20. [CrossRef]
15. Sonkawadea, R.G.; Kantb, K.; Muralithara, S.; Kumara, R.; Ramola, R.C. Natural radioactivity in common building construction and radiation shielding materials. *Atmos. Environ.* **2008**, *42*, 2254–2259. [CrossRef]
16. Moura, C.L.; Artur, A.C.; Bonotto, D.M.; Guedes, S.; Martinelli, C.D. Natural radioactivity and radon exhalation rate in Brazilian igneous rocks. *Appl. Rad. Isot.* **2011**, *69*, 1094–1099. [CrossRef]
17. Jasaitis, D.; Chadysiene, R.; Peciuliene, M.; Vasiliauskiene, V. Research on change of natural ionizing radiation in car parking places. *Rom. J. Phys.* **2016**, *61*, 1567–1576.
18. Perna, A.F.N.; Paschuk, S.A.; Corrêa, J.N.; Narloch, D.C.; Barreto, R.C.; Del Claro, F.; Denyak, V. Exhalation rate of radon-222 from concrete and cement mortar. *Nukleonika* **2018**, *63*, 65–72. [CrossRef]
19. Roelofs, L.M.M.; Scholten, L.C. The effect of aging, humidity and fly-ash additive on the radon exhalation from concrete. *Health Phys.* **1994**, *67*, 206–271. [CrossRef]
20. Yu, K.N.; Young, E.C.M.; Chan, T.F.; Lo, T.; Balendran, R.V. The variation of radon exhalation rates from concrete surfaces of different ages. *Build. Environ.* **1996**, *31*, 255–257. [CrossRef]
21. Taylor-Lange, S.C.; Stewart, J.G.; Juenger, M.C.G.; Siegel, J.A. The contribution of fly ash toward indoor radon pollution from concrete. *Build. Environ.* **2012**, *56*, 276–282. [CrossRef]
22. Leonardi, F.; Bonczyk, M.; Nuccetelli, C.; Wysocka, M.; Michalik, B.; Ampollini, M.; Tonnarini, S.; Rubin, J.; Niedbalska, K.; Trevisi, R. A study on natural radioactivity and radon exhalation rate in building materials containing norm residues: Preliminary results. *Constr. Build. Mater.* **2018**, *173*, 172–179. [CrossRef]
23. Stajic, M.; Nikezic, D. Measurement of radon exhalation rates from some building materials used in Serbian construction. *J. Radioanal. Nucl. Chem.* **2015**, *303*, 1943–1947. [CrossRef]
24. Dabayneh, K.M. ^{222}Rn concentration level measurements and exhalation rates in different types of building materials used in Palestinian buildings. *Isot. Radiat. Res. J.* **2008**, *40*, 277–289.
25. Bala, P.; Kumar, V.; Mehra, R. Measurement of radon exhalation rate in various building materials and soil samples. *J. Earth Syst. Sci.* **2017**, *126*, 1–8. [CrossRef]
26. Hussain, R.O.; Hussain, H.H. Investigation the Natural Radioactivity in Local and Imported Chemical Fertilizers. *Braz. Arch. Biol. Technol.* **2011**, *54*, 777–782. [CrossRef]
27. ICRP. International Commission on Radiological Protection. Available online: http://icrpaedia.org/Dose_limits (accessed on 30 April 2021).
28. Lithuanian Hygiene Norm HN 85: 2011. Natural Exposure. Radiation Protection Standards. Available online: https://e-seimas.lrs.lt/portal/legalAct/lt/TAD/TAIS.408807 (accessed on 30 April 2021). (In Lithuanian).
29. European Commission. *Radiological Protection Principles Concerning the Natural Radioactivity of Building Materials. Radiation Protection 112*; Directorate General Environment, Nuclear Safety and Civil Protection: Luxembourg, 1999; Available online: https://op.europa.eu/en/publication-detail/-/publication/988f3243-5259-43a5-b621-fbff662deeb0/language-en (accessed on 30 April 2021).
30. Righi, S.; Bruzzi, L. Natural radioactivity and radon exhalation in building materials used in Italian dwellings. *J. Environ. Radioact.* **2006**, *88*, 158–170. [CrossRef]
31. Mujahid, S.A.; Rahim, A.; Hussain, S.; Farooq, M. Measurements of natural radioactivity and radon exhalation rates from different brands of cement used in Pakistan. *Radiat. Prot. Dosim.* **2008**, *130*, 206–212. [CrossRef]
32. United Nations Scientific Committee on the Effects of Atomic Radiation. *Sources and Effects of Lonizing Radiation. Report of the United Nations Scientific Committee on the Effects of Atomic Radiation to the General Assembly*; United Nations: New York, NY, USA, 2000.
33. Organization for Economic Cooperation and Development (OECD). *Exposure to Radiation from Natural Radioactivity in Building Materials*; Report by a Group of Experts of the OECD Nuclear Energy Agency; OECD: Paris, France, 1979.
34. Varshney, R.; Mahur, A.K.; Sonkawade, R.G.; Suhail, M.A.; Azam, A.; Prasad, R. Evaluation and analysis of ^{226}Ra, ^{232}Th, ^{40}K and radon exhalation rate in various grey cements. *Indian J. Pure Appl. Phys.* **2010**, *48*, 473–477.
35. Ibraheem, A.A.; El-Taher, A.; Alruwaili, M.H. Assessment of natural radioactivity levels and radiation hazard indices for soil samples from Abha, Saudi Arabia. *Res. Phys.* **2018**, *11*, 325–330. [CrossRef]
36. Mehdizadeh, S.; Faghihi, R.; Sina, S. Natural radioactivity in building materials in Iran. *Nukleonika* **2011**, *56*, 363–368.

37. El-Taher, A. Gamma spectroscopic analysis and associated radiation hazards of building materials used in Egypt. *Radiat. Prot. Dosim.* **2010**, *138*, 166–173. [CrossRef] [PubMed]
38. Beretka, J.; Matthew, P.J. Natural radioactivity of Australian building materials, waste and by-products. *Health Phys.* **1985**, *48*, 87–95. [CrossRef]
39. Ademola, A.K.; Belloa, A.K.; Adejumobi, A.C. Determination of natural radioactivity and hazard in soil samples in and around gold mining area in Itagunmodi, south-western, Nigeria. *J. Rad. Res. Appl. Sci.* **2014**, *7*, 249–255. [CrossRef]
40. Ptiček Siroci, A.; Stanko, D.; Sakač, N.; Dogančic, D.; Trojko, T. Short-Term Measurement of Indoor Radon Concentration in Northern Croatia. *Appl. Sci.* **2020**, *10*, 2341. [CrossRef]

Article

Evaluation of the Radiological and Chemical Risk for Public Health from Flour Sample Investigation

Francesco Caridi [1,*], Giuseppe Acri [2,*], Alberto Belvedere [3], Vincenza Crupi [4], Maurizio D'Agostino [3], Santina Marguccio [3], Maurizio Messina [3], Giuseppe Paladini [1], Valentina Venuti [1,*] and Domenico Majolino [1]

[1] Dipartimento di Scienze Matematiche e Informatiche, Scienze Fisiche e Scienze Della Terra, Università degli Studi di Messina, V.le F. Stagno D'Alcontres, 31-98166 Messina, Italy; gpaladini@unime.it (G.P.); dmajolino@unime.it (D.M.)

[2] Dipartimento di Scienze Biomediche, Odontoiatriche, e Delle Immagini Morfologiche e Funzionali, Università degli Studi di Messina, c/o A.O.U. Policlinico "G. Martino" Via Consolare Valeria, 1-98125 Messina, Italy

[3] Agenzia Regionale Protezione Ambientale Calabria (ARPACal), Dipartimento di Reggio Calabria, via Troncovito SNC, 89135 Reggio Calabria, Italy; a.belvedere@arpacal.it (A.B.); m.dagostino@arpacal.it (M.D.); s.marguccio@arpacal.it (S.M.); m.messina@arpacal.it (M.M.)

[4] Dipartimento di Scienze Chimiche, Biologiche, Farmaceutiche e Ambientali, Università degli Studi di Messina, V.le F. Stagno D'Alcontres, 31-98166 Messina, Italy; vcrupi@unime.it

* Correspondence: fcaridi@unime.it (F.C.); gacri@unime.it (G.A.); vvenuti@unime.it (V.V.)

Citation: Caridi, F.; Acri, G.; Belvedere, A.; Crupi, V.; D'Agostino, M.; Marguccio, S.; Messina, M.; Paladini, G.; Venuti, V.; Majolino, D. Evaluation of the Radiological and Chemical Risk for Public Health from Flour Sample Investigation. *Appl. Sci.* **2021**, *11*, 3646. https://doi.org/10.3390/app11083646

Academic Editors: Elza Bontempi and Raffaele Marotta

Received: 22 March 2021
Accepted: 16 April 2021
Published: 18 April 2021

Publisher's Note: MDPI stays neutral with regard to jurisdictional claims in published maps and institutional affiliations.

Copyright: © 2021 by the authors. Licensee MDPI, Basel, Switzerland. This article is an open access article distributed under the terms and conditions of the Creative Commons Attribution (CC BY) license (https:// creativecommons.org/licenses/by/ 4.0/).

Abstract: Flour investigation, in terms of physical and chemical pollutants and mineral content, is of great interest, in view of its high consumption for nutritional purposes. In this study, eleven types of flour (five samples for each one), coming from large retailers and employed by people for different cooking food purposes, were investigated through high-purity germanium (HPGe) gamma spectrometry, in order to estimate natural (^{40}K) and anthropogenic (^{137}Cs) radioisotope specific activity and thus, to assess the radiological risk due to the flour ingestion. Inductively-coupled plasma mass spectrometry (ICP-MS) and inductively-coupled plasma emission spectroscopy (ICP-OES) were also employed to evaluate any possible heavy metal contamination and the mineral composition, and to perform multivariate statistical analysis to deduce the flour authenticity. The evaluation of dose levels due to flour ingestion was performed, for the age category higher than 17 years, taking into account the average yearly consumption in Italy and assuming this need to be satisfied from a single type of flour as a precaution. All obtained results are under the allowable level set by Italian legislation (1 mSv y^{-1}), thus excluding the risk of ionizing radiation effects on humans. As far as heavy metal contamination is concerned, Cd and Pb concentrations turned out to be lower than the threshold values, thus excluding their presence as pollutants. Finally, the multivariate statistical analysis allowed to unambiguously correlate flour samples to their botanical origin, according to their elemental concentrations.

Keywords: flour; natural and anthropogenic radioactivity; heavy metals contamination; mineral concentration; high-purity germanium gamma spectrometry; inductively-coupled plasma mass spectrometry; inductively-coupled plasma emission spectroscopy; effective dose; ingestion

1. Introduction

Natural radioactivity occurs in the environment due to the presence of cosmogenic and primordial radionuclides in the Earth's crust [1]. The first radionuclides were produced by cosmic-rays' interaction with atomic nuclei in the atmosphere, while primordial radioisotopes were generated by the nucleo-synthesis process during the Earth's formation [2]. Anthropogenic radioactivity is due to radionuclides, such as ^{137}Cs, mainly derived from nuclear accidents and global nuclear tests conducted between the mid-1940s and the 1980s [3].

Human beings can be exposed to ionizing radiations through external gamma rays, the inhalation of radon and other radioactive nuclides, and ingestion of radioisotopes through food and water [4]. In particular, for the latter, the natural radioactivity in food comes mainly from ^{40}K; uranium and thorium daughter products are usually present in traces [4–8].

The presence in food of anthropogenic radionuclides, as well as of heavy metals, is a significant issue, involving contamination of the food chain and harm to public health [9]. The danger associated to heavy metals is especially severe, because they are not chemically or biologically degradable [7]. Once released into the environment, mainly due to industrial or mining activities, they can remain for hundreds of years, polluting the soil and accumulating in plants and organic tissues. Moreover, their concentration in living beings increases as they move up the food chain [10].

Among all sources of the food chain contamination, pollution of the soil (from which foods are produced) due to the radioactive fall-out, residual muds, chemical fertilizers, and pesticides used in agriculture appear to be the most significant [11]. Having this contamination in so many different sources, there is a wide range of foods potentially contaminated by anthropic radionuclides and heavy metals, including products of plant origin, such as cereals, rice, wheat, edible roots, mushrooms, etc., as well as animal origin foods, such as fish, crustaceans, mollusks, etc. [6].

Flour is a plant origin foodstuff consumed daily by inhabitants of Italy [12]. The average annual consumption of flour is of about 85 kg per person, taking into consideration its use to produce bread, pizza, and baked goods, so the analysis of flour in terms of chemical and radioactive contamination is extremely important to safeguard human health [13]. The consumption of contaminated food increases the amount of radioactivity and chemical contamination inside an individual, and therefore increases the health risks associated with radiation exposure and heavy metal pollution. The exact health effects depend on the type and quantity of ingested radionuclides and metals [14].

Consumers have an increasing interest towards safe foodstuffs and protection [15,16]. For this reason, studies focused on food authenticity and traceability are in constant increase to preserve costumers against fraud and commercial disputes [17]. In particular, botanical and geographical origins of various foodstuffs have been verified by developing quali-/quantitative methods with subsequent multivariate analysis [18,19].

In this article, eleven different types of flour (five samples for each one), i.e., wholemeal, semolina, rice, coconut, almond, chestnut, Mallorcan wheat, oat, corn, rye, and pistachio, coming from large retailers and employed by people for different alimentary purposes, were analyzed. The analysis was to identify and quantify, on the one hand, natural (^{40}K) and artificial (^{137}Cs) gamma-emitting radionuclides with HPGe gamma spectrometry, in order to evaluate any possible radioactive contamination and estimate the effective dose due to the flour ingestion. On the other hand, heavy metals and minerals were estimated by ICP-MS and ICP-OES, in order to assess any possible chemical pollution, through a comparison between experimental concentrations and threshold limits set by Italian legislation [20], and to deduce the flour authenticity, correlating botanical origin, with chemical composition.

The schematic block diagram of Figure 1 summarizes what was performed in the present study.

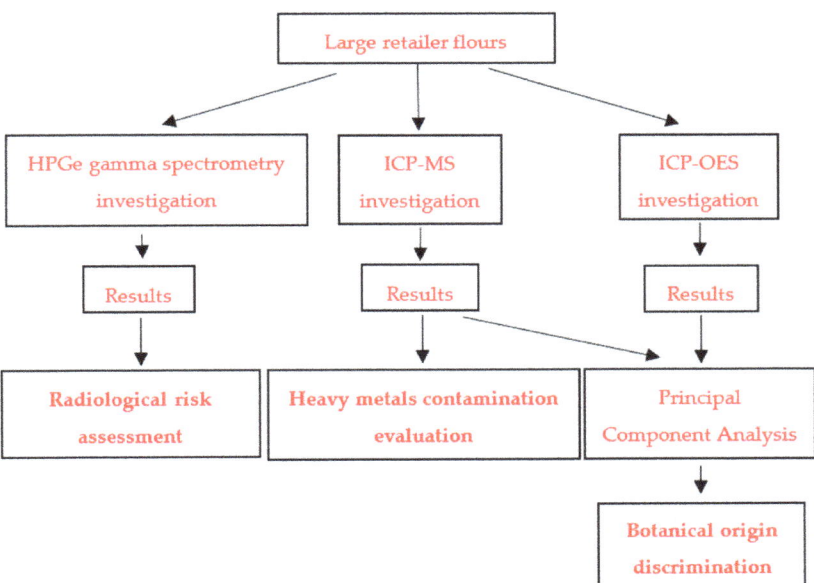

Figure 1. Schematic block diagram.

2. Materials and Methods

2.1. Sample Description

Five samples for each type of flour (wholemeal, semolina, rice, coconut, almond, chestnut, Mallorcan wheat, oat, corn, rye, and pistachio) were analyzed in this study.

Wholemeal flour is a powdered substance, a basic food ingredient derived from the stone grinding of the whole wheat grain. It has a dusty consistency and is aimed toward mixing with liquid and/or fatty ingredients (water, oil or eggs) to give rise to many doughs of typically Mediterranean origin, such as bread and pasta. The benefits for human health deriving from the use of this flour mainly consist of the reduction of cardiovascular risk and arteriosclerosis, overweightness and obesity, and diabetes risk, as well as anti-inflammatory action [21].

Semolina flour is produced by grinding durum wheat. It is typical of the southern regions of Italy, such as Puglia and Sicily, and other areas of the southern and eastern Mediterranean. Semolina flour is mainly used for the production of bread and pasta, but also for typical sweets. It can be used for biscuits and cakes, as well as pizzas and focaccias. It is rich in fibers, vitamins, and minerals, and has a relatively low glycemic index, thanks to the presence of complex carbohydrates. It also contains antioxidants, particularly beneficial in counteracting cellular aging. It is gluten-rich, though, and therefore not suitable for the diet of people with celiac disease [22,23].

Rice flour is obtained from the ground seeds of the *Oryza sativa* plant, i.e., rice. It is one of the most-used alternative flours in gluten-free cuisine, being suitable for the preparation of many recipes. As an example, it is excellent in the dough of biscuits, cakes, pies, pizzas, bread, and home-made pasta, because despite having a poor aptitude for leavening, it gives a pleasant crispness. This flour is recommended for cardiovascular health, due to its very low fat and cholesterol content, and low sodium content as well. It can be part of the diet of hypertensive patients. Rice flour also provides a high content of minerals, such as calcium and iron compounds, and vitamins [24].

Coconut flour is the powder obtained by grinding dried coconut pulp. It is a fairly versatile ingredient, so it can be used for different preparations, taking into account its tendency to absorb a lot of liquids. This means that the dishes containing it are and remain more humid than those made with other flours. For this reason, coconut flour is highly appreciated, especially in gluten-free cuisine, where the products tend to dry out very quickly. This kind of flour has several health benefits, since it is a rich source of fiber and protein, does not contain gluten, and has a low glycemic index [25].

Almond flour is a product easily obtained by grinding shelled and peeled almonds. It is used, as is, for the preparation of baked goods, especially sweets, or in combination with sugar for the preparation of the well-known almond and marzipan paste, rich ingredients of granita or artisanal ice cream, as well as malleable pastes for the decoration of cakes or biscuits. It is gluten-free, a source of vegetable protein, and contains magnesium and iron. It is also source of good fats, helps to reduce cholesterol, is a source of energy for the body, and has restorative properties [26].

Chestnut flour is the product of the drying and subsequent grinding of chestnuts. It is a very versatile ingredient, which can be useful for the preparation of both sweet and savory recipes. Beyond some traditional recipes, this flour is nowadays used quite rarely in the kitchen, while in the past it represented a staple food, replacing the fine wheat flour in poor cuisine. This flour is rich in proteins, fiber, and vitamins, and is useful for the intestinal bacterial flora and against cholesterol [27].

Mallorcan flour is obtained by the stone-grinding of Mallorca wheat, a variety of ancient Sicilian wheat produced from organic farming, and characterized by a low gluten index and by being a source of fiber. The stone grinding is followed by a sieving, which gives it its typical characteristics. This flour is used in the recipes of typical Sicilian sweets, wafers, white breads, and breadsticks. It has a lot of protein, mineral salts, and vitamins content, and excellent bread-making qualities. It is also an easily digestible food, with a low gluten content [28].

Oat flour is a product obtained by grinding the seeds of oats, preceded by the separation of the bran, which is rich in cellulose indigestible for the human body. With this flour, it is possible to prepare various types of food products, from appetizers to desserts, including bread, pizza, porridge, pasta, quiche, sweet cakes, and savory desserts. It is an excellent source of carbohydrates, fiber, protein, and fats, and is also rich in micronutrients, such as vitamins, minerals, and lecithin [29].

Corn flour is a dried cornmeal. It is a common staple food and is ground to coarse, medium, and fine consistency. This flour, obtained by grinding the seeds of *Zea mais*, is suitable for celiacs and used for the preparation of polenta and as a thickener. rich in carotenoids and has an antioxidant action. It is suitable for celiacs and is used for the preparation of polenta, and as a thickener. It is also used for the preparation of flans, Mexican tortillas, crèpes, pasta, and desserts [30].

Rye flour is produced by grinding the seeds of *Secale cereale*. It is rich in soluble fibers, but it tends to absorb large quantities of water, thus hindering baking. Rye-based dough is not very elastic and almost devoid of resistance, because it contains little gluten. The bread made from it is very dark, with a characteristic flavor. Rye flour can also be used for the preparation of sweets, biscuits or cakes, pasta, buns, and fried foods. From a nutritional point of view, it provides a high amount of energy [31].

Pistachio flour is obtained by chopping shelled pistachios until a not-too-fine grain is obtained, with an irregular shape and intense color. It is deal as a base for the preparation of cakes and desserts in general, sauces for pasta, and main courses of meat and fish. This flour is rich in mineral salts, is a source of vegetable proteins, contains B vitamins and carotenoids, is rich in antioxidants, protects eyesight, and prevents aging [32].

All the investigated types of flour are reported in Table 1, together with their identification code (ID) and typology.

Table 1. List of investigated types of flour, together with their identification code (ID) and typology.

Sample ID	Sample Typology
S1	Wholemeal flour
S2	Semolina flour
S3	Rice flour
S4	Coconut flour
S5	Almond flour
S6	Chestnut flour
S7	Mallorcan wheat flour
S8	Oat flour
S9	Corn flour
S10	Rye flour
S11	Pistachio flour

2.2. Gamma Spectrometry Analysis and Radiological Hazard Effects Assessment

For the gamma spectrometry investigations, samples were packed in a 20 mL polyethylene plastic vial to reach a geometry homogeneity around the detector; then, the respective net weights were measured and recorded. After this preparation step, they were counted for 70,000 s, and spectra were analyzed in order to obtain the activity concentration of ^{137}Cs and ^{40}K, through the evaluation of their γ-lines at 661.66 keV and 1460.81 keV, respectively. A positively-biased Ortec HPGe detector (GEM) (FWHM of 1.85 keV; peak-to-Compton ratio of 64:1; relative efficiency of 40% at the 1.33 MeV ^{60}Co γ-line), placed inside lead wells to shield the background radiation environment, was employed for the analysis. A photo of the experimental setup is reported in Figure 2.

Figure 2. HPGe gamma spectrometry setup.

A multipeak Marinelli geometry gamma source (AK-5901) of 1 L capacity, covering the energy range 59.54–1836 keV, customized to reproduce the exact geometries of samples in a water-equivalent epoxy resin matrix, was employed for efficiency and energy calibrations. The ANGLE 4 code was employed for the efficiency transfer factor calculations to the 20 mL vial sample holder geometry [33]. For data acquisition and analysis, Gamma Vision (Ortec) software was used [34].

The activity concentration (C) of each detected radionuclide was calculated according to the following [35,36]:

$$C = \frac{N_E}{\varepsilon_E t \gamma_d M} \quad (1)$$

where N_E indicates the net area of the radioisotope photopeak; ε_E and γ_d are the efficiency and yield of the photopeak, respectively; M is the mass sample (g); and t is the lifetime (s).

The resulting uncertainty of each measurement, with coverage factor $k = 2$, was calculated, taking into account the uncertainty of the counting estimation, of the calibration source, of the efficiency calibration, of the background subtraction, and of the γ-branching ratio [37].

The quality of the gamma spectrometry experimental results was certified by the Italian Accreditation Body (ACCREDIA) [38].

This implies the continued verification (with annual periodicity) of the maintenance of the gamma spectrometry method performance characteristics.

The repeatability of the results, in particular, is verified over time with the double test method. A certified reference material (also containing the radionuclides ^{40}K and ^{137}Cs) is analyzed twice, with the active concentration of the radionuclide of interest defined as x_1 (first measurement) and x_2 (second measurement). The probability level $p = 0.95$ is considered. The following formula is applied:

$$|x_1 - x_2| \leq \sqrt{2} \cdot s_r \cdot t$$

where t is the Student variable, and s_r is the standard deviation of repeatability obtained in the validation phase.

To evaluate radiological hazard effects, the effective dose for flour ingestion was calculated [39]:

$$D_{ing}\left(\frac{\text{Sv}}{\text{y}}\right) = h_{ing,K-40} \times J_{ing,K-40} \qquad (2)$$

where $h_{ing,K-40}$ is the coefficient of the effective dose for the insertion unit for ingestion of ^{40}K (Sv Bq^{-1}), and $J_{ing,K-40}$ is the intake of ^{40}K (Bq year^{-1}) [40]. The latter value is obtained by multiplying the yearly flour consumption for the mean activity concentration of the investigated radionuclide experimentally measured.

2.3. ICP-MS and ICP-OES Analysis

For the analysis, approximately 0.5–1.0 g of sample, together with 5 mL of ultrapure (for trace analysis) HNO$_3$ (67–69%) and 1 mL of hydrogen peroxide (H$_2$O$_2$), as well as 5 mL of ultrapure water, were directly introduced into a 100 mL TFM vessel. Acid digestion was performed using a Milestone microwave system, Ethos 1, in four steps: 5 min at 1000 W and 85 °C, 10 min at 1000 W and 145 °C, 4 min at 1000 W and 180 °C, 15 min at 1000 W, and cooling [41]. The mixture was filtered and filled up to 100 mL with distilled H$_2$O.

ICP-MS calibration solutions for the analytes measured at 1, 5, 10, 100, and 200 ppb for As, Be, Cd, Cu, Pb, and Zn, as well as at 0.2, 0.5, 1.0, 2.0, and 3.0 ppb for Hg, were prepared by opportune dilutions of two different reference materials (o2si Multi-element aqueous RM 100 mL 20 μg mL^{-1}, and o2si Single-element Mercury Hg aqueous RM 100 mL 1007 μg mL^{-1}) in 0.5 % (v/v) HNO$_3$ and 0.5% (v/v) HCl [42]. Internal standardization was applied, with an internal standard at 20 ppb, added on-line via a T-piece before the nebulizer. For the ICP-MS measurements a Thermo Scientific iCAP Qc ICP-MS was used [43] (see Figure 3).

The sample introduction system consisted of a cooled (3 °C) Peltier, a baffled cyclonic spray chamber, a PFA nebulizer, and a quartz torch with a 2.5 mm i.d. removable quartz injector. The instrument operated in a single collision cell mode, with kinetic energy discrimination (KED), using pure He as collision gas. All samples were presented for analysis using a Cetac ASX-520. The iCAP Qc ICP-MS operated in a single KED mode using 1550 W forward power, 0.98 L min^{-1} nebulizer gas, 0.8 L min^{-1} auxiliary gas, 14.0 L min^{-1} cool gas flow, 4.5 mL min^{-1} He collision cell gas, 45 s each for sample uptake/wash time, optimized dwell times per analyte (0.1 s, except 0.5 s for As), one point per peak, and three repeats per sample.

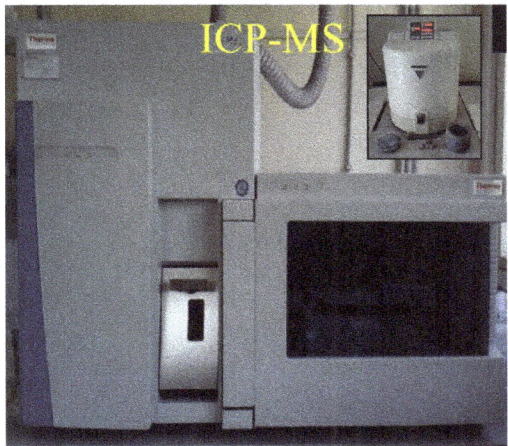

Figure 3. ICP-MS experimental setup.

For the ICP-OES measurements, a Perkin Elmer Optima 2100 DV was employed [44] (see Figure 4).

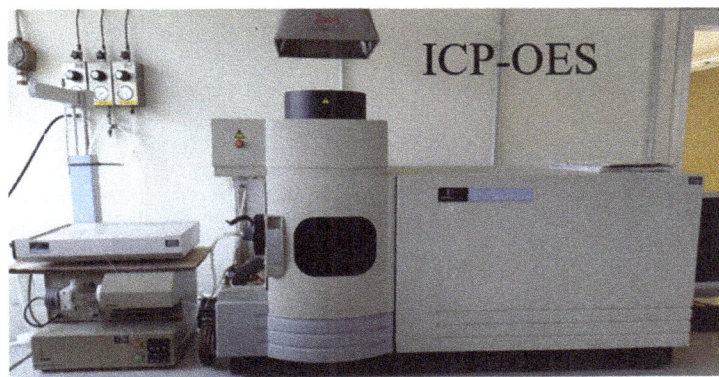

Figure 4. ICP-OES experimental setup.

The operating conditions were 1450 W RF power, 15 L min^{-1} plasma gas flow rate, 0.2 L min^{-1} auxiliary gas flow rate, 0.8 L min^{-1} nebulizer gas flow rate, 1.5 L min^{-1} sample flow rate, 50 s read delay, CCD detector, and nitrogen purge gas, with 589.592 nm (Na), 285.213 nm (Mg), 317.933 nm (Ca) wavelengths.

2.4. Multivariate Statistical Analysis

The Microcal Origin software for Windows (Northampton, MA, United States, ver. 2018) was used for all statistical calculations [45]. A statistical analysis was conducted, starting on a multivariate matrix, where variables were the average concentrations of detected elements (P, Mg, Ca, Na, Fe, Zn, Mn, Cu, Ni), and the cases were the eleven analyzed flour samples.

With the aim of unambiguously correlating flour samples to their botanical origin, according to their elemental concentrations, an exploratory method (principal components analysis, PCA) was performed. It ensures the reduction of the data dimensionality, whereas the combinations of variables identified by the PCs provide the greatest contribution to sample variability. Before the elaboration, the appropriateness of the data set was preliminarily checked by the Bartlett test (sphericity test), as already reported in a previous work [46].

3. Results and Discussion

3.1. Radioactivity Analysis

The activity concentration of ^{40}K in the investigated flour samples, as calculated by Equation (1), is reported in Table 2 as mean value ± standard deviation for each type of flour.

Table 2. The activity concentration (mean value ± standard deviation) of ^{40}K and ^{137}Cs in the analyzed flour samples.

Sample ID	Activity Concentration (Bq kg^{-1})	
	^{40}K	^{137}Cs
S1	285 ± 46	<4.1
S2	144 ± 26	<3.9
S3	155 ± 30	<5.1
S4	345 ± 51	<9.8
S5	248 ± 40	<2.9
S6	443 ± 68	<2.6
S7	70 ± 15	<2.2
S8	152 ± 29	<6.7
S9	99 ± 19	<5.1
S10	300 ± 41	<6.4
S11	370 ± 56	<7.2

The highest value refers to chestnut flour. This may reasonably reflect the different composition of the two investigated flours, reported to have 847 mg and 171 mg of potassium per 100 g of sample [47,48], respectively.

Regarding ^{137}Cs, its activity concentration in all analyzed samples, reported in Table 2, turned out to be lower than the minimum detectable activity value, thus excluding an anthropogenic radioactive contamination of the investigated samples.

3.2. The Annual Effective Dose for Food Ingestion

Table 3 reports the estimation of the annual effective dose due to the ingestion of investigated samples, D_{ing}, as calculated by Equation (2), for the age category higher than 17 years.

Table 3. Annual effective dose due to the ingestion of investigated samples, D_{ing}, for the age category higher than 17 years, together with its percentage with respect to worldwide average natural dose to humans (2.4 mSv y^{-1}).

Sample ID	D_{ing} (mSv y^{-1})	Percentage (%) with Respect to Worldwide Average Natural dose to Humans (2.4 mSv y^{-1})
S1	0.15	6.2
S2	0.07	2.9
S3	0.08	3.3
S4	0.18	7.5
S5	0.13	5.4
S6	0.23	9.6
S7	0.04	1.6
S8	0.08	3.3
S9	0.05	2.1
S10	0.15	6.2
S11	0.19	7.9

Reported values take into account the average yearly consumption of flour in Italy, assumed to be of about 85 kg, taking into consideration its use to produce bread, pizza, and baked goods [49,50], making the hypothesis that this need was satisfied from a single type of flour. For each type of investigated flour, Table 3 also shows the percentage values of the aforementioned doses with respect to the total (external + internal) natural radioactivity value for humans, expressed in terms of effective dose, equal to 2.4 mSv y^{-1} [51]. Noteworthily, the calculated annual effective doses for all investigated flour types were under the threshold level of 1 mSv y^{-1} imposed by the legislation [51] (see Figure 5).

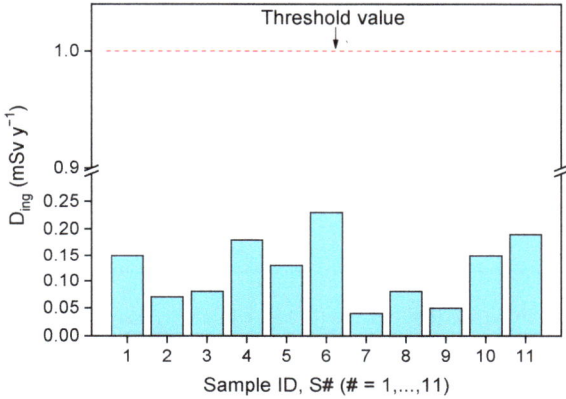

Figure 5. D_{ing} for all investigated samples, compared to the threshold level imposed by legislation.

Therefore, no risk to humans due to ionizing radiations can be associated with the flour ingestion.

3.3. Heavy Metal Analysis

Table 4 reports Cd and Pb mean concentrations (mg kg^{-1}) for each type of investigated flour, as obtained through ICP-MS analysis.

Table 4. Cd and Pb mean concentrations in investigated flour samples.

	Heavy Metal Concentration (mg kg^{-1})	
Sample ID	**Cd**	**Pb**
S1	0.010	0.17
S2	0.010	0.08
S3	0.020	0.08
S4	0.020	0.11
S5	0.003	0.08
S6	0.070	0.10
S7	0.010	0.15
S8	0.030	0.17
S9	0.004	0.18
S10	0.010	0.07
S11	0.010	0.08
Contamination threshold EU Reg. 1881/06	0.100–0.200	0.20

As can be seen from the table, the experimental values are lower than the contamination thresholds established by the commission regulations [52]. Therefore, Cd and Pb cannot be considered as pollutants, and are generally expected not to cause severe effects on human health.

3.4. Elemental and Chemometric Analysis

Table 5 reports the elemental composition of the analyzed flour samples.

Table 5. Average mineral content, determined by ICP-OES and ICP-MS, for each investigated flour type.

Sample ID	Mineral Concentration (mg kg^{-1})								
	P	Mg	Ca	Na	Fe	Zn	Mn	Cu	Ni
S1	3652	1159	357	41	133	36	36	7	0.6
S2	1439	478	227	42	17	14	7	4	0.4
S3	1045	240	54	1	5	12	8	3	0.5
S4	2173	2976	8318	118	17	14	6	6	0.7
S5	2204	1105	1204	64	20	16	6	7	0.9
S6	1015	505	573	4607	19	8	28	6	1.4
S7	808	172	272	78	18	8	6	2	0.5
S8	2610	1140	864	40	44	24	38	6	2.5
S9	717	1106	353	97	10	6	1	1	0.2
S10	4497	1247	1161	132	29	26	9	11	0.9
S11	4413	722	827	51	29	26	9	11	1.0

In particular, macro- (P, Mg, Ca) and micro-inorganic minerals (Na, Fe, Zn, Mn, Cu, Ni) determined by ICP-OES and ICP-MS were tabulated; their average concentrations were in good agreement with values reported in literature [53].

As reported [48], the presence of inorganic minerals in flour samples is strictly correlated with the plant or fruit of origin. In order to unambiguously establish this correlation, PCA was conducted, considering nine variables and eleven cases. Preliminarily, the measure of sampling adequacy and Bartlett's test of sphericity were carried out to verify the suitability of the data for factor analysis. Test results suggest that the correlation matrix was factored and appropriate for PCA. By using the Kaiser criterion, two principal components (PC1 and PC2) with eigenvalues exceeding one were extracted, representing the 40.57% and 23.72% of total variance, respectively.

PCA results reveal the presence of four different groups, reported in the bi-plot of Figure 6.

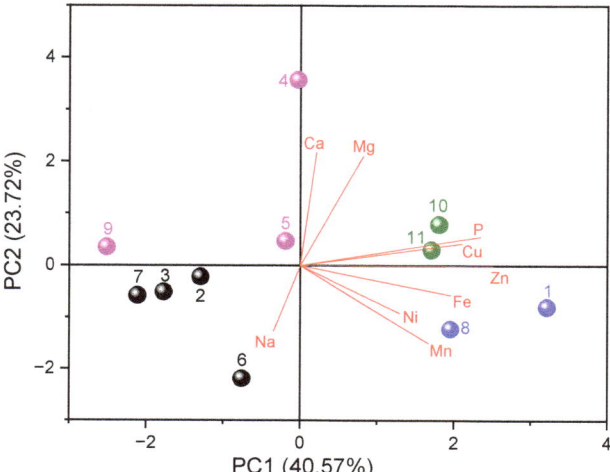

Figure 6. Results of the PCA (bi-plot) for all analyzed samples.

The groups appear to be comparable to each other in terms of macro- and micro-element concentration. Specifically, four groups were recognized: group I (containing samples S10 and S11, green points) and IV (containing samples S1 and S8, blue points) refer to flours that turned out to be positively correlated, as far as PC1 is concerned, with Ca, Mg, P, Cu, Zn, Fe, Ni, and Mn, and negatively correlated with Na. Regarding PC2, flours in group I exhibited a positive correlation with values of Cu, P, Mg, and Ca contents, and a negative correlation with other variables. The opposite occurred for flours in group IV. Continuing on, group II (containing samples S4, S5, and S9, purple points) and III (containing samples S2, S3, S6, and S7, black points) refers to flours that turned out to be negatively correlated, as far as PC1 is concerned, with Ca, Mg, P, Cu, Zn, Fe, Ni, and Mn, and positively correlated with Na. Regarding PC2, flours in group II exhibited a positive correlation with the values of the Cu, P, Mg, and Ca contents, and a negative correlation with other variables. The opposite occurs for flours in group III.

The differences in the average concentrations of P, Mg, Ca, Na, Fe, Zn, Mn, Cu, and Ni revealed among the identified groups strictly depend on the compositional features of the plant or fruit from which the analyzed flours derive. In the light of this, the obtained results could potentially be helpful to the producers to warn against food fraud, ensure flour quality, and inform the customers about sensitive parameters to be used potentially in the traceability process, in order to build up several fingerprints able to ensure the healthy effects of these products.

4. Conclusions

In this article, radiation levels, metals contamination, and inorganic mineral content in flours were measured; this is extremely important, due to their high consumption by the population for nutritional use.

The specific activity of the main natural radionuclide present in flour, ^{40}K, was measured using HpGe gamma spectrometry, with the aim of estimating the health risk for the age category higher than 17 years by the assessment of the effective dose due to flour ingestion. The coefficient of the effective dose for ingestion reported by Italian Legislative Decree 101/20 was employed. The estimation of the annual effective dose was found to be in the range 0.04–0.23 mSv y^{-1}, about 1.6–9.6% of the total natural radioactivity value for humans (2.4 mSv y^{-1}) and under the threshold level (1 mSv y^{-1}), thus excluding the risk of ionizing radiation effects on humans. The ^{137}Cs activity concentration was lower than the minimum detectable activity value for all analyzed samples, thus excluding its presence as pollutant.

As far as the heavy metal (Cd and Pb) concentration is concerned, it was lower than the contamination threshold value, thus excluding their presence as contaminants.

The PCA multivariate statistical analysis, performed starting from the inorganic minerals content in the investigated samples, showed how it is possible to discriminate among them, with a strict dependance on the compositional features of the plant or fruit from which the analyzed flours derive, thus representing a powerful tool to guarantee the product authenticity to the consumers.

Author Contributions: Conceptualization, F.C. and V.V.; methodology, F.C. and V.C.; validation, D.M.; formal analysis, G.A., M.D., A.B., S.M. and M.M.; investigation, F.C., G.A., G.P. and V.V.; resources, F.C., V.C. and D.M.; data curation, F.C.; writing—original draft preparation, F.C.; supervision, D.M., V.C. and V.V. All authors have read and agreed to the published version of the manuscript.

Funding: This research received no external funding.

Institutional Review Board Statement: Not applicable.

Informed Consent Statement: Not applicable.

Data Availability Statement: Not applicable.

Conflicts of Interest: The authors declare no conflict of interest.

References

1. Caridi, F.; Marguccio, S.; D'Agostino, M.; Belvedere, A.; Belmusto, G. Natural radioactivity and metal contamination of river sediments in the Calabria region, south of Italy. *Eur. Phys. J. Plus* **2016**, *131*, 1–10. [CrossRef]
2. Caridi, F.; D'Agostino, M.; Marguccio, S.; Belvedere, A.; Belmusto, G.; Marcianò, G.; Sabatino, G.; Mottese, A. Radioactivity, granulometric and elemental analysis of river sediments samples from the coast of Calabria, south of Italy. *Eur. Phys. J. Plus* **2016**, *131*, 1–8. [CrossRef]
3. Ravisankar, R.; Chandrasekaran, A.; Vijayagopal, P.; Venkatraman, B.; Senthilkumar, G.; Eswaran, P.; Rajalakshmi, A. Natural radioactivity in soil samples of Yelagiri Hills, Tamil Nadu, India and the associated radiation hazards. *Radiat. Phys. Chem.* **2012**, *81*, 1789–1795. [CrossRef]
4. Fadlalla, H.E. Radioactivity Levels of Basic Foodstuffs Anddose Estimates in Sudan. Master's Thesis, University of Khartoum, Khartoum, Sudan, 2005; p. 60.
5. Mlwilo, N.A.; Mohammed, N.K.; Spyrou, N.M. Radioactivity levels of staple foodstuffs and dose estimates for most of the Tanzanian population. *J. Radiol. Prot.* **2007**, *27*, 471–480. [CrossRef]
6. Caridi, F.; Messina, M.; Belvedere, A.; D'Agostino, M.; Marguccio, S.; Settineri, L.; Belmusto, G. Food Salt Characterization in Terms of Radioactivity and Metals Contamination. *Appl. Sci.* **2019**, *9*, 2882. [CrossRef]
7. Ramachandran, T.; Mishra, U. Measurement of natural radioactivity levels in Indian foodstuffs by gamma spectrometry. *Int. J. Radiat. Appl. Instrum.* **1989**, *40*, 723–726. [CrossRef]
8. Júnior, J.A.S.; Cardoso, J.J.R.F.; Silva, C.M. Radioactivity levels of basic foodstuffs and dose estimates in Sudan. *J. Radioanal. Nucl. Chem.* **2006**, *269*, 451–455. [CrossRef]
9. Caridi, F.; Pappaterra, D.; Belmusto, G.; Messina, M.; Belvedere, A.; D'Agostino, M.; Settineri, L.; Agostino, D. Radioactivity and Heavy Metals Concentration in Italian (Calabrian) DOC Wines. *Appl. Sci.* **2019**, *9*, 4584. [CrossRef]
10. Albergamo, A.; Bua, G.D.; Rotondo, A.; Bartolomeo, G.; Annuario, G.; Costa, R.; Dugo, G. Transfer of major and trace elements along the "farm-to-fork" chain of different whole grain products. *J. Food Compos. Anal.* **2018**, *66*, 212–220. [CrossRef]
11. Di Bella, G.; Naccari, C.; Bua, G.D.; Rastrelli, L.; Lo Turco, V.; Potortì, A.G.; Dugo, G. Mineral composition of some varieties of beans from Mediterranean and Tropical areas. *Int. J. Food Sci. Nutr.* **2016**, *67*, 239–248. [CrossRef]
12. Sette, S.; D'Addezio, L.; Piccinelli, R.; Hopkins, S.; Le Donne, C.; Ferrari, M.; Mistura, L.; Turrini, A. Intakes of whole grain in an Italian sample of children, adolescents and adults. *Eur. J. Nutr.* **2015**, *56*, 521–533. [CrossRef]
13. Dona, A.; Dourakis, S.; Papadimitropoulos, B.; Maravelias, C.; Koutselinis, A. Flour Contamination as a Source of Lead Intoxication. *J. Toxicol. Clin. Toxicol.* **1999**, *37*, 109–112. [CrossRef]
14. Caridi, F.; Marguccio, S.; Belvedere, A.; D'Agostino, M.; Belmusto, G. The Natural Radioactivity in Food: A Comparison Between Different Feeding Regimes. *Curr. Nutr. Food Sci.* **2019**, *15*, 493–499. [CrossRef]
15. Mottese, A.F.; Fede, M.R.; Caridi, F.; Sabatino, G.; Marcianò, G.; Ravenda, P.; Gaetano, A.D.; Dugo, G. Fingerprint of PGI Mantova Cucumis melo by ICP-MS and Chemometric Analysis. *Curr. Nutr. Food Sci.* **2020**, *17*, 94–104. [CrossRef]
16. Acri, G.; Sansotta, C.; Ruello, E.V.; Denaro, L.; Salmeri, F.M.; Testagrossa, B. The Use of Time Domain NMR in Food Analysis: A Review. *Curr. Nutr. Food Sci.* **2020**, *16*, 1–9. [CrossRef]
17. Mottese, A.F.; Fede, M.R.; Caridi, F.; Sabatino, G.; Marcianò, G.; Calabrese, G.; Albergamo, A.; Dugo, G. Chemometrics and innovative multidimensional data analysis (MDA) based on multi-element screening to protect the Italian porcino (Boletus sect. Boletus) from fraud. *Food Control* **2020**, *110*, 107004. [CrossRef]
18. Caridi, F.; D'Agostino, M.; Belvedere, A.; Mottese, A.F. Multi-element Analysis and Geographical Origin Classification of Italian (Calabrian) Wines. *Curr. Nutr. Food Sci.* **2020**, *16*, 1259–1264. [CrossRef]
19. Acri, G.; Testagrossa, B.; Vermiglio, G. FT-NIR analysis of different garlic cultivars. *J. Food Meas. Charact.* **2015**, *10*, 127–136. [CrossRef]
20. Italian Legislation D.Lgs. 101/20. Available online: http://www.gminternational.net/en/legislative-decree-101-of-31-07-20-transposes-in-italy-the-directive-2013-597-euratom-on-the-controls-on-ionizing-radiation-which-is-the-impact/ (accessed on 18 April 2021).
21. Gómez, M.; Gutkoski, L.C.; Bravo-Núñez, Á. Understanding whole-wheat flour and its effect in breads: A review. *Compr. Rev. Food Sci. Food Saf.* **2020**, *19*, 3241–3265. [CrossRef]
22. Jafarzadeh, S.; Alias, A.K.; Ariffin, F.; Mahmud, S. Physico-mechanical and microstructural properties of semolina flour films as influenced by different sorbitol/glycerol concentrations. *Int. J. Food Prop.* **2018**, *21*, 983–995. [CrossRef]
23. Panasiti, I.; Costa, S.; Caminiti, L.; Crisafulli, G.; Pajno, G.B.; Pellegrino, S.; Testagrossa, B.; Acri, G. Association of wheat Allergy and Coeliac Disease Through Pediatric and Adult Age: A Review of Literature. *Curr. Nutr. Food Sci.* **2020**, *16*, 1–6. [CrossRef]
24. Wu, T.; Wang, L.; Li, Y.; Qian, H.; Liu, L.; Tong, L.; Zhou, X.; Wang, L.; Zhou, S. Effect of milling methods on the properties of rice flour and gluten-free rice bread. *LWT* **2019**, *108*, 137–144. [CrossRef]
25. Prasanna Priyantha Gunathilake, K.D.; Yalegama, C.; Kumara, A.A.N. Use of coconut flour as a source of protein and dietary fiber in wheat bread. *Asian J. Food Agro-Ind.* **2009**, *2*, 382–391.
26. Martínez, M.L.; Marín, M.A.; Gili, R.D.; Penci, M.C.; Ribotta, P.D. Effect of defatted almond flour on cooking, chemical and sensorial properties of gluten-free fresh pasta. *Int. J. Food Sci. Technol.* **2017**, *52*, 2148–2155. [CrossRef]
27. Littardi, P.; Paciulli, M.; Carini, E.; Rinaldi, M.; Rodolfi, M.; Chiavaro, E. Quality evaluation of chestnut flour addition on fresh pasta. *LWT* **2020**, *126*, 109303. [CrossRef]

28. Ciudad-Mulero, M.; Barros, L.; Fernandes, A.; Ferreira, I.C.F.R.; Callejo, M.; Matallana-González, M.; Fernández-Ruiz, V.; Morales, P.; Carrillo, J.M. Potential Health Claims of Durum and Bread Wheat Flours as Functional Ingredients. *Nutrients* **2020**, *12*, 504. [CrossRef]
29. Rasane, P.; Jha, A.; Sabikhi, L.; Kumar, A.; Unnikrishnan, V.S. Nutritional advantages of oats and opportunities for its processing as value added foods—A review. *J. Food Sci. Technol.* **2013**, *52*, 662–675. [CrossRef] [PubMed]
30. Gwirtz, J.A.; Garcia-Casal, M.N. Processing maize flour and corn meal food products. *Ann. N. Y. Acad. Sci. USA* **2013**, *1312*, 66–75. [CrossRef]
31. Stępniewska, S.; Słowik, E.; Cacak-Pietrzak, G.; Romankiewicz, D.; Szafrańska, A.; Dziki, D. Prediction of rye flour baking quality based on parameters of swelling curve. *Eur. Food Res. Technol.* **2017**, *244*, 989–997. [CrossRef]
32. Martínez, M.L.; Fabani, M.P.; Baroni, M.V.; Huaman, R.N.M.; Ighani, M.; Maestri, D.M.; Wunderlin, D.; Tapia, A.; Feresin, G.E. Argentinian pistachio oil and flour: A potential novel approach of pistachio nut utilization. *J. Food Sci. Technol.* **2016**, *53*, 2260–2269. [CrossRef]
33. Caridi, F.; D'Agostino, M.; Belvedere, A.; Marguccio, S.; Belmusto, G. Radon radioactivity in groundwater from the Calabria region, south of Italy. *J. Instrum.* **2016**, *11*, P05012. [CrossRef]
34. Caridi, F.; Marguccio, S.; Durante, G.; Trozzo, R.; Fullone, F.; Belvedere, A.; D'Agostino, M.; Belmusto, G. Natural radioactivity measurements and dosimetric evaluations in soil samples with a high content of NORM. *Eur. Phys. J. Plus* **2017**, *132*, 56. [CrossRef]
35. Caridi, F.; Santangelo, S.; Faggio, G.; Gnisci, A.; Messina, G.; Belmusto, G. Compositional and Mineralogical Analysis of Marine Sediments from Calabrian Selected Areas, Southern Italy. *Int. J. Environ. Res.* **2019**, *13*, 571–580. [CrossRef]
36. Caridi, F.; Testagrossa, B.; Acri, G. Elemental composition and natural radioactivity of refractory materials. *Environ. Earth Sci.* **2021**, *80*, 1–6. [CrossRef]
37. Caridi, F.; Messina, M.; D'Agostino, M. An investigation about natural radioactivity, hydrochemistry, and metal pollution in groundwater from Calabrian selected areas, southern Italy. *Environ. Earth Sci.* **2017**, *76*, 668. [CrossRef]
38. Caridi, F.; D'Agostino, M.; Belvedere, A. Radioactivity in Calabrian (Southern Italy) Wild Boar Meat. *Appl. Sci.* **2020**, *10*, 3580. [CrossRef]
39. Caridi, F.; Belvedere, A.; Agostino, M.D.; Marguccio, S.; Marino, G.; Messina, M.; Belmusto, G. An investigation on airborne particulate radioactivity, heavy metals and polycyclic aromatic hydrocarbons composition in Calabrian selected sites, Southern Italy. *Indian J. Environ. Prot.* **2019**, *39*, 321–326.
40. Caridi, F.; D'Agostino, M. Evaluation of drinking water radioactivity content and radiological risk assessment: A new methodological approach. *J. Instrum.* **2020**, *15*, P10016. [CrossRef]
41. Hassan, N.M.; Rasmussen, P.E.; Dabek-Zlotorzynska, E.; Celo, V.; Chen, H. Analysis of Environmental Samples Using Microwave-Assisted Acid Digestion and Inductively Coupled Plasma Mass Spectrometry: Maximizing Total Element Recoveries. *Water Air Soil Pollut.* **2007**, *178*, 323–334. [CrossRef]
42. Bednar, A.; Kirgan, R.; Jones, W. Comparison of standard and reaction cell inductively coupled plasma mass spectrometry in the determination of chromium and selenium species by HPLC–ICP–MS. *Anal. Chim. Acta* **2009**, *632*, 27–34. [CrossRef]
43. Thermo Fisher iCAP Q Operating Manual. Available online: https://vdocuments.mx/icap-q-operating-manual-thermo-fisher-scientific-us-assistance-thermo-fisher-scientific.html (accessed on 18 April 2021).
44. *Perkin Elmer Optima 2100 DV ICP-OES Spectrometer User Manual*; Perkin Elmer: Waltham, MA, USA, 2012.
45. Seifert, E. OriginPro 9.1: Scientific Data Analysis and Graphing Software—Software Review. *J. Chem. Inf. Model.* **2014**, *54*, 1552. [CrossRef] [PubMed]
46. Caridi, F.; Di Bella, M.; Sabatino, G.; Belmusto, G.; Fede, M.R.; Romano, D.; Italiano, F.; Mottese, A.F. Assessment of Natural Radioactivity and Radiological Risks in River Sediments from Calabria (Southern Italy). *Appl. Sci.* **2021**, *11*, 1729. [CrossRef]
47. Dulger, D.; Mete, M. Chestnut flour and applications of utilization. *Int. J. Food Eng. Res.* **2017**, *3*, 9–16.
48. Araujo, R.G.O.; Macedo, S.M.; Korn, M.D.G.A.; Pimentel, M.F.; Bruns, R.E.; Ferreira, S.L.C. Mineral composition of wheat flour consumed in Brazilian cities. *J. Braz. Chem. Soc.* **2008**, *19*, 935–942. [CrossRef]
49. *Italmopa I Nuovi Trend del Consumo di Pane in Italia*; Fiera Internazionale Sigep & AB-Tech: Rimini, Italy, 2020.
50. Frazzoli, R. I consumi alimentari extradomestici. *Ind. Aliment.* **2007**, *46*, 481–482.
51. United Nations Scientific Committee on the Effects of Atomic Radiation. *Sources and Effects of Ionizing Radiation: Report to the General Assembly, with Scientific Annexes*; UNSCEAR: Vienna, Austria, 2000; Volume I, ISBN 92-1-142238-8.
52. Commission Regulation (EC) N. 1881/06. 2006. Available online: http://extwprlegs1.fao.org/docs/pdf/eur68134.pdf (accessed on 18 April 2021).
53. Morris, E.D. Mineral Elements in Wheat, Flour, and Bread. *Nutr. Rev.* **2009**, *22*, 223. [CrossRef]

Article

Assessment of Natural Radioactivity and Radiological Risks in River Sediments from Calabria (Southern Italy)

Francesco Caridi [1,*], Marcella Di Bella [2,3], Giuseppe Sabatino [1], Giovanna Belmusto [4], Maria Rita Fede [5], Davide Romano [1,2], Francesco Italiano [2] and Antonio Francesco Mottese [1]

[1] Department of Mathematics and Informatics, Physics and Earth Sciences (MIFT), University of Messina, Viale F. Stagno d'Alcontres 31, 98166 Messina, Italy; gsabatino@unime.it (G.S.); davide.romano@unime.it (D.R.); amottese@unime.it (A.F.M.)
[2] Istituto Nazionale di Geofisica e Vulcanologia (INGV), Sezione di Palermo, Via Ugo La Malfa 153, 90146 Palermo and Milazzo Office, Via dei Mille 46, 98057 Milazzo (ME), Italy; mdibella@unime.it (M.D.B.); francesco.italiano@ingv.it (F.I.)
[3] Stazione Zoologica Anton Dohrn (SZN), Villa Comunale, 80121 Napoli, Italy
[4] Environmental Protection Agency of Calabria, Italy (ARPACal), Department of Reggio Calabria, Via Troncovito SNC, 89135 Reggio Calabria, Italy; gbelmusto@arpacal.it
[5] Department of Biomedical and Dental Sciences and Morphofunctional Imaging SASTAS Section, University of Messina, Viale Annunziata, 98168 Messina, Italy; f_mariarita@yahoo.it
* Correspondence: fcaridi@unime.it

Citation: Caridi, F.; Di Bella, M.; Sabatino, G.; Belmusto, G.; Fede, M.R.; Romano, D.; Italiano, F.; Mottese, A.F. Assessment of Natural Radioactivity and Radiological Risks in River Sediments from Calabria (Southern Italy). *Appl. Sci.* **2021**, *11*, 1729. https://doi.org/10.3390/app11041729

Academic Editor: Richard Kouzes

Received: 20 January 2021
Accepted: 11 February 2021
Published: 15 February 2021

Publisher's Note: MDPI stays neutral with regard to jurisdictional claims in published maps and institutional affiliations.

Copyright: © 2021 by the authors. Licensee MDPI, Basel, Switzerland. This article is an open access article distributed under the terms and conditions of the Creative Commons Attribution (CC BY) license (https://creativecommons.org/licenses/by/4.0/).

Abstract: This study was developed to carry out a comprehensive radiological assessment of natural radioactivity for river sediment samples from Calabria, southern Italy, and to define a baseline background for the area on a radiation map. In the studied area, elevated levels of natural radionuclides are expected, due to the outcropping acidic intrusive and metamorphic rocks from which the radioactive elements derive. To identify and quantify the natural radioisotopes, ninety river sediment samples from nine selected coastal sampling points (ten samples for each point) were collected as representative of the Ionian and the Tyrrhenian coastline of Calabria. The samples were analyzed using a gamma ray spectrometer equipped with a high-purity germanium (HPGe) detector. The values of mean activity concentrations of ^{226}Ra, ^{232}Th and ^{40}K measured for the studied samples are (21.3 ± 6.3) Bq kg^{-1}, (30.3 ± 4.5) Bq kg^{-1} and (849 ± 79) Bq kg^{-1}, respectively. The calculated radiological hazard indices showed average values of 63 nGy h^{-1} (absorbed dose rate), 0.078 mSv y^{-1} (effective dose outdoors), 0.111 mSv y^{-1} (effective dose indoors), 63 Bq kg^{-1} (radium equivalent), 0.35 (H_{ex}), 0.41 (H_{in}), 0.50 (activity concentration index) and 458 μSv y^{-1} (Annual Gonadal Equivalent Dose, AGED). In order to delineate the spatial distribution of natural radionuclides on the radiological map and to identify the areas with low, medium and high radioactivity values, the Surfer 10 software was employed. Finally, the multivariate statistical analysis was performed to deduce the interdependency and any existing relationships between the radiological indices and the concentrations of the radionuclides. The results of this study, also compared with values of other locations of the Italian Peninsula characterized by similar local geological conditions, can be used as a baseline for future investigations about radioactivity background in the investigated area.

Keywords: natural radioactivity; river sediments; gamma spectroscopy; radiological risks; background radioactivity; multivariate statistics

1. Introduction

Radioactivity naturally occurs in the environment. Aside from the cosmic radiation which bombards the earth from the outside of the atmosphere, the predominant natural source of human exposure to radiation doses is due to the terrestrial radiation which includes radionuclides of ^{238}U, ^{232}Th, ^{235}U series and ^{40}K [1].

It is established that the abundance of these primordial radionuclides depends on the local environment's geology [2,3]. Moreover, natural and anthropogenic events such as flooding, radionuclide uptake by plants and the use of fertilizers, usually provoke an alteration in the distribution of the abundance levels of the radionuclides in the environment [4–6].

Studies of natural radiation are needed to establish reference levels, especially in areas where the hazard of radioactive exposure may be higher due to the lithological features of the geological context.

In this framework, central and southern Calabria (Southern Italy) can be considered as "risky" areas, since granitoids and metamorphic rocks that represent sources of radionuclides widely outcrop along the Serre and the Aspromonte Massifs. Moreover, recent studies highlighted the presence of heavy minerals, such as monazite and zircons, in the Calabrian rocks [7], which might contain high amounts of radioactive U and Th.

In this study, fluvial deposits from nine different selected sites from the Ionian and Tyrrhenian coastline of Calabria were analyzed. River sediments, consisting of mineral particles with different size and chemical composition, are considered reliable long-term indicators of river pollution by radionuclides, because water pollution components are deposited in the sediments [8]. Major sources of natural radionuclides in sediments have different possible origins, like weathering and recycling by erosion of terrestrial minerals and rocks (igneous or metamorphic) containing ^{40}K and radionuclides of uranium and thorium radioactive series, and also rainfall and other depositional phenomena such as landslides and precipitations [9]. The main aim of this paper is to identify and quantify natural gamma-emitting radionuclides and to evaluate the radiological hazard effects [10]. For this purpose, High-Purity Germanium (HPGe) gamma spectrometry was used to measure the ^{226}Ra (in secular equilibrium with ^{238}U), ^{232}Th and ^{40}K activity concentration [11]. Statistical and radiological maps were produced in order to detect the relationship among values and to identify the most hazardous zone.

Moreover, since sandy natural materials were widely used in the field of civil construction, a series of radiological indices were calculated to evaluate the potential hazard connected with the building use of these materials.

2. Geological Setting

The investigated river sediments come from the Ionian and Tyrrhenian seaboard of the Calabrian coastline (Figure 1), and they derive from the dismantling of the Serre Massifs and Aspromonte due to erosion processes. These Massifs belong to the Calabria-Peloritani Orogen (CPO), which is the peri-Mediterranean orogenic Alpine nappe system that comprises the whole Calabria and the north-eastern sector of Sicily [12]. It includes the Sila and Catena Costiera Massifs in northern Calabria, the Serre and Aspromonte Massifs in central and southern Calabria and the Peloritani Mountains in Sicily [12].

The Serre Massif (Central Calabria) is characterized by outcrops of granitoids and Variscan metamorphic rocks. A thin early Mesozoic sedimentary cover is present only along the Ionian margin. According to recent studies [12–14], the Serre Massif represents a nearly complete continental crust section, which is divided into lower, middle and upper crustal portions. The lower one is composed of granulitic and migmatitic complexes, whereas the middle one is made up by late-Variscan acidic granitoid rocks, such as tonalites, granodiorites and granites. Conversely, the upper crustal portion consists of high- to low-grade metapelites (Mammola and Stilo-Pazzano complexes) [13,14].

The Aspromonte Massif (Calabria), together with the Peloritani Mountains (Sicily), constitutes the southern sector of the CPO (Calabria Peloritani Orogen). This Massif was generated by the juxtaposition of three different tectonic units. The Madonna di Polsi Unit is the lowermost unit and it is composed of greenschist to amphibolite facies metamorphic rocks showing only Alpine metamorphism. The higher-most unit is represented by the Stilo Unit, made up of phyllites, schists and paragneisses derived from the variscan metamorphism of Paleozoic sediments. The Aspromonte Unit, which is sandwiched between the Stilo and Madonna di Polsi Unit, exhibits high-grade metamorphites and late-variscan granitoids [12–14].

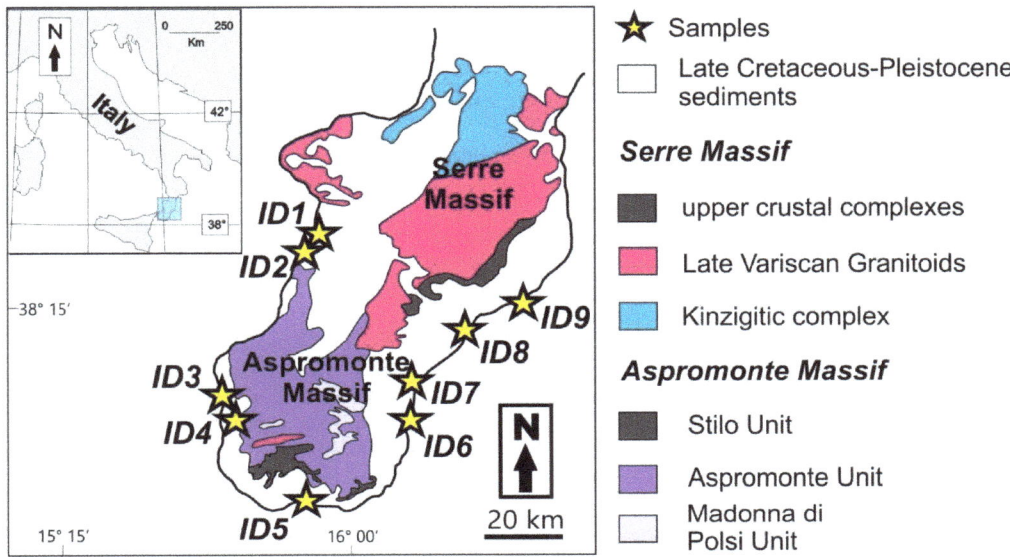

Figure 1. Geological sketch map of central-southern Calabria; yellow stars: sampling sites.

Paleozoic and early Mesozoic rocks of both Serre and Aspromonte Massif are covered by sedimentary deposits ranging in age from the Late Cretaceous to the Pleistocene.

3. Materials and Methods

3.1. Samples Collection and Preparation

Ninety samples of river sediments, around 1 kg each, were collected in nine selected sites of the Ionian and Tyrrhenian coast of Calabria for subsequent laboratory gamma spectrometric measurements. Locations, coordinates and labels of the collected samples are indicated in Figure 1 and in Table 1.

Table 1. Labels and Global Positioning System (GPS) locations of the sampling sites.

Site ID	Sampling Site	GPS Position	
		Latitude	Longitude
1	Gioia Tauro–Budello river	38.43	15.9075
2	Gioia Tauro–Petrace river	38.4202778	15.8839
3	Reggio Cal.–Gallico river	38.1730556	15.6506
4	Reggio Cal.–Calopinace river	38.1005556	15.6897
5	Bova Marina–Amendolea river	37.928333	15.8878
6	Africo–Laverde river	38.9291667	16.8338
7	Bovalivo–Bonamico river	38.1275	16.1591
8	Siderno–Novito river	38.2505556	16.2794
9	Caulonia–Allaro river	38.3480556	16.4727

Samples were collected with a metal sampler and stored in labeled plastic boxes. Adequate care was taken to prevent their contamination, particularly during transportation to the laboratory. Samples were oven-dried for 24 h at 110 °C until moisture was completely removed and constant mass was attained. They were grounded and further homogenized by passing them through a 2 mm sieve using a sieve shaker. After, they were successfully inserted in Marinelli hermetically sealed containers of 1 L capacity. After 40 days, the secular radioactive equilibrium between ^{226}Ra and their daughter products was attained and samples were ready for gamma spectrometry counting.

3.2. Gamma Spectrometry Measurements

Specific activity measurements of the investigated samples were performed by using a high-purity germanium (HPGe) detector (Ortec, Oak Ridge, TN, USA) for gamma spectrometry analysis.

In order to reduce statistical uncertainty, samples were counted for 70,000 seconds and spectra were analyzed in order to obtain the activity concentration of ^{226}Ra, ^{232}Th and ^{40}K. The ^{226}Ra-specific activity was calculated through a weighted average of ^{214}Pb and ^{214}Bi (in secular equilibrium) specific activities. The ^{232}Th activity concentration was determined by using the 911.21 and 968.97 keV ^{228}Ac γ-ray lines; for ^{40}K, the evaluation was performed from its γ-line at 1460.8 keV. The experimental setup was composed by a positive biased Ortec HPGe detector (GEM) (Full Width at Half Maximum, FWHM) of 1:85 keV, peak to Compton ratio of 64:1, relative efficiency of 40% at the 1:33 MeV ^{60}Co-line), placed inside lead wells to shield the background radiation environment. Efficiency and energy calibrations were performed using a multipeak Marinelli geometry gamma source (AK-5901) of 1 L capacity, covering the energy range, 59.54–1836 keV, customized to reproduce the exact geometries of samples in a water-equivalent epoxy resin matrix [15].

The Gamma Vision (Ortec) software was used for data acquisition and analysis [16].

The activity concentration (Bq kg^{-1}) of the investigated radionuclides was calculated using the following formula [17]:

$$C = \frac{N_E}{\varepsilon_E t \gamma_d M} \qquad (1)$$

where N_E indicates the net area of a peak at energy E, ε_E and γ_d are the efficiency and yield of the photopeak at energy E respectively, M is the mass of the sample (kg) and t is the live time (s).

The measurement uncertainty is a combined standard one at coverage factor k = 2, taking into account the following components: uncertainty counting statistics, uncertainty in nuclear data library, uncertainty due to calibration efficiency and uncertainty about the quantity of the sample [18].

The quality of the gamma spectrometry experimental results was certified by the Italian Accreditation Body (ACCREDIA) [19]. This implies the continued verification (with annual periodicity) of the maintenance of the gamma spectrometry method performance characteristics.

In particular, with regard to the blanks, they are generally determined by acquiring an empty lead well spectrum or an ultrapure water sample in the sample holder of the desired geometry (for determination of natural-emitting gamma radionuclides) or, in the case of samples requiring a material of support (e.g., atmospheric particulate aspirated on filter), by acquiring the support of clean sampling, under the same geometric conditions as the sample. The measurement of the blanks is performed on a quarterly basis.

Regarding the precision and accuracy assessment, we proceed as follows:

For the precision, with the double test method, the repeatability of the method is verified over time. A certified reference material (also containing the radionuclides K-40, Ra-226 and Th-232) is analyzed twice, with the activity concentration of the radionuclide of interest defined as X_1 (first measurement) and X_2 (second measurement). The probability level p = 0.95 is considered. The following formula is applied:

$$|x_1 - x_2| \leq \sqrt{2} \cdot s_r \cdot t \qquad (2)$$

where t is the Student variable and s_r is the standard deviation of repeatability obtained in the validation phase.

For the accuracy, it is evaluated by comparing the reference (certified sample) and the measured values of the radionuclide of interest, taking into account the uncertainty. This is done using the u-test, with the following acceptability criterion:

$$u_{test} = \frac{\text{measured} - \text{reference}}{\sqrt{u_{meas}^2 - u_{ref}^2}} \leq 2 \tag{3}$$

where u_{meas}^2 and u_{ref}^2 are the uncertainties of the measured and reference values, respectively.

3.3. Radiological Indices

3.3.1. Absorbed Gamma Dose Rate

The absorbed gamma dose rate calculation is the first major step to evaluate the health risk [20]. It was estimated as follows [21]:

$$D \, (nGy \cdot h^{-1}) = 0.462 \cdot C_{Ra} + 0.604 \cdot C_{Th} + 0.0417 \cdot C_K \tag{4}$$

where C_{Ra}, C_{Th} and C_K are the mean activity concentrations (Bq kg^{-1}) of ^{226}Ra, ^{232}Th and ^{40}K in the river sediments, respectively.

3.3.2. The Annual Effective Dose Equivalent

Annual estimated average effective dose equivalent (AEDE) received by an individual was calculated using the following equations with an outdoor occupancy of 20% and 80% for indoors [22]:

$$\text{AEDE (outdoor)} \, (mSv \cdot y^{-1}) = \text{absorbed dose} \, (nGy \cdot h^{-1}) \times 8760 \cdot h \times 0.7 \cdot Sv \cdot Gy^{-1} \times 0.2 \times 10^{-6} \tag{5}$$

$$\text{AEDE (indoor)} \, (mSv \cdot y^{-1}) = \text{absorbed dose} \, (nGy \cdot h^{-1}) \times 8760 \cdot h \times 0.7 \cdot Sv \cdot Gy^{-1} \times 0.8 \times 10^{-6} \tag{6}$$

3.3.3. Radium Equivalent Activity

The activity concentrations of the radionuclides measured in the analyzed samples do not give a direct measure of the γ-radiation dose incurred by the population. To estimate the gamma radiation dose due to activity concentrations of ^{226}Ra, ^{232}Th and ^{40}K in the river samples, especially when used as components of building construction, the radium equivalent activity is regularly utilized.

It is an index which describes the activities of ^{226}Ra, ^{232}Th and ^{40}K in a single activity term. The gamma energy doses from these radionuclides in river sediments are different even if they are present in the same amount. Radium equivalent activity (Ra$_{eq}$) estimated in Bq kg^{-1} is evaluated with conditions that 1 Bq kg^{-1} of ^{226}Ra or 1.43 Bq kg^{-1} of ^{232}Th or 0.077 Bq kg^{-1} of ^{40}K produce equal gamma dose rate.

The radium equivalent activity was calculated as [23]:

$$Ra_{eq} \, (Bq \cdot kg^{-1}) = C_{Ra} + 1.43 \, C_{Th} + 0.077 \cdot C_K \tag{7}$$

3.3.4. Hazard Indices

External and internal radiation hazard indices were defined to limit the radiation dose to 1 mSv y^{-1} [24].

The external hazard index (H$_{ex}$) was calculated using the given equation:

$$H_{ex} = (C_{Ra}/370 + C_{Th}/259 + C_K/4810) \leq 1 \tag{8}$$

It must be lower than the unity for the radiation hazard to be negligible.

The internal hazard index (H_{in}) gives the internal exposure to carcinogenic radon and its short-lived progeny and it is given by the following formula:

$$H_{in} = (C_{Ra}/185 + C_{Th}/259 + C_K/4810) \leq 1 \qquad (9)$$

3.3.5. Activity Concentration Index

Another radiation hazard, called the activity concentration index (I), has been defined by the European Commission [25] and it is given below:

$$I = (C_{Ra}/300 + C_{Th}/200 + C_K/3000) \qquad (10)$$

The activity concentration index is correlated with the annual dose rate due to the excess external gamma radiation caused by superficial material. Values of $I \leq 1$ correspond to a criterion of 1 mSv y^{-1} [25]. Thus, this index should be used only as a screening tool to identify materials that might be of concern to be used as construction materials [26].

3.3.6. Annual Gonadal Equivalent Dose (AGED)

Some organs exhibit high sensitivity to radiation as they are highly susceptible to harmful effects of radiation. The gonads, the active bone marrow and the bone surface cells are considered to be the organs of importance due to their high radiosensitivity. The annual gonadal equivalent dose (AGED) due to the specific activities of ^{226}Ra, ^{232}Th and ^{40}K is evaluated using the following formula [27]:

$$AGED\ (\mu Sv \cdot y^{-1}) = 3.09 \cdot C_{Ra} + 4.18 \cdot C_{Th} + 0.314 \cdot C_K \qquad (11)$$

where C_{Ra}, C_{Th} and C_K are the mean activity concentrations of ^{226}Ra, ^{232}Th and ^{40}K, respectively.

3.4. Delineation of Radiological Map

Surfer 10 software was employed to generate a radiological map for the study area [28]. The software uses the kriging interpolation method, used in geostatistics to predict the value of a random variable over a spatial region. Using the values of radiological measurements at all the sampling sites with different geographic coordinates, kriging allows the prediction of the radiological values throughout the regions where there are no experimental observations in the entire study area.

This method is widely employed in hydrogeology and environmental science, among others.

3.5. Statistical Analysis

The XLSTAT statistical software for Windows was used for all statistical calculations [29].

With the aim to individuate the presence of the relationships among the original variables (Pearson correlation analysis), an exploratory method (Principal Component Analysis, PCA) was performed. The PCA elaboration ensures the reduction of the data dimensionality, whereas the combinations of variables identified by the PCs provide the greatest contribution to sample variability. However, before the elaboration, the logarithmic transformation of the dataset was conducted and the appropriateness of the dataset was preliminarily checked by the Kaiser–Meyer–Olkin (KMO) test and the Bartlett test (sphericity test), as already reported in our previous work [30].

4. Results and Discussion

4.1. ^{226}Ra, ^{232}Th and ^{40}K Activity Concentration in the River Sediments, Spatial Distribution and Classification of Hazard Regions

The activity concentrations of the three naturally occurring ^{226}Ra, ^{232}Th and ^{40}K radionuclides in river sediments across the study area were determined for the sampling points reported in Table 1.

The obtained results are reported in Table 2. As shown in the Table, the highest average concentration, (31.3 ± 8.3) Bq kg^{-1}, of ^{226}Ra was obtained for samples from the site ID8 (Siderno–Novito river), whereas the lowest mean value, (14.5 ± 4.9) Bq kg^{-1}, was detected for sediments from the site ID1 (Gioia Tauro–Budello river). Concerning ^{232}Th, samples from the site ID8 are characterized by the highest average concentration, (43.5 ± 4.9) Bq kg^{-1}, while those from the site ID2 (Gioia Tauro–Petrace river) have the lowest mean value, (20.3 ± 2.9) Bq kg^{-1}. Sediments from the site ID1 show the highest average concentration of ^{40}K, with (1088 ± 98) Bq kg^{-1}, while the lowest mean concentration of (643 ± 53) Bq kg^{-1} was obtained for samples from the site ID 6 (Africo–Laverde river).

Table 2. Activity concentrations of ^{226}Ra, ^{232}Th and ^{40}K in the investigated sampling sites.

Scheme 226.	No. of Samples	^{226}Ra (Bq kg^{-1})		^{232}Th (Bq kg^{-1})		^{40}K (Bq kg^{-1})	
		Range	Mean	Range	Mean	Range	Mean
1	10	10.2–23.6	14.5 ± 4.9	16.5–48.6	22.7 ± 3.2	961–1450	1088 ± 98
2	10	13.6–22.9	18.2 ± 4.4	17.5–23.8	20.3 ± 2.9	949–1028	1009 ± 88
3	10	15.1–19.6	16.2 ± 4.3	37.2–41.5	39.5 ± 4.8	712–918	815 ± 77
4	10	15.1–18.8	16.5 ± 6.8	22.5–26.3	24.1 ± 2.9	591–811	722 ± 84
5	10	19.1–21.7	20.6 ± 2.3	20.3–46.8	27.8 ± 3.9	678–762	702 ± 66
6	10	19.3–29.4	26.2 ± 7.5	25.1–36.5	32.5 ± 9.2	528–691	643 ± 53
7	10	23.6–31.8	26.5 ± 9.5	28.2–43.5	34.5 ± 5.6	608–749	715 ± 60
8	10	26.6–33.9	31.3 ± 8.3	38.2–48.6	43.5 ± 4.9	871–942	917 ± 86
9	10	17.8–26.8	21.9 ± 8.5	25.3–33.8	27.7 ± 3.4	1002–1079	1030 ± 98
Overall	90	10.2–33.9	21.3 ± 6.3	16.5–48.6	30.3 ± 4.5	528–1450	849 ± 79

Across all sampling locations, the activity concentration values of ^{226}Ra ranged between 10.2 and 33.9 Bq kg^{-1}, with overall mean value of 21.3 ± 6.3 Bq kg^{-1}, that of ^{232}Th varied from 16.5 to 48.6 Bq kg^{-1} and the overall average value is (30.3 ± 4.5) Bq kg^{-1}. The ^{40}K ranged between 528 and 1450 Bq kg^{-1}, with an overall average value of (849 ± 79) Bq kg^{-1}.

The average values of ^{226}Ra, ^{232}Th and ^{40}K obtained in this study, for each sampling site, were compared with the world average value reported in Reference [1]. All the average values of ^{226}Ra are lower than that of the world average (35 Bq kg^{-1}). For ^{232}Th, the mean values are lower than that of the world average (30 Bq kg^{-1}) except for samples from the sites ID3 (39.5 ± 4.8 Bq kg^{-1}), ID6 (32.5 ± 9.2 Bq kg^{-1}), ID7 (34.5 ± 5.6 Bq kg^{-1}) and ID8 (43.5 ± 4.9 Bq kg^{-1}). The average concentration of ^{40}K is higher than the 420 Bq/kg average concentration reported in Reference [1] for all the analyzed samples.

Contour maps, showing the spatial distributions of ^{226}Ra, ^{232}Th and ^{40}K, are presented in Figure 2.

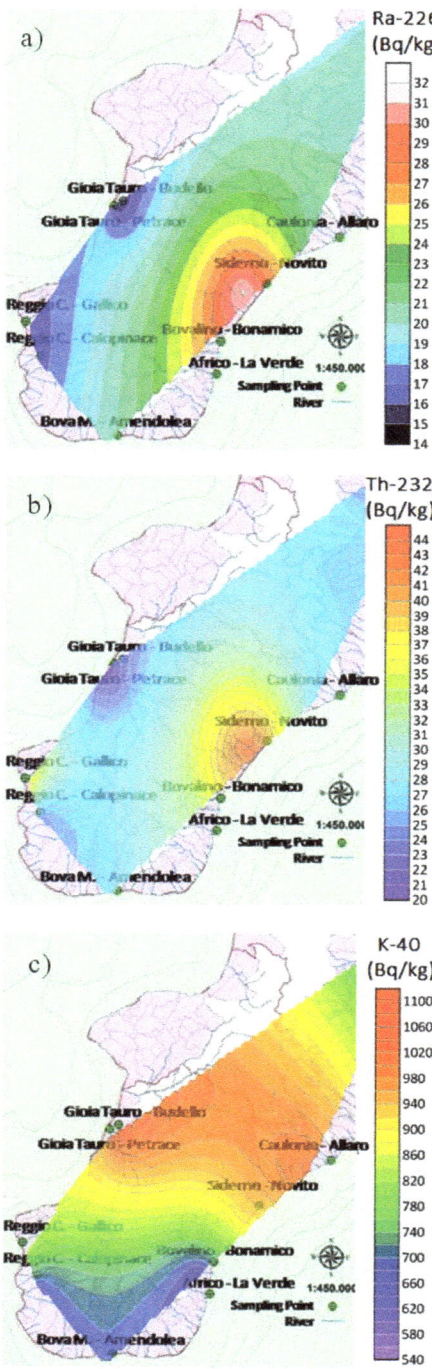

Figure 2. Contour maps showing the spatial distributions of (**a**) ^{226}Ra, (**b**) ^{232}Th and (**c**) ^{40}K in the investigated region.

As can be seen in the ^{226}Ra map (Figure 2a), there are four distinct regions. The activity concentration of ^{226}Ra in these regions was classified as low (C_{Ra} < 15 Bq kg^{-1}), moderate (15 Bq kg^{-1} < C_{Ra} < 20 Bq kg^{-1}), high (20 Bq kg^{-1} < C_{Ra} < 25 Bq kg^{-1}) and very high (C_{Ra} > 25 Bq kg^{-1}), which are deep blue, light blue, green and yellow (and red) areas on the map. In the case of ^{232}Th, two regions of very low and moderately low activity concentrations were identified. As seen from Figure 2b, the southern part of the study area as well as the mid-west and the northern part exhibit low activity concentrations of ^{232}Th with typical activities concentrations less than 33 Bq kg^{-1}. Otherwise, the middle-east zone of the study area exhibits high activity, higher than 35 Bq kg^{-1}. The delineated map of ^{40}K (Figure 2c) shows two distinct zones of concentration. The blue zone in the southern part belongs to the low-concentration region (lower than 700 Bq kg^{-1}). Whereas, other areas are classified as high-concentration zones (higher than 700 Bq kg^{-1}).

4.2. Dose Assessment and Hazard Indices

Table 3 reports the calculated average values of adsorbed and effective doses together with the hazard indices. The absorbed gamma dose rate was estimated using Equation (4). Measured values range from 52 to 79 nGy h^{-1}, with an average value of 63 nGy h^{-1}. This average value is near the world mean value of 60 nGy/h [1], although 66% of the analyzed samples showed values that are in excess than the world mean. The variability of the adsorbed and effective doses is attributable to the different lithologic components of the considered areas.

Table 3. Radiological indices in the investigated sampling sites.

Scheme 1.	Absorbed Dose Rate (nGyh^{-1})	Effective Dose Outdoors (mSv y^{-1})	Effective Dose Indoors (mSv y^{-1})	Ra$_{eq}$ (Bq kg^{-1})	H$_{ex}$	H$_{in}$	I	Annual Gonadal Equivalent Dose (AGED) (μSvy^{-1})
1	66	0.081	0.323	66	0.35	0.39	0.52	481
2	63	0.077	0.084	63	0.33	0.39	0.50	457
3	66	0.080	0.088	65	0.36	0.41	0.52	471
4	52	0.064	0.070	52	0.28	0.33	0.42	378
5	56	0.068	0.075	55	0.30	0.36	0.44	400
6	58	0.072	0.079	58	0.33	0.40	0.46	418
7	63	0.077	0.085	63	0.35	0.43	0.50	450
8	79	0.097	0.106	79	0.44	0.53	0.63	566
9	70	0.086	0.094	69	0.38	0.44	0.55	506
Mean	63	0.078	0.111	63	0.35	0.41	0.50	458

Equation (5) was used to evaluate the annual outdoor effective dose due to the activities of ^{226}Ra, ^{232}Th and ^{40}K in the analyzed samples. The obtained values range from 0.064 to 0.097 mSv y^{-1}, with an average value of 0.078 mSv y^{-1}. In a similar way, the annual indoor effective dose (Equation (6)) ranges from 0.070 to 0.323 mSv y^{-1}, with a mean value of 0.111 mSv y^{-1}. The total average annual effective dose is therefore of 0.189 mSv y^{-1}. This value is lower than the worldwide average of annual effective dose (0.48 mSv y^{-1} [1]). The mean value is also lower than 1 mSv y^{-1}, which is set as the maximum limit by Reference [31].

The radium equivalent activity (Ra$_{eq}$) was calculated using Equation (7) in order to determine the suitability of the samples when they are used as components in building materials. The obtained Ra$_{eq}$ values vary from 52 to 79 Bq kg^{-1} with an average value of 63 Bq kg^{-1}, which is lower than 370 Bq kg^{-1} set as the upper limit for building materials [29]. This indicates that the investigated samples may not be hazardous if used in the field of civil construction. The minimum value of radium equivalent activity was obtained for the river sediments come from the site ID4 (Reggio Cal.–Calopinace river), while the maximum one characterizes the samples collected at the site ID8 (Siderno–Novito river).

The external and internal hazard indices, given by Equations (8) and (9), are lower than the unity for all investigated samples, thus the radiological risks can be considered negligible.

The activity concentration index, calculated with Equation (10), is again lower than the unity for all analyzed samples. Thus, these river sediments are not be of concern to be used as construction materials.

The obtained values of annual gonadal equivalent dose (AGED), calculated by Equation (11), range from 378 (site ID4) to 566 µSv y^{-1} (site ID8), with an average of 458 µSv y^{-1}, for the investigated samples. These values are higher than the world average value for AGED, for sediments, which in the literature was found to be 300 µSv y^{-1} [32].

4.3. Statistical Features

The radiological parameters obtained from the measured activity concentrations of ^{40}K, ^{226}Ra and ^{232}Th were subjected to Pearson's correlation analysis, with the aim to deduce the interdependency and identify any existing relationships between the radiological indices and the concentrations of the radionuclides. This will help in making valid assessments concerning the nature and distribution of these radionuclides in the study area. The results of the Pearson's correlation coefficients are presented in Table 4. Among the negative correlations, the most interesting are those between ^{40}K and ^{226}Ra (-0.287) and between ^{40}K and ^{232}Th (-0.305), while a perfect positive correlation is found between absorbed dose rate and effective dose outdoors (1.00), and between Ra$_{eq}$ and absorbed dose rate (1.00) and effective dose outdoors (1.00). The correlations of the three radionuclides are positive and in agreement with all the radiological parameters considered in this study at $p < 0.01$, except for correlations between ^{226}Ra and H$_{in}$ (0.739) and between ^{232}Th and H$_{in}$ (0.719), obtained at $p < 0.05$.

Table 4. Pearson correlation matrix among the considered variables.

Variables	^{226}Ra	^{232}Th	^{40}K	Absorbed Dose Rate (nGy h^{-1})	Effective Dose Outdoors (mSv y^{-1})	Effective Dose Indoors (mSv y^{-1})	Ra$_{eq}$ (Bq kg^{-1})	H$_{ex}$	H$_{in}$	Gamma index I	AGED µSv y^{-1}
^{226}Ra	1	0.649	−0.287	0.468	0.465	−0.378	0.468	0.559	0.739	0.464	0.417
^{232}Th	0.649	1	−0.305	0.546	0.536	−0.281	0.546	0.666	0.719	0.553	0.494
^{40}K	−0.287	−0.305	1	0.595	0.603	0.607	0.596	0.465	0.301	0.591	0.647
Absorbed Dose Rate (nGy/h)	0.468	0.546	0.595	1	1.000	0.236	1.000	0.988	0.936	0.999	0.998
Effective Dose outdoors (mSv/y)	0.465	0.536	0.603	1.000	1	0.245	1.000	0.986	0.933	0.998	0.998
Effective Dose indoors (mSv/y)	−0.378	−0.281	0.607	0.236	0.245	1	0.237	0.148	0.002	0.223	0.275
Ra$_{eq}$ (Bq/kg)	0.468	0.546	0.596	1.000	1.000	0.237	1	0.988	0.936	0.999	0.998
H$_{ex}$	0.559	0.666	0.465	0.988	0.986	0.148	0.988	1	0.970	0.988	0.976
H$_{in}$	0.739	0.719	0.301	0.936	0.933	0.002	0.936	0.970	1	0.935	0.912
Gamma index I	0.464	0.553	0.591	0.999	0.998	0.223	0.999	0.988	0.935	1	0.996
AGDE (µSv/y)	0.417	0.494	0.647	0.998	0.998	0.275	0.998	0.976	0.912	0.996	1

Bold values refer to $p < 0.05$.

Moreover, ^{226}Ra and ^{232}Th are negatively correlated with the annual effective dose equivalent indoors (-0.378 and -0.281, respectively). The radiological parameters are positively and significantly correlated with each other, showing direct relationships.

In order to better define the relationships among the specific activities of ^{226}Ra, ^{232}Th and ^{40}K, the PCA multivariate statistical method was carried out. The geological feature of sediments is the most important variable, neglecting the others (erosive power of rivers, solid transport, selective erosion, weathering, etc.), which is useful to evaluate the degree of relationship between the isotopic specific activities and the samples' geolocation. Results of the PCA allow to group the sampling sites in four clusters that seem to be comparable to each other (Figure 3) in terms of activity concentration of ^{226}Ra, ^{232}Th and ^{40}K. Specifically, sites ID1 and ID2 show positive correlations with ^{40}K-specific activity but negative linear relationships with ^{226}Ra and ^{232}Th ones, whereas sites IDs 3, 4 and 5 are negatively correlated to the activity concentrations of ^{226}Ra, ^{232}Th and ^{40}K. The sites ID6 and ID7 show instead a positive correlation with values of ^{226}Ra- and ^{232}Th-specific activities, and exhibit a negative correlation with ^{40}K. Finally, sites ID8 and ID9 show positive correlations of the three investigated radionuclides' activity concentrations. We believe that the differences of ^{226}Ra-, ^{232}Th- and ^{40}K-specific activities among the identified clusters mainly depend on the compositional/mineralogical features of rocks from which the analyzed river sediments derive. The sediments collected along the rivers located in the Tyrrhenian side (ID1 and ID2) record the chemical fingerprint of the granitoid rocks from the Serre Massif. On the contrary, the Ionian river sediments (ID6, ID7, ID8 and ID9) reflect the chemical and mineralogical composition of the outcropping Late Cretaceous and Cenozoic terrigeous sediments. Moreover, the ID6 and ID7 rivers are characterized by a component provided by the erosion of the Aspromonte Unit, whereas clasts from the upper crustal complexes (Stilo-Pazzano and Mammola) and from granitoids supply the ID8 and ID9 rivers. Regarding the rivers on the western and southern margin of the Aspromonte Massif (ID3, ID4 and ID5), the main lithologies occurring within the drainage basins come from the Aspromonte and the Stilo Units.

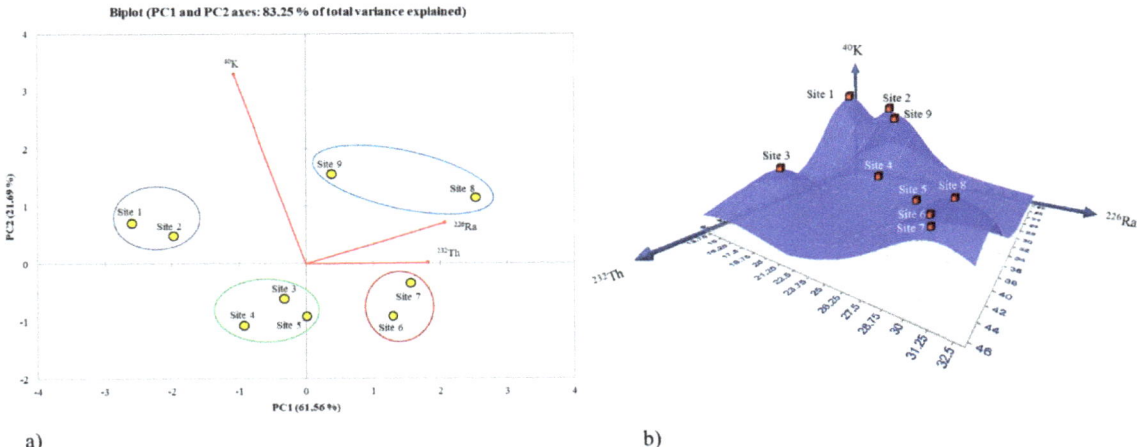

Figure 3. Two-dimensional (2D) plots of the first two Principal Components (PCs) obtained through Principal Component Analysis (PCA) elaboration starting from ^{40}K, ^{232}Th and ^{226}Ra activity concentrations (**a**). Mean concentration three-dimensional (3D) map of ^{40}K, ^{232}Th and ^{226}Ra into the investigated sites (**b**).

5. Conclusions

The activity concentration and the distribution of natural terrestrial radionuclides ^{226}Ra, ^{232}Th and ^{40}K for river sediments from selected locations of the Calabrian coastline (Southern Italy) were measured using HPGe gamma spectrometry. The obtained average values of the absorbed dose rate in air, AEDE (outdoor and indoor), Ra_{eq}, H_{ex} and H_{in}, I and AGDE are comparable with average worldwide ranges and they fell within the maximum recommended values.

The background radiation maps for the study area evidence that the Tyrrhenian side shows, in general, the lowest activity concentrations of ^{226}Ra and ^{232}Th, whereas the Ionian zone is characterized by the highest ones. Concerning the ^{40}K, an increasing of the specific activity was defined from south to north. Multivariate statistical analysis allowed to assess the nature and distribution of natural radionuclides in the investigated area and highlighted the relationships between chemical/mineralogical features of the local outcropping lithologies.

Data provided in this study will serve to contribute as a reference database for future researches in the area, and also as a pilot scheme to provide a comprehensive background radiation map for Italy, which is not yet available.

Author Contributions: Conceptualization, F.C.; methodology, F.C. and A.F.M.; validation, F.C. and G.S.; formal analysis, F.C.; investigation, F.C., A.F.M., G.S., M.D.B., M.R.F., D.R. and F.I.; resources, G.S. and G.B.; data curation, F.C. and A.F.M.; writing—original draft preparation, F.C.; supervision, G.B. All authors have read and agreed to the published version of the manuscript.

Funding: This research received no external funding.

Institutional Review Board Statement: Not applicable.

Informed Consent Statement: Not applicable.

Conflicts of Interest: The authors declare no conflict of interest.

References

1. United Nations Scientific Committee on the Effects of Atomic Radiation (UNSCEAR). *Sources and Effects of Ionizing Radiation. Report of the United Nations Scientific Committee on the Effects of Atomic Radiation to the General Assembly*; United Nations: New York, NY, USA, 2000.
2. Baeza, A.; Del Rio, M.; Jimenez, A.; Miro, C.; Paniagua, J. Influence of geology and soil particle size on the surface-area/volume activity ratio for natural radionuclides. *J. Radioanal. Nucl. Chem.* **1995**, *189*, 289–299. [CrossRef]
3. Tzortzis, M.; Tsertos, H.; Christofides, S.; Christodoulides, G. Gamma-ray measurements of naturally occurring radioactive samples from Cyprus characteristic geological rocks. *Radiat. Meas.* **2003**, *37*, 221–229. [CrossRef]
4. Navas, A.; Soto, J.; Machin, J. Edaphic and physiographic factors affecting the distribution of natural gamma-emitting radionuclides in the soils of the Arnas catchment in the Central Spanish Pyrenees. *Eur. J. Soil Sci.* **2002**, *53*, 629–638. [CrossRef]
5. Pulhani, V.A.; Dafauti, S.; Heqde, A.G.; Sharma, R.M.; Mishra, U.C. Uptake and distribution of natural radioactivity in wheat plants from soil. *J. Environ. Radioact.* **2005**, *79*, 331–346. [CrossRef]
6. Chandrajith, R.; Seneviratna, S.; Wickramaarachchi, K.; Attanayake, T.; Aturaliya, T.N.C.; Dissanayake, C.B. Natural radionuclides and trace elements in rice field soils in relation to fertilizer application: Study of a chronic kidney disease area in Sri Lanka. *Environ. Earth Sci.* **2010**, *60*, 193–201. [CrossRef]
7. Fornelli, A.; Piccarreta, G.; Del Moro, A.; Acquafredda, P. Multi-stage melting in the lower crust of the Serre (southern Italy). *J. Petr.* **2002**, *43*, 2191. [CrossRef]
8. Sabatino, G.; Di Bella, M.; Caridi, F.; Italiano, F.; Romano, D.; Magazù, S.; Gnisci, A.; Faggio, G.; Messina, G.; Santangelo, S.; et al. Radiological assessment, mineralogy and geochemistry of the heavy-mineral placers from the Calabrian coast (South Italy). *J. Instrum.* **2019**, *14*, P05015. [CrossRef]
9. El-Gamal, A.; Nasr, S.; El-Taher, A. Study of the spatial distribution of natural radioactivity in the upper Egypt Nile river sediments. *Radiat. Meas.* **2007**, *42*, 457–465. [CrossRef]
10. Caridi, F.; Marguccio, S.; Belvedere, A.; D'Agostino, M.; Belmusto, G. A methodological approach to a radioactive sample analysis with low-level γ-ray spectrometry. *J. Instrum.* **2018**, *13*, P09022. [CrossRef]
11. Caridi, F.; Marguccio, S.; Belvedere, A.; D'Agostino, M.; Belmusto, G.; Durante, G.; Trozzo, R.; Fullone, F. Natural radioactivity measurements and dosimetric evaluations in soil samples with a high content of NORM. *Eur. Phys. J. Plus* **2017**, *132*, 56. [CrossRef]
12. Cirrincione, R.; Fazio, E.; Fiannacca, P.; Ortolano, G.; Pezzino, A.; Punturo, R. The Calabria-Peloritani Orogen, a composite terrane in Central Mediterranean; Its overall architecture and geodynamic significance for a pre-Alpine scenario around the Tethyan basin. *Periodico di Mineralogia* **2015**, *84*, 701–749. [CrossRef]
13. Caggianelli, A.; Liotta, D.; Prosser, G.; Ranalli, G. Pressure-temperature evolution of the late Hercyian Calabria continental crust: Compatibility with post-collisional extensional tectonics. *Terra Nova* **2007**, *19*, 502. [CrossRef]
14. Angì, G.; Cirrincione, R.; Fazio, E.; Fiannacca, P.; Ortolano, G.; Pezzino, A. Metamorphic evolution of preserved Hercynian crustal section in the Serre massif (Calabria-Peloritani Orogen, southern Italy). *Lithos* **2010**, *115*, 237. [CrossRef]
15. Caridi, F.; D'Agostino, M.; Belvedere, A.; Marguccio, S.; Belmusto, G.; Gatto, M.F. Diagnostics techniques and dosimetric evaluations for environmental radioactivity investigations. *J. Instrum.* **2016**, *11*, C10012. [CrossRef]
16. Caridi, F.; D'Agostino, M.; Messina, M.; Belvedere, A.; Marguccio, S.; Belmusto, G.; Marcianò, G.; Grioli, L. Lichens as environmental risk detectors. *Eur. Phys. J. Plus* **2017**, *132*, 189. [CrossRef]

17. Caridi, F.; Belvedere, A.; D'Agostino, M.; Marguccio, S.; Marino, G.; Messina, M.; Belmusto, G. An investigation on airborne particulate radioactivity, heavy metals and polycyclic aromatic hydrocarbons composition in Calabrian selected sites, southern Italy. *Ind. J. Environ. Protect.* **2019**, *39*, 321–326.
18. Caridi, F.; Messina, M.; Belvedere, A.; D'Agostino, M.; Marguccio, S.; Settineri, L.; Belmusto, G. Food salt characterization in terms of radioactivity and metals contamination. *Appl. Sci.* **2019**, *9*, 2882. [CrossRef]
19. Caridi, F.; D'Agostino, M.; Belvedere, A. Radioactivity in Calabrian (Southern Italy) wild boar meat. *Appl. Sci.* **2020**, *10*, 3580. [CrossRef]
20. Ramasamy, V.; Suresh, G.; Meenakshisundaram, V.; Ponnusamy, V. Horizontal and vertical characterization of radionuclides and minerals in river sediments. *Appl. Rad. Isot.* **2011**, *69*, 184–195. [CrossRef] [PubMed]
21. Caridi, F.; Pappaterra, D.; Belmusto, G.; Messina, M.; Belvedere, A.; D'Agostino, M.; Settineri, L. Radioactivity and heavy metals concentration in Italian (Calabrian) DOC wines. *Appl. Sci.* **2019**, *9*, 4584. [CrossRef]
22. Caridi, F.; Messina, M.; Faggio, G.; Santangelo, S.; Messina, G.; Belmusto, G. Radioactivity, radiological risk and metal pollution assessment in marine sediments from Calabrian selected areas, southern Italy. *Eur. Phys. J. Plus* **2018**, *133*, 65. [CrossRef]
23. Torrisi, L.; Visco, A.M.; Campo, N.; Caridi, F. Pulsed laser treatments of polyethylene films. *Nucl. Instrum. Methods Phys. Res. Sect. B Beam Interact. Mater. Atoms* **2010**, *268*, 3117–3121. [CrossRef]
24. Beretka, J.; Matthew, P.J. Natural radioactivity of Australian building materials, waste and by-products. *Health Phys.* **1985**, *48*, 87–95. [CrossRef]
25. Official Journal of the European Union. *Council Directive 2013/59/Euratom*; Official Journal of the European Union: Luxembourg, 2015.
26. Ravisankar, R.; Vanasundari, K.; Chandrasekaran, A.; Rajalakshmi, A.; Suganya, M.; Vijayagopal, P.; Meenakshisundaram, V. Measurement of natural radioactivity in building materials of Namakkal, Tamil Nadu, India using gamma-ray spectrometry. *Appl. Rad. And Isot.* **2012**, *70*, 699–704. [CrossRef] [PubMed]
27. Darwish, D.A.E.; Abul-Nasr, K.T.M.; El-Khayatt, A.M. The assessment of natural radioactivity and its associated radiological hazards and dose parameters in granite samples from South Sinai, Egypt. *J. Radiat. Res. Appl. Sci.* **2015**, *8*, 17–25. [CrossRef]
28. Surfer 10 Software. Available online: https://www.goldensoftware.com/products/surfer (accessed on 17 November 2020).
29. XLSTAT: Statistical Software & Data Analysis Add-On for Excel. Available online: https://www.xlstat.com/en/ (accessed on 16 November 2020).
30. Mottese, A.F.; Sabatino, G.; Di Bella, M.; Fede, M.R.; Caridi, F.; Parisi, F.; Marcianò, G.; Caccamo, M.T.; Italiano, F.; Yuce, G.; et al. Environmental screening for the assessment of potentially toxic elements content in PGI soils from the Mediterranean region (Italy and Turkey). *Environ. Earth Sci.* **2020**, *79*, 499. [CrossRef]
31. International Commission on Radiological Protection (ICRP). 1990 Recommendations of the International Commission on Radiological Protection. ICRP Publication 60. *Ann. ICRP* **1991**, *21*, 1–3.
32. Chandrasekaran, A.; Ravisankar, R.; Senthilkumar, G.; Thillaivelavan, K.; Dhinakaran, B.; Vijayagpal, P.; Bramha, S.N.; Venkatraman, B. Spatial distribution and lifetime cancer risk due to gamma radioactivity in Yelagiri Hills, Tamilnadu, India. *Egypt J. Basic Appl. Sci.* **2014**, *1*, 38–48. [CrossRef]

MDPI
St. Alban-Anlage 66
4052 Basel
Switzerland
www.mdpi.com

Applied Sciences Editorial Office
E-mail: applsci@mdpi.com
www.mdpi.com/journal/applsci

Disclaimer/Publisher's Note: The statements, opinions and data contained in all publications are solely those of the individual author(s) and contributor(s) and not of MDPI and/or the editor(s). MDPI and/or the editor(s) disclaim responsibility for any injury to people or property resulting from any ideas, methods, instructions or products referred to in the content.

www.ingramcontent.com/pod-product-compliance
Lightning Source LLC
LaVergne TN
LVHW070605100526
838202LV00012B/573